Writing the Austrian Traditions

Relations between Philosophy and Literature

Edited by

Wolfgang Huemer

and

Marc-Oliver Schuster

Wirth-Institute for Austrian and Central European Studies
University of Alberta
Edmonton, Alberta
2003

Gedruckt mit Unterstützung des Bundesministeriums für Bildung, Wissenschaft und Kultur in Wien (BMBWK)

Printed in Canada by University of Toronto Press
First published in 2003 by Wirth-Institute for Austrian and Central European Studies (University of Alberta; Edmonton, Alberta)

Copyright © 2003 Wolfgang Huemer and Marc-Oliver Schuster

All rights reserved. No part of this publication may be reproduced, stored in a retrieval system, or transmitted, in any form or by any means, electronic, mechanical, photocopying, or otherwise, without the prior written permission of the editors.

Original design of the photomontage on the front page: James Retallack
  Upper left: Thomas Bernhard's desk in his workspace (Ohlsdorf, Austria; 1988)
  Upper right: Front page of the *Manifesto* of the Vienna Circle
  Lower left: Ludwig Wittgenstein, the Fellowship Portrait (1930)
  Lower right: Coffeehouse in *fin-de-siècle* Vienna

For the use of photographs on the front page, we gratefully acknowledge the friendly permission of the following persons and institutions:
  Upper left: Erika Schmied
  Upper right: Friedrich Stadler
  Lower left: Suhrkamp Verlag

National Library of Canada Cataloguing in Publication

Writing the Austrian traditions : relations between philosophy and literature / edited by Wolfgang Huemer and Marc-Oliver Schuster.

Essays originally presented as papers at the conference Writing the Austrian traditions, held at Woodsworth College, University of Toronto, May 12-14, 2000.
Includes bibliographical references and index.
ISBN 1-55195-097-9

1. Philosophy, Austrian—Congresses. 2. Austrian literature—History and criticism—Congresses. 3. Philosophy in literature—Congresses. 4. Literature—Philosophy—Congresses. I. Huemer, Wolfgang, 1968- II. Schuster, Marc-Oliver, 1968- III. Wirth Institute for Austrian and Central European Studies.

B3181.W75 2003   193   C2003-906956-7

TABLE OF CONTENTS

Preface i

Wendelin Schmidt-Dengler
The Austrian Plato 1

Fred Wilson
The Vienna Circle and Freud 13

Rudolf Haller
Wittgenstein – Poetry and Literature 37

John Gibson
Reality & The Language of Fiction 49

Newton Garver
The "Silence" of Wittgenstein and Kraus 67

Barry Smith
Kraus on Weininger, Kraus on Women, Kraus on Serbia 81

Dale Jacquette
David Lewis on Meinongian Logic of Fiction 101

Wolfgang Huemer
Phenomenological Reduction and Aesthetic Experience:
Husserl Meets Hofmannsthal 121

Mark E. Blum
The "Soft Law" of Austrian Historical Logic
since the Enlightenment in the Arts and Sciences 131

Randall R. Dipert
Mathematics in Musil 143

Jill Scott
Oedipus Endangered: Atrean Incest and Ethical Relations in Musil's
Der Mann ohne Eigenschaften 160

Marc Grzeskowiak
A Symposium as Ornament? Hermann Broch's *Schlafwandler Trilogie*
and the Discourse of Art and Philosophy in the Modern Novel 181

Franz Josef Czernin
SONNETS 191

Index 205

Contributors 211

PREFACE

Austrians tend to be preoccupied with the idiosyncrasies of their own mentality. The Austrian soul (*die österreichische Seele*) and its various crises of identity have been the objects of all kinds of analyses, ranging from Erwin Ringel's psychological inquiries to Helmut Qualtinger's satirical caricatures, whose black humour is typical of the entertainment seen in the Austrian cabaret. The reasons for this self-questioning obsession are manifold and partially roorted in the multiculturalism of the Austro-Hungarian Empire. Vienna of the *fin de siècle* was not only the capital but also the cultural meeting place for intellectuals from all corners of the Empire. This creative atmosphere was characterized by the exchange of ideas among various schools, circles, groups, and individuals, and nourished by Vienna's thriving coffeehouse culture. The decline and eventual dissolution, in 1918, of the Habsburg Monarchy, reactivated once again the problematic issue of Austrian identity, an identity defined mainly in contrast to Germany, its neighbour to the north.

Numerous scholars have tried both to define and to account for the existence of Austrian traditions in various cultural fields. The extensive work of philosophers such as Rudolf Haller and Barry Smith has substantiated the claim, expressed earlier by Otto Neurath in the manifesto of the Vienna Circle, that there are distinct Austrian traditions in philosophy. Literary critics such as Claudio Magris, Ulrich Greiner, and Robert Menasse investigated similar claims about typically Austrian features in literature.

We invited leading experts on these topics to participate in an international conference, *Writing the Austrian Traditions* (May 12-14, 2000 at Woodsworth College, University of Toronto), in order to discuss some of the significant connections between Austrian literary and philosophical traditions. The articles collected in the present volume emerged from this conference.

In the opening article "The Austrian Plato," Wendelin Schmidt-Dengler gives an overview of Austrian responses to Plato and Platonism by drawing on overlapping philosophical, literary, and philological discourses. He includes examples from such writers as Franz Grillparzer, Heinrich Gomperz, Hermann Broch, and Karl Popper, all of whom are representative of Austrian literary and intellectual history. The mainly anti-idealistic responses pertained to artistic and philosophical questions rather than to systematic philosophical issues. Against the background of the enduring seductiveness of Plato's thought, Schmidt-Dengler argues, the Austrian responses apparently strive to avoid a thorough discussion of Plato's metaphysics.

Fred Wilson argues for a more careful assessment of Freud's work, given recent criticism of the unscientific aspects of Freud's psychoanalytic method, in his article "The Vienna Circle and Freud." He discusses the examination of psychoanalysis in the works of Gustav Bergmann, who was one of the younger members of the Vienna Circle, and of Egon Brunswik, who was closely associated with this group. On the whole, both accepted the scientific claims of Freud despite some negative tendencies in psychoanalysis such as the teleological thinking so characteristic of German Romantic philosophy. After commenting on Adolf Grünbaum's work on the methodological status of psychoanalysis, Wilson suggests that Freud provided reasonable grounds to consider his theory scientific even according to the criteria proposed by the Vienna Circle. The relationships between the Freudians in Vienna and the Vienna Circle were not merely personal; similar cultural and ethical aims on both sides situated them in broader philosophical contexts. Wilson concludes by looking at their shared background, which includes Nietzsche, neo-Kantian philosophy, and the traditions of Enlightenment and humanism.

In his article "Wittgenstein – Poetry and Literature," Rudolf Haller explores the philosopher's attitudes toward literature and art. According to Haller, Wittgenstein remained critical of cultural modernity; neither his writings nor his reading list renders examples of modern(ist) literature. Economic and social modernization as well as cultural and intellectual modernity from the turn of the century to the 1930s provide the background for his anti-modernistic responses. Haller emphasizes that Wittgenstein's conservative taste in poetry and music should not be mistaken for political neo-conservativism. Wittgenstein's exposure to the journals *Die Fackel* and *Der Brenner*, and his interest in Trakl, Anzengruber, Dostoevskii, and Tolstoi prove that to split Wittgenstein into the analytic philosopher, on the one hand, and the artist striving for perfection of form, on the other, is misleading. Haller states that unification of such a split character is a precondition for interpreting Wittgenstein's views of culture. His concerns for language and, specifically, for form and style, are consistent with his views on life and life-form which, in turn, are bound up with questions of morality, faith, religious experience, and mysticism.

John Gibson shows in his article "Reality & The Language of Fiction," how we can use Wittgenstein's theory of language in the context of the theory of literature. The prevalent trend in many contemporary theories of literature, Gibson argues, is to conceive of literary language as a self-referential use of language, one which does not and cannot reach beyond the "world of the text" to touch the nature and reality of the world of the reader of literary texts. The late Wittgenstein demonstrates that since language provides our point of contact with reality, it is by examining the structure of language, of linguistic convention and practice, that we investigate our linguistic connection to reality. Literature, Gibson argues, is capable of providing this sort of Wittgensteinian investigation. Accordingly, the popular idea that we can segregate a literary text from reality is theoretically flawed, since literature's use of a common social language reveals a way of understanding how it can weave our world into the very words it uses to construct its fictional worlds.

Newton Garver argues in his article "The 'Silence' of Wittgenstein and Kraus" that Wittgenstein's famous slogan to keep silent whereof one cannot speak is more than the climactic expression of his philosophical program in his early book, the *Tractatus*. Wittgenstein's silence is instead a life-long practice, an activity rather than a mere absence of speaking, related to Goethe's phrase "In the beginning was the deed." Garver points out that this understanding of silence as an activity rather than an absence could also account for Wittgenstein's admiration of the Quakers, a religious group whose practices have various parallels to Wittgenstein's philosophical program. His views on silence as well as his life-long silence about political matters, Garver argues, were strongly influenced by Karl Kraus, an extremely productive writer who, nevertheless, found silence the most effective reaction to some of the political developments in his lifetime, notably in his comment "I cannot think of anything to say about Hitler."

Barry Smith discusses three interrelated topics at the heart of the thinking of Karl Kraus in his contribution "Kraus on Weininger, Kraus on Women, Kraus on Serbia." In the first part of his paper Smith gives a concise outline of Otto Weininger's position on sex, value, and morality. Smith shows that Weininger's ethics is strongly influenced by Kant, and that Weininger formulates an extreme version of Kantian ethics, which he then applies to the distinction between male and female. In the second part of his paper, Smith argues that Kraus turns Weininger's work on its head: Kraus, like Weininger, accepts the basic distinction between male and female aspects, but whereas Weininger detests female aspects and believes every person has a moral obligation to try to become more man and less woman, Kraus loves women precisely for their female aspects and criticises the attempts of some women to become man, as in the case of Alice Schalek, an Austrian war correspondent he disparages as a "male-female perversion."

Concentrating on the theory of fiction, Dale Jacquette, in his article on "David Lewis on Meinongian Logic of Fiction," defends Meinong's position against objections raised by David Lewis. Meinongian semantic domains admit existent and nonexistent objects, including objects ostensibly referred to in works of fiction, and permit reference and true predication of constitutive properties to existent and nonexistent objects alike. Lewis proposes an alternative to Meinong's object theory that considers the truth of a sentence in a work of fiction only within an explicit story-context. Jacquette argues that Lewis-style modal story-contexting is not incompatible with a Meinongian logic of fiction and suggests that it needs to be combined with a Meinongian semantics of fiction in order to avoid both Lewis's objections to Meinongian object theory and Meinongian objections to Lewis's story-context-prefixing.

A particular form of the relation between philosophy and literature, namely the actual meeting of a writer and a philosopher, is the topic of Wolfgang Huemer's contribution to this volume. Huemer discusses a letter Edmund Husserl wrote Hugo von Hofmannsthal shortly after Hofmannsthal had visited him. In this letter, Husserl compares the phenomenological reduction to Hofmannsthal's theory of aesthetic experience. The letter was written at a time when Husserl was just beginning to develop the phenomenological reduction and was still struggling with a way to introduce this new method. Huemer analyses why Husserl does not continue to use this comparison to introduce his new ideas. He shows that while the comparison had clear limitations for Husserl's early version of the phenomenological reduction, a comparison with Hofmannsthal's later aesthetic theory, especially his *Lord Chandos Letter*, could have provided Husserl with a strong tool to introduce his later version of the phenomenological method.

In his article "The 'Soft Law' of Austrian Historical Logic since the Enlightenment in the Arts and Sciences," Mark E. Blum approaches the distinctive features of Austrian historical reasoning as in contrast to German traditions. National historical logics respond to political-social experience and are interpretive norms that structure the understanding of how events of public and private life are ordered causally over time. Blum characterizes Austrian historical logic, which arose with the Habsburg authority in Europe, as a morphological logic that functions like a family dynasty. With its sense of an evolving form bridging times and places, this type of logic privileges the non-dramatic, non-dialectical, or the Gestalt. Examples from writers, philosophers, and political scientists support his claim that Austrian historical logic favors models of the "one in the many," of interdependence and empathy.

In his article on "Mathematics in Musil," Randall R. Dipert focuses on mathematics as an important leitmotif in Robert Musil's work. He points out that Musil's view of mathematical metaphysics lies close to his "secular mysticism," but is notably different from the views of his contemporaries, such as Thomas Mann or Hermann Broch. Musil's views are even further removed from the outright hostility toward scientific and excessively rational thinking, a hostility that flourished in the shadow of Heidegger and that came to be regarded as informing Nazism. Dipert argues that the traditional interpretation of Musil, according to which Musil is seen as a kind of literary exponent of logical positivism, is profoundly mistaken.

Jill Scott argues in her contribution "Oedipus Endangered: Atrean Incest and Ethical Relations in Musil's *Der Mann ohne Eigenschaften*" that Musil's masterpiece threatens the psychoanalytical master narrative of Freud's Oedipus. Without staging a direct polemic, *Mann ohne Eigenschaften* has the Atrean myth of Electra usurp the singular, masculine-gendered subject position of the Oedipal model. In addition, the Electra myth serves as a platform for a critically engaged dialog with Ernst Mach's theories of the provisional ego and sensation body. Tacitly referring, among others, to Johann Jacob Bachofen and Friedrich Nietzsche, the novel gives rise to a new ideal of femininity and an alternative relational ethics.

The state of morality in an epochal "Zerfall der Werte" is a core topic of Hermann Broch's cultural-philosophical *Schlafwandler Trilogie*, which is a fine example of the late modernist novel in German-language literature. In his article "A Symposium as Ornament? Hermann Broch's *Schlafwandler Trilogie* and the Discourse of Art and Philosophy in the Modern Novel," Mark Grzeskowiak considers how Broch's conception of a new type of novel based on unity is achieved in *Die Schlafwandler* and how it relates to modernist architectural debates around the *fin de siècle*. The passage "Symposion oder Gespräch über die Erlösung" from the trilogy's third part "Huguenau oder die Sachlichkeit" is singled out for the distinction between the ornament (which has contextual function) and decoration (which is purely aesthetic). If the whole trilogy, like this passage, is decorative, then the question about the novel's status as (late) modernist might have to be reviewed in light of postmodernism.

We are extremely pleased that we can conclude this collection of studies with recent examples from the poetic work of Franz Josef Czernin. The contemporary Austrian writer is known for his diverse literary interests and techniques ranging from the traditional to the experimental. With publication beginning in 1978, his extensive work includes theoretical-critical texts and is informed by a highly self-reflective position. Austrian language criticism and Wittgensteinian philosophy are just two of the contexts that Czernin competently and creatively engages with philosophical questions about language, poetics, and realism. Czernin both thematizes and applies such questions to his literary work without reducing poetic speech to a mere vehicle of theoretical claims.

Acknowledgments

We wish to thank the Department of Philosophy as well as the Department of Germanic Languages and Literatures (both at the University of Toronto), and especially Prof. Mark Thornton, Prof. James Retallack, Suzanne Puckering, and Kristin Perry for their continuous support in preparing the conference.

We also thank the Austrian Embassy and Trade Commission, the Austrian Canadian Council, the Austrian Federal Ministry of Education, Science and Culture (BMBWK), the Connaught Foundation, and the Joint Initiative for German and Eastern European Studies (University of Toronto) for their contributions to our initiative.

Special thanks go to Prof. Franz A.J. Szabo from the Wirth-Institute/Canadian Centre for Austrian and Central European Studies (University of Alberta) for making it possible to print the present volume.

Finally, we are heavily indebted to Barbara Bulcock, who read the entire manuscript and made numerous valuable suggestions.

Marc-Oliver Schuster
Wolfgang Huemer

THE AUSTRIAN PLATO

Wendelin Schmidt-Dengler
University of Vienna

I.

It is not my intention to give Austrian philosophy or literature any credit for special achievements as far as the discussion of Platonism is concerned. On the contrary, Austrian writers and thinkers have tended to steer clear of Plato and thus more or less ignore a thinker and artist whom one cannot avoid if one is to deal with thought and art at all. The responses of Austrian authors to Plato's works seem to me, on the whole, interesting, particularly as strategies of avoidance that are, in turn, revealing in the sense that they determine one's own position. In the discussion on Plato, the philosophical, the aesthetic, the literary, and even the philological discourses would seem to overlap, and therefore the following paper should also be regarded as a minor contribution to the history of these four disciplines and thus as shedding light on a context which is by no means insignificant for Austrian literary and intellectual history. I hasten to add that the point is not to discuss individual aspects of Platonism, but instead to present an overall picture, and to focus on those points that have aroused the interest of a variety of writers.

II.

Plato's place is marked also by controversy in the history of German philosophy and literature. Hölderlin, for example, praised him in a hymn as a person who created paradise, and then condemned him in *Hyperion* as an enemy of poets. In his novel *Aristipp*, Wieland portrays him as a liar who has betrayed the legacy of Socrates through his reports. And we are familiar with the negative views that Nietzsche expressed on the creator of a theory of ideas and his mentor Socrates. The contours of this dispute cannot be dealt with here even generally. Suffice it to say that German literature and philosophy tended to regard Plato as an incontrovertible fact involving the creation of a self-sufficient system and theory of ideas that has left us with the unavoidable point of departure for any discussion of metaphysics. Similar coherence will hardly be found among the views expressed by Austrian writers, although his name and his achievements – even if there is no express mention of them – play a key role for many of them, although it is a role that is scarcely discernible on the surface.

Writing the Austrian Traditions: Relations between Philosophy and Literature.
Ed. Wolfgang Huemer and Marc-Oliver Schuster. Edmonton, Alberta:
Wirth-Institute for Austrian and Central European Studies, 2003. pp. 1-11.

III.

As is evident from his diaries, Franz Grillparzer read Plato throughout his life. There are entries on Plato from 1820 all the way up to the year of his death in 1862. He read Plato primarily in the original; later in life, due to his failing eyesight, he turned to German translations.[1] The point of departure for Grillparzer's scepticism toward philosophy and German philosophy in particular arises due to the neglect of psychology in German thinking, on the one hand, and Grillparzer's admiration of the physicist and perspicacious psychologist Lichtenberg on the other: "O Lichtenberg Lichtenberg, why were you snatched so early from your fatherland!" he laments in 1809.[2] And in 1816, he jots down the following from the *Spectator*: "Our disputants put me in mind of the scuttle-fish, that when he is unable to extricate himself, blackens all the water about him until he becomes invisible" and concludes the entry with the question: "Philosophers?"[3] In his notes on Plato and Aristotle his chief aim is to find the basis among the Greek philosophers for the works of Kant and Hegel, and with respect to the latter, he writes: "In the final analysis, this Hegelian system is, indeed, based on Platonic ideas."[4] It is worth noting that this is the only place where Grillparzer makes any reference at all to the theory of ideas. The purpose of his notes is apparently not so much to emphasize the general, but instead the particular. Thus, in *Phaedrus* he does not perceive much more than the sublime criticism of a speech by Lysias rather than a treatise on rhetoric and beauty or – as Schleiermacher assumed – dialectics. There is only one lesson to be drawn from Grillparzer's selective perception: rhetoric without dialectics is a futile undertaking. Naturally, Plato did, in Grillparzer's view, advance far beyond the topic under discussion – as in the case of every major writer the actual reason for writing is taken up only to go to a point beyond.[5] Grillparzer never tries to pin Plato down to a system; he appears only to have taken note of the aporias, which concerned him most. In a note he made in 1862 we read:

> The main task of Socrates, one which Plato continued in his dialogs, was obviously the following: to get the Athenians – such a wonderful people, the likes of which have never again been known in history, who, however, because of their sanguine temperament had a flaw, which was to undertake the most important things only in response to a whim, to some kind of feeling or passion – used to thinking, used to the investigation he calls dialectics. For that reason, the inquiry is always carried out with painstaking precision, the result, however, is lacking, although in philosophy the result ought indeed to be the main issue.[6]

On repeated occasions, Grillparzer mentions the "hogwash" which he compares to the verbose speech in tragedies; his explanation for this, and he is likely right, is the tendency of the Athenians toward "Räsonnement."[7] The form of these dialogs is, in his eyes, superior to their philosophical validity. Philosophy appears to be less a matter of teaching or theory that is capable of being transformed into a state of the highest abstraction, than an activity, a working with and on words. The achievement of Plato is precisely the work on language: "Plato [is] entirely modern in the emotional dissection of the original notions."[8] It is not the definition that is fascinating, but the dissection; not the result, but the process of analysis.

It is safe to say that for Grillparzer Plato was the only recognized authority among the philosophers. Everything that philosophy has otherwise to show for itself is preformed in him and his work.[9] Grillparzer is more interested in the procedure. Thus, it is not without reason that he takes note of the "stationary" element that distinguishes the tragedies of Aeschylus and transforms itself into garrulousness in the works of Sophocles and Euripides.[10] Grillparzer's interest is focused neither on epistemology nor on the ethical or political maxims. What concerns him is the formal quality of this thinking which seems to be self-sufficient in its aimlessness. Philosophy appears to have been a therapy for the Athenians, and it is precisely the inconclusiveness of the dialogs which leads Grillparzer to esteem the "divine Plato."[11] It is as if he wanted to overlook the consequences of Plato's train of thought simply in order to better appreciate the rhetorical and psychological dimension. And because these dialogs present themselves as works of art, they have validity and permanence for Grillparzer, who also claims to see life in the Age of Antiquity mirrored there in a highly concrete fashion. What Plato's philosophy loses in validity from a theoretical standpoint tends to become more binding from a practical point of view.

IV.

In nineteenth-century Austrian philosophy Plato obviously plays a less significant role than does Aristotle. When Theodor Gomperz wrote his *Greek Thinkers* he appears to have approached Plato with major reservations. Accordingly, the *Greek Thinkers* deserve attention solely by virtue of their influence on a wide range of personalities. For Karl Popper, for instance, they became an important authority. Benito Mussolini, for his part, gave them careful study,[12] and Sigmund Freud ranked them among the ten most important books in his life.[13]

Theodor Gomperz's son Heinrich wrote extensively about the reservations his father had about Plato. His father spent more than three years working on the sections on Plato, but it seems that during the course of this work he clearly changed his mind about the Greek philosopher. According to the son, the material simply became too much for his father, whose difficulties were also increased by a certain inability to relate to the key points of Platonic thought (theory of ideas, immortality, religious-conservative attitude).[14] Theodor Gomperz had certainly given credit to Plato, Heinrich Gomperz said, but he had given a condescending smile to the theory of ideas and had argued that the idea of immortality and the uplifting power of virtue was not supported by good arguments and that the ideal state was scarcely within the realm of human capabilities. But his father had, Heinrich Gomperz went on, identified Plato as the discoverer of association of ideas, regarding him as a precursor of the emancipation of women and praising him as the originator of an electoral process for the representation of minorities. All in all, his father had not succeeded in presenting the unity of Plato's thought, but, at the same time, had never tried to press the wide range of thoughts into the Procrustean bed of a system.

Theodor Gomperz saw himself forced to expose the fallacies of Platonism, and this was not to be without consequence. On the other hand, the Platonic dialogs seemed to him to be the place for "free, unconditional dialog, inquiry, and research."[15] The fact that he supported the philosophy of experience of someone like Democritus and condemned the theory of ideas is typical of philologists at the end of the nineteenth century. But the fact that he succumbed to the "spell of Plato" is equally understandable – as is the fact that he changed his mind about Plato while he was working on the book. Grillparzer, for his part, simply ignored the theory of ideas; it appeared to him to be relatively uninteresting, and he did not concern himself with the unity of Platonic thought either. Theodor Gomperz distanced himself from the theory of ideas, and he also lost sight of this unity of thought. Instead, he became more and more interested in the formal qualities of the individual dialogs, especially in the procedure Plato used to present his arguments.

Crucial to the intellectual development of Theodor Gomperz was his close association with British philology, philosophy, and social sciences. He dealt very intensively with the works of George Grote and John Stuart Mill. Mill's review of Grote's book on Plato found its way into the German edition of Mill's writings, for which Gomperz was responsible. The review appeared in the twelfth and final volume, and it had been translated by none other than the young doctor of medicine Siegmund [sic!] Freud.[16] Freud had been given the job of translation at the recommendation of Brentano.[17] The bias against the metaphysicist Plato is clearly evident in Mill's writings; however, this rejection of the philosopher goes hand in hand with a re-evaluation of the dialectician:

> The real merits, however, of the Platonic dialectics are not dependent on this religious and metaphysical superstructure; and before we follow Plato farther on that slippery ground, we must dwell a little on the debt mankind owe to him for this, incomparably his greatest gift.[18]

On repeated occasions Mill attempts – in concordance with Grote – to emphasize Plato's importance as a dialectician rather than as a moralist, although he is aware that Plato was, first and foremost, definitely a moralist.[19] At the same time both scholars are conscious of the inconsistencies of Platonic thought, especially in respect of the definition of virtue.[20] The previously admired theory of ideas thus met its death "in a fog of mystical Pythagoreanism."[21]

Anglo-Saxon criticism of Plato tends to focus on the dialog *Theaetetus* because it concerns the essential question as to what "knowledge" is. I will not here go into Plato's complex line of argumentation against the celebrated epigram of Protagoras "homo-mensura" and George Grote's defense of it, but what is important in this context is that, while Grote and Mill indeed recognize that the course of the dialog is inconclusive, at the same time they consider the questions it raises as essential to philosophy itself. Grote concludes – and in so doing wins approval from Mill – that the following is the key to Gomperz's approach: All of Plato's critics are preoccupied with the notion that they are dealing with a body of ideas and a ready-made system,

> even when professedly modifying it. Their admiration for Plato is not satisfied unless they conceive him in the professorial chair as a teacher, surrounded by a crowd of learners, all under the obligation (incumbent on learners generally) to believe what they hear. Reasoning upon such a basis, the Platonic dialogues present themselves to me as a mystery. They exhibit neither identity of the teacher, nor identity of the matter taught: the composer (to use various Platonic comparisons) is Many, and not One – he is more complex than Typhôs.[22]

Gomperz tries to provide a precise analysis of the various attempts to define what constitutes knowledge: The fact that the source of our knowledge is sensual perception makes this dialog in particular important and interesting for philosophical debate even in the twentieth century.[23] Here, again, it is not so much the right answer or the result that is significant, it is the procedure that Socrates uses. First of all, in the *Theaetetus* there is repeated reference to the fact that no positive results in any shape or form can be expected from this dialog. Furthermore, Socrates presents himself as a helpful intermediary:

> It is not as critic that Socrates is introduced, but as *accoucheur*, for the son of the "esteemed and portly" midwife Phaenarete assists into the world the thoughts of the youthful Theaetetus, whose portrait is painted in the most sympathetic colours. It is only because at these intellectual births some discrimination is required between mere phantoms and genuine offspring, that it becomes incumbent on Socrates to test the thoughts of which Theaetetus is delivered, and decide whether they can live or no.[24]

It is significant that the disputant is given a degree of freedom, which must not be mistaken for arbitrariness, although it definitely does considerably limit the position of authority held by Socrates. The dialog *Theaetetus* was especially important to Austrian philosophers in many other cases, and for that reason will be mentioned again in the following.

Theodor Gomperz also devoted a good deal of attention to the dialog *Phaedrus*. As Grillparzer already observed, its issue is that of overcoming the pure rhetoric of Lysias; Socrates can counter with a language far superior to the flowery speech of Lysias and others like him. However, there is more substance to this dialog, for Plato also wanted to overcome what poetic writing otherwise consists of; he would turn his back on it here, even if it was supported by

> the two pillars of dialectic and psychology. Himself one of the greatest among authors, if not the greatest of all, he mounts here to a height from which he looks down upon all authorship and all rhetoric, recognizes and sets forth all their weaknesses and drawbacks with incomparable depth of insight.[25]

This dialog allows Gomperz to pay tribute to Plato's procedure, one which rejects every dogmatic commitment and makes writing itself debatable. Schleiermacher described the necessity for the reader to become actively involved in the text in order to open its secrets.[26] Of course, we are talking here about the philologist's Plato and not the philosopher's Plato. Heinrich Gomperz repeatedly appears to censure his father for not investigating thoroughly the philosophical aspects of Plato's dialogs. Nevertheless, the father's attempts are indeed impressive at every phase of the work because he succeeds in defending in discursive fashion the variety of Platonic thought against any attempt at a one-sided approach. He views Plato's works as a process and makes no attempt to overlook the fallacies. In his eyes, Plato is the "great original thinker" who, when "he has trodden the path of error to the end, [...] is nearer to the truth than if he had halted half-way."[27] Had he not read Grote and Mill, who both had drawn attention to those qualities in Plato's work that were worthy of praise and beyond all metaphysical concern, Theodor Gomperz probably would never have reached this far in his judgment on Plato.

V.

A special variation in the reception of Plato in Austria is worth mentioning. In 1897 the young Heinrich Gomperz published a work entitled *Grundlegung der Neusokratischen Philosophie*, in which he characterized Plato as "the most noble, the richest, and the most reliable source" for understanding Socrates.[28] In it he tells of a strange group, which took seriously the Socratic maxim that a good person could suffer no evil. Accordingly, the members of this group thought bad marks in school were not to be taken seriously. The group's motto was: "Paidias charin" – "for the love of the game." Adherents to this neo-Socratic teaching held the view that everything is merely a game and that all human activity has no serious purpose, but is instead part of a game. For Gomperz, the *Paidia* offers a way to transform the world altogether. All activity will be merely for the sake of the game:

> It will happen [...] that the simplest farmer will no longer respond to the question "Why do you till the soil?" by saying, "In order to make a living!" Instead, he will reply: "*paidias charin.*" And the wisest scholar will no longer respond to the question "Why do you ponder?" by saying, "In order to benefit mankind." He, too, will reply: "*paidias charin.*" Thus man will become similar to God, who, when asked "Why did you create the world?" could only respond by saying, "For the sake of the game, *paidias charin.*"[29]

A rather simple solution to social and theological problems by a man from a family of good standing! Socratic irony here undergoes transformation into Viennese decadence. Socrates, the Platonic Socrates, becomes the advocate of a new code of conduct, which can deliver humanity from evil by avoiding all worldly interests.

Of course, this pronouncement is not to be taken completely seriously, and the jocular tone, paradoxically, clearly offers an opportunity to do justice to Platonism in all its complexity. What appears here to be a joke is a clear indication of the degree to which the Socratic teachings were internalized. What, on the one hand, could be regarded as a game or *paidia* could, on the other hand, be interpreted as an inclination toward experimentation, something which is revocable, something which opens up possibilities and then again can be revoked. There is, however, a deeper significance to the fact that the *décadents* in Vienna chose Socrates of all people as their patron saint. This becomes especially apparent when one looks to Nietzsche who regarded Socrates as the buffo, the harlequin, the epitome of the *décadent*. Plato, on the other hand, is considered the artist par excellence, but this is only the case if the ethical and political substance, which constitutes Platonism, is disregarded. If the only thing that is important is *paidia*, the game, then one can either have a good laugh with this adaptation of Socrates on the part of *Jung Wien* or else even dismiss it as being irrelevant. However, this perspective is revealing in terms of the mentality that lies behind it: once again, philosophy no longer appears as a system or even as a reliable science, but instead as an activity with no strings attached. In the case of Heinrich Gomperz, philosophy is not brought down from the heavens to the people as it were. It is, instead, freed from the shackles of dogmatism and academia and transformed into a concept of art.

I must confess that when one looks at these things with the strict tradition of thought in mind then the approaches of the young Heinrich Gomperz do seem somewhat outrageous and juvenile. It is a naïve utopia devised by a young man from a well-to-do home for whom it is possible to solve all social and ethical problems by taking a detour through a very subjectively adapted Socratic philosophy. Of course it is difficult to distinguish between irony and seriousness (of intent). However, this ambiguity is what gives the text its particular appeal as a departure from accepted academic practice. At the same time, it demonstrates that henceforth philosophizing can be possible not only in the hallowed halls of academia, but that it can also find its way back onto the street and into day-to-day life. It shows that the problems of the workday in particular would be easier to master if people were capable of philosophical observation. Having said that, it is conceivable that someone who heard all this talk about everything being for the sake of a game could interpret it as downright dangerous cynicism.

VI.

The "spell of Plato" exerted a lasting influence especially around the turn of the century. There was scarcely a thinker whose attention was not drawn to him. Wittgenstein frequently mentions the *Theaetetus* – something which comes as no real surprise. And he always cites the same passage concerning the object of "to imagine"; Wittgenstein does not reproduce the text verbatim, but instead appears to paraphrase it,[30] thus making it difficult to trace precisely the link to Plato. Typically, it is a matter of semantics: for example, the word "vorstellen" (to imagine) has entirely different aspects of contextual meaning than the word "to kill."

For Ernst Mach, Plato's allegory of the cave is a successful example of how effective the popular notion of an antithesis between appearance and reality can be. He considers the allegory to be "a pregnant and poetical fiction" that was, however, "not thought out to its final consequences" and therefore exerted "an unfortunate influence on our world-view": "The universe, of which nevertheless we are a part, became completely separated from us, and was removed an infinite distance away."[31] This is where the criticism of metaphysics sets in. Plato seems to have the right approach, but the consequences of his failure to carry through with the allegory are fatal.

The most radical criticism of Plato comes from Karl Popper, whose reception of Plato merits special mention not so much because of its philosophical substance but because of the tenacity with which the demystification takes place. Popper cites R.H.S. Crossman's *Plato To-Day* from the year 1937 but also makes reference to George Grote and Theodor Gomperz: "This interesting book [i.e., Crossman's *Plato To-Day*] (like the works of Grote and Th. Gomperz) has greatly encouraged me to develop my rather unorthodox views on Plato, and to follow them up to their rather unpleasant conclusions."[32] With amazing over-meticulousness Popper gathers together every small detail he can find to use against Plato. Even Gomperz is taken to task for succumbing to the spell of Plato. In this manner, the book becomes, in a very impressive way, a commitment to the importance that the author attaches to Plato, while, at the same time, the book is a settling of accounts on Plato's political attitude and his thinking generally. And Popper readily admits to this – albeit at the end of an appendix that includes his response to Levinson's critique:

> Yet I do not wish to end this long discussion without reaffirming my conviction of Plato's overwhelming intellectual achievement. My opinion that he was the greatest of all philosophers has not changed. Even his moral and political philosophy is, as an intellectual achievement, without parallel, though I find it morally repulsive, and indeed horrifying.[33]

Popper's commitment to the spell of Plato could hardly be more succinct. The philosopher Plato is blamed for forming the theory, which paved the way for fascism, National Socialism, and Stalinism. Popper is, like Gomperz, no longer concerned about determining the possibilities of error or erroneous actions themselves and then committing himself to them. For him Plato becomes the most consistent dogmatist of an anti-enlightenment and mystifying attitude. Unfortunately, it is not apparent from this book – in which polemics has such a dominant place – where precisely the overwhelming achievement of the Greek thinker could, indeed, lie; this aspect very obviously distinguishes Popper from Gomperz. He simply continues, as far as I can see, Plato's train of thought. The more idealistic Plato's portrayal of his ruler, the more negative it becomes politically, Popper claims:

> The great importance which Plato attaches to a philosophical education of the rulers must be explained by other reasons – by reasons which must be purely political. The main reason I can see is the need for increasing to the utmost the authority of the rulers. If the education of the auxiliaries functions properly, there will be plenty of good soldiers [...]. Thus Plato's philosophical education has a definite political function. *It puts a mark on the rulers, and it establishes a barrier between the rulers and the ruled.*[34]

Popper is the last of a line of Austrian thinkers who have typically regarded Plato in an anti-idealistic light. Even the attempt to make the best people into rulers is contrary, as Popper sees it, to Plato's claim that he is seeking an ideal state. The empirical method is mobilized against the Utopia, which is not regarded by Popper as a principle that gives us grounds for hope and keeps us alive and well. Instead, it is depicted as a constraint that leads to destruction.

VII.

Contrary to Popper's own intention, I, for my part, cannot read his text as a fundamental refutation of Plato. I see it as more of an attempt at liberation. With an enthusiasm that demands respect and a persistence that is irritating, these people go after Plato as if that were the way to clean up the house of European thought. It is entirely legitimate to ask whether this effort could not have been directed also toward making the complexity of Platonic thought somewhat more vivid. This is especially true in the case of Theodor Gomperz, whose critical discussion did, after all, lead to a far more varied result. Popper's autobiography does, indeed, clearly reveal how important Plato was to him as a thinker in cases where the focus was not on political issues.[35]

Hermann Broch took a gentler, almost nostalgic approach to the farewell to Plato. One of his essays, from 1932, is entitled "Leben ohne Platonische Idee" ("Life without the Platonic Idea"). In it, however, he scarcely makes reference to any one of Plato's individual works. But he does argue that Platonism must be regarded as a decisive point in the development of the human race. It appears as the product of the disintegration of religion and, accordingly, the intellectual becomes the guardian of the Platonic idea. At this point, according to Broch, the Platonic is no longer universally binding: "The rule of the intellect passes over to the rule of the worldly, and this marks the beginning of that strange process through which the universally binding character of reasoning, too, is handed over to worldly matters."[36]

The end of Platonism apparently coincides with the end of large fields of philosophy; philosophy itself, insofar as it is identical with ethics and metaphysics, is no longer valid.[37] The intellectual and the hero – this too is a product of the decline of religious (or Platonic) thought – concur, according to Broch, in their rejection of Platonism.[38] Philosophy, and here in particular Platonism itself, has been replaced by a new manner of thinking, "since that which can be scientifically proven takes places exclusively within the tautology of the logical and mathematical."[39] It is highly likely that Broch had the Vienna Circle in mind when he wrote this passage. He assumed that this philosophy was also determined by the desire for a savior, a bringer of salvation, and that "the new Platonic freedom would one day arise out of the darkest constraint of rational reason: the 'irrational ratio': the present state of the world."[40] Whatever Broch may have meant by this, the important point is that the Platonic idea has had its day and that this is utterly deplorable. The end of the Platonic era can be likened to the period of Advent, which is waiting for a new religion, one for which "philosophy is not only a post-but also a pre-religion."[41] The present is regarded as a transitional period, and it is by no means certain whether "the philosophical striving will find its new shape in the bare mathematical formulas or else whether it will be restricted for the time being to poetic expression."[42] Broch, whose text is to be found at the end of a long farewell to Plato, leaves us with this perspective. The farewell is by no means easy and has caused most of those mentioned here sorrow and difficulty. Theodor Gomperz, Popper, and Broch are all looking for an escape from Plato's cave and, at the same, have the feeling they are losing the protection they need.

But do Austrian writers try to escape the cave to which they seem to be confined by the Platonic allegory? Hans Blumenberg provided us with good evidence of the mutations of the cave allegory in the works of Wittgenstein.[43] But as compelling as the allegory may be, it is just as disturbing as the concept of the totalitarian state. It is not because Plato wanted to see all the writers banned from his state that many thinkers have tried to free themselves from this concept. It is because the suggestive power of Plato's thought is so attractive. The kind of literature, which sees itself as committed to such idealistic views and would like to slave away on concrete objects, will not find any hospitality in Plato's works.

Heimito von Doderer, writing on his theory of the novel in 1959, decreed that, for him, idealism was useless. The novelist was, he added, "least of all an idealist, and, for him, Plato's cave allegory is as useless as Kant's *Ding an sich*."[44] This is a brief, but succinct rejection of Plato and his allegory. It well illustrates the dividing line between the complex of Platonic thought and Platonic imagery on the one hand and literary writing on the other. It is precisely at the site of such seismic faults that powerful movements and tremors become noticeable, and that is where Philosophy and Literature have to set up shop – even if it happens to be dangerous.

---

[1] Franz Grillparzer, *Sämtliche Werke: Ausgewählte Briefe, Gespräche, Berichte. Dritter Band*, ed. Peter Frank and Karl Pörnbacher, Munich: Carl Hanser, 1964, p. 1150.
[2] *Ibid.*, p. 1145; here and in the following, my translations.
[3] *Ibid.*, p. 1145.
[4] *Ibid.*, p. 1155.
[5] *Ibid.*, p. 1149.
[6] *Ibid.*, p. 1149f.
[7] *Ibid.*, p. 351.
[8] *Ibid.*, p. 1150.
[9] See Friedrich Kainz, *Grillparzer als Denker: Der Ertrag seines Werks für die Welt- und Lebensweisheit*, Vienna: Verlag der Österreichischen Akademie der Wissenschaften, 1975; Josef Nadler, *Franz Grillparzer*, Vienna: Bergland, 1952. Kainz does not fully take into account Plato's influence, whereas Nadler overestimates it.
[10] Grillparzer, *Sämtliche Werke*, p. 320f.
[11] *Ibid.*, p. 351.
[12] Robert A. Kann, ed., *Theodor Gomperz: Ein Gelehrtenleben im Bürgertum der Franz-Josefs-Zeit. Auswahl seiner Briefe und Aufzeichnungen, 1869-1912, erläutert und zu einer

Darstellung seines Lebens verknüpft von Heinrich Gomperz, Vienna: Verlag der österreichischen Akademie der Wissenschaften, 1974, p. 381.
[13] *Ibid.*, p. 18.
[14] *Ibid.*, p. 301f.
[15] *Ibid.*, p. 184.
[16] John Stuart Mill, *Über Frauenemancipation. Plato. Arbeiterfrage. Socialismus*, Leipzig: Fues' Verlag (R. Reisland), 1880 (= *John Stuart Mill's Gesammelte Werke*. Autorisirte Übersetzung unter Redaction von Professor Dr. Theodor Gomperz. Zwölfter Band. Vermischte Schriften III).
[17] See Kann, *Theodor Gomperz*, p. 106f.
[18] John Stuart Mill, *Collected Works. Volume XI: Essays on Philosophy and the Classics*, Toronto: University of Toronto Press, 1978, p. 406.
[19] *Ibid.*, p. 415.
[20] *Ibid.*, p. 419.
[21] *Ibid.*, p. 421.
[22] *Ibid.*, p. 429f.
[23] Theodor Gomperz, *Griechische Denker: Eine Geschichte der antiken Philosophie*, Vol. 2. Berlin: Walter de Gruyter, 1973 (reprint), p. 433; English edition entitled *Greek Thinkers: A History of Ancient Philosophy*, Vols. II and III, London: John Murray, 1964.
[24] Gomperz, *Greek Thinkers*, Vol. III, p. 157.
[25] *Ibid.*, p. 21.
[26] *Ibid.*, p. 22.
[27] *Ibid.*, p. 265.
[28] Heinrich Gomperz, *Grundlegung der Neusokratischen Philosophie*, Leipzig/Vienna: Franz Deuticke, 1897, p. 9.
[29] *Ibid.*, p. 131f.
[30] See Ludwig Wittgenstein, *Philosophische Grammatik*. Ed. Rush Rhees. Frankfurt a.M.: Suhrkamp, 1969, p. 137, p. 164; and Ludwig Wittgenstein, *Das Blaue Buch. Eine Philosophische Betrachtung. Zettel*. Frankfurt a.M.: Suhrkamp, 1970, p. 303.
[31] Ernst Mach, *The Analysis of Sensations and the Relation of the Physical to the Psychical*, New York: Dover Publications, 1959, p. 11f.
[32] Karl R. Popper, *The Open Society and Its Enemies*. One-volume edition. London: Routledge, 1995, p. 583.
[33] *Ibid.*, p. 226.
[34] *Ibid.*, p. 148; original italics.
[35] Karl R. Popper, *Ausgangspunkte: Meine intellektuelle Entwicklung*. Hamburg: Hoffmann and Campe, 1979, p. 87.
[36] Hermann Broch, *Philosophische Schriften 1. Kritik*. Frankfurt a.M.: Suhrkamp, 1977, p. 47; my translations.
[37] *Ibid.*, p. 49.
[38] *Ibid.*, p. 49.
[39] *Ibid.*, p. 49.
[40] *Ibid.*, p. 51.
[41] *Ibid.*, p. 52.
[42] *Ibid.*, p. 52.
[43] Hans Blumenberg, *Höhlenausgänge*. Frankfurt a.M.: Suhrkamp, 1989, pp. 752-792.
[44] Heimito von Doderer, *Die Wiederkehr der Drachen. Aufsätze, Traktate, Reden*. Munich: Biederstein, 1970, p. 166; my translation.

THE VIENNA CIRCLE AND FREUD

Fred Wilson

University of Toronto

Gustav Bergmann was one of the last of the Vienna Circle to flee. In 1938 Otto Neurath had already been in Amsterdam for several years, and there he arranged for funds to enable his younger colleague to obtain passage to New York. He asked in return only that Bergmann write a memoir of his time as a member of the circle. These recollections have recently been published.[1] Bergmann mentions how in the young left culture of Vienna there was a coming together of sympathizers with the program of the Circle and a number of young Freudians (p. 199). Bergmann was a member of both these groups. Arne Naess, in his somewhat later memoir,[2] describing the meetings of the Circle from the viewpoint of an invited *Ausländer*, also notes how there was cooperation between some of the Freudians and members of the Circle (p. 14ff).[3] So there were personal connections. But the regard in which members of the Vienna Circle held Freud can best be gauged by an anecdote that Bergmann once told,[4] though it does not occur in the memoir. While in Amsterdam waiting for his passage to the United States, Bergmann was despairing of what was happening in Europe. Neurath attempted to reassure him, somewhat at least. "Don't worry," Neurath said, "in 200 years Hitler will be just another mad dictator who lived at the time of Freud." Neurath had no doubt underestimated the evil that had been descending upon Europe and the world. But that is not the point, which is rather that when Neurath, the Marxist and positivist, had to choose a figure as representing not the evil but the greatness of our century, he chose Freud.

Given the criticisms that have more recently been made of Freud's work, and given that the Vienna Circle was a champion of scientific method and of the methodological unity of science,[5] it would seem an odd choice: it would seem that in fact Freud had succeeded in pulling the wool as it were over the eyes of the positivists, misleading them into believing that what he was doing was in fact scientific. I do not, however, think that it is so easy. Gustav Bergmann, who was one of the younger members of the Vienna Circle, had himself undergone analysis in the 1920s – though he never met Freud himself, he did know Anna Freud – and he was later to write a detailed critique and evaluation of psychoanalysis. Furthermore, Egon Brunswik, not a member of the circle, but close to it, wrote the monograph on psychology for Neurath's *International Encyclopedia of Unified Science*;[6] in the latter he provided a critical account of psychoanalysis.

Writing the Austrian Traditions: Relations between Philosophy and Literature.
Ed. Wolfgang Huemer and Marc-Oliver Schuster. Edmonton, Alberta:
Wirth-Institute for Austrian and Central European Studies, 2003. pp. 13-35.

What I propose to do is first to look at psychoanalysis and the psychoanalytic method, to see whether these stand up to the sort of scrutiny upon which the Vienna Circle rightly insisted. In this examination, I will begin with the work of Bergmann and Brunswik, but then go on to comment on some of the recent work of Adolf Grünbaum.[7] I shall suggest that Freud has in fact provided good grounds for accepting his theories, in broad outline at least, and that they pass any sort of reasonable test that the Vienna Circle might have proposed. I shall then go on to look at the broader context, at the shared background in Nietzsche and neo-Kantian philosophy, and at the cultural aims of the Vienna Circle and how Freud's views fit into that framework.

– A –

I. Bergmann and Brunswik

Freud himself acknowledged the impact of Darwinism on his thought and on his approach to the mind. In speaking of Darwinism, I am thinking not so specifically of Darwin's own theories, but rather that broader stream of thought that became a characteristic frame of reference for so much in the nineteenth century. In particular, there came with this frame of reference an emphasis upon *functions*.[8] In psychology the group that most directly took up this theme were the American functionalists. These psychologists were inspired by John Dewey's study in "The Reflex Arc Concept in Psychology."[9] Dewey's emphasis on functions derived as much from his background in Hegelianism and German Romantic philosophy as it did from Darwin. But those who took up Dewey's themes soon dropped the metaphysical trappings and simply looked at the person as an animal whose organs performed certain functions enabling it to survive and reproduce. The mind was one of those organs, and by turning to functions they began to think of psychology as dealing with behavior and not just what could be grasped by our inner consciousness.

The functionalists were not yet behaviorist, but they did make behavior a central part of psychology, and it was not long before the next generation of psychologists became simply behaviorists. They were led by John B. Watson,[10] who was many things besides a behaviorist. He favored classical conditioning over re-inforcement – the latter seemed too close to teleology and all the bad metaphysical theories of mind such as that which one could find, for example, in Dewey. He favored peripheral theories for bodily localization rather than central theories – it seemed easier to get rid of minds if the central nervous system played but a minor role in explaining behavior. But no one is now troubled by re-inforcement theories of learning: metaphysical teleology no longer is a worry for psychologists. As for the issue of peripheral vs. central theories, it too is no longer an issue: with cognitive science the balance has shifted to the central nervous system, but in general psychologists simply take it to be a matter of fact that functions have their bodily locations. Above all, Watson was a metaphysical behaviorist – he simply denied that there are any conscious states. The latter theory is just silly, to use the felicitous expression of C.D. Broad.[11] Watson himself recognized the point when he argued on the one hand that there are no conscious states and on the other that they are to be identified with certain bodily states.[12]

Psychologists now for the most part do not deny conscious states; they simply ignore them, proceeding to study behavior and to explain it in the same sort of causal terms that are used to explain the behavior of stones or trees. Psychologists are now simply methodological behaviorists: psychology has become an objective science, methodologically the same as any other science.[13] To be sure, there is nothing particularly non-scientific about introspection. In principle the data obtained by introspection could be treated in straightforward scientific fashion.[14] What was non-scientific was the insistence that somehow by their nature conscious products escaped the same sort of causal analysis that applied to stones and trees. Scientific psychology had by the end of the century abandoned these mystical ideas. The point is not that behaviorism made psychology into a science but that it made it into an objective science. Psychology was already most of the way there; the parallelistic hypothesis had become common among late nineteenth-century introspectionists, and according to this there was always a physical state of the system parallel to any conscious state. Once this was granted, then there was no need to try to explain behavior in terms of mental states: the parallel physical state sufficed. In that sense, psychology was already prepared for methodological behaviorism.[15] We can therefore see that Watson, however important he was historically, made only a small step when he transformed psychology into an objective science of human behavior.

Bergmann[16] and Brunswik[17] both emphasize the close connection of Freud's work in psychology with that of the American functionalists.[18] Both also emphasize that methodologically there is a close fit, in principle at least, between the psychoanalytic approach to human behavior and that of the methodological behaviorists. It is clear that with its emphasis on the unconscious, psychoanalysis can hardly adopt the introspective methods of the older psychology. At the same time, however, psychoanalysis by the nature of what it is trying to do carries on some of the spirit of the older views, insofar as it must rely for much of its data upon verbal reports of dreams and of purposely uninhibited streams of ideas ("free association").

Brunswik notes how psychology had previously concentrated on sensation, or, what is the same, on peripheral processes. It was only with psychoanalysis that a determined attempt was made to investigate central processes (p. 714). At the same time, however, he criticizes psychoanalysis for its narrow view of functions. In particular, it focuses its attention on proximate effects, tending to ignore the importance of distal effects (p. 678, p. 715). The latter are for the most part social factors. Brunswik is thus criticizing Freud for not taking sufficiently into account social variables. Brunswik therein finds himself strangely allied with what Bergmann called the "nicifiers" such as Karen Horney, who wanted to de-emphasize the sexual in favor of the social. It is a strange criticism, however. As Ernest Jones once remarked, "It would not be a gross exaggeration to say that psycho-analysis is essentially a detailed study of the relations between a child and his parents."[19] The social is thus hardly ignored by psychoanalysis. The point becomes even more evident when one realizes that the socialization of the child, the making of the child fit for society, takes place in the context of the family: it is through the parents that social values and social skills are passed on to future generations.

Bergmann makes a different point. He does not downplay the importance of functions. But functions are merely effects, and, in the case of minds, acquired effects.[20] What science aims at is *causal explanation*, where to speak of causes is to speak, as Ernest Jones had made clear, in Humean fashion, of regularities. Jones contrasts the older concept of causality with that of correlation or regularity. "Psychological science," he states, "any more than any other, cannot do without the latter concept, and in its postulate of orderly relationship subsisting between phenomena must therefore be as deterministic as the rest of science."[21] The ideal is to understand functions as originating within a causal context. Focusing on functions establishes the temptation to teleological thinking, and to the idea that to understand is to grasp the function. As Bergmann puts it, "The disadvantage inherited from the Darwinian outlook I see in the propensity to teleological thinking and in the tendency to take teleological patterns for scientific explanation."[22] This is a temptation to which Freud and the psychoanalysts too often succumbed, Bergmann argues. He cites in particular the so-called death wish or death instinct.[23] The endpoint becomes a goal or terminus which in turn becomes explanatory. There is the same temptation in the Deweyan side of American functionalism. What is important from the viewpoint of explanation is not functions but rather the causes of those functions. This led the American functionalists almost directly, by way of Watson, into learning theory. This of course is the point of the slogan that psychology seeks "stimulus-response" relations.

It was Bergmann's argument that if one looked carefully at psychoanalytic theory, then there was nothing incompatible with that and learning theory in experimental psychology (p. 365ff). The first training of libidinal hungers occurs at an early stage of infancy, long before there is any significant development of language. But the process is complicated by the development of language, that is, by the development of the human symbolic apparatus (p. 367). The point is that symbols can in the case of humans start the same train of events as the thing symbolized: ideas are potent. The complexities of the human personality cannot be understood apart from the many roles language plays in learning. These are complexities far beyond the skills of the experimental psychologist to grasp – though in principle at least there is no reason to suppose that these complexities are not the cumulative result of rather simple learning processes.

At the same time, however, if one does want to come to grips with such complexities, if one does want to put them into some sort of causal story, then one must perforce work in ways that take for granted the complexities of the symbolic apparatus of language. This means, on the one hand, that the methods will hardly be those of the controlled experiment. Other means must be found to explore the complexities. It means, on the other hand, that the theorizing will in fact and inevitably be relatively loose. In terms of theory, one could reasonably expect nothing much better than what Freud and the psychoanalysts have provided.

The verdict of the Vienna Circle, then, as represented by Bergmann and Brunswik, was that on the whole one should be prepared to accept the scientific claims of Freud. There were to be sure negative tendencies. In particular there was the tendency to lapse into the sort of teleological thinking that was characteristic of German Romantic philosophy. But those awkward details aside, they were prepared to accept the claim of psychoanalytic theory that it passed the verifiability test: one could take it for granted that it was reasonable to claim that it was scientific.[24]

II. Grünbaum

The great British psychologist Henry Maudsley[25] recognized the limits of introspectionist psychology.[26] As a psychiatrist he was clear that there are often unconscious forces at work in or on the human mind. He therefore proposed that one use the method Cuvier had developed in anatomy, the comparative method.[27] What he proposed comparing were the sane and the insane.[28] But in order to do this, one already has to have some method for exploring the mind of the non-normal person. The best that Maudsley could suggest was some retreat to physiology. But exactly how physiology was to do the job remained unclear indeed. It was a program, not a practical method for undertaking practical research.[29] In the end, he failed to provide a serious method of research for the non-normal.[30]

It was Freud's genius to have discovered a method for dealing with, if not the insane, then at least the non-normal.[31] It built on the fact that even the insane have a set of symbols: their language. Their symbols may not be normal; their language may be confused and confusing in many ways. But it is for all that language. As we look back on the history, the method is not all that surprising. Psychologists had used the method of association to investigate sensory phenomena. This method involved the mind attending to associations connected to a stimulus and inferring from these the genetic antecedents of conscious events. The theory goes back to practices recorded by Aristotle.[32] Orators had learned about association and had used the technique to help them in remembering the topics they wished to present in their speeches. Aristotle recorded this knowledge in his three laws of association. With Hobbes and Locke these laws were recalled in the seventeenth century, and they became a central part of psychological theory, of learning theory specifically, a place which they retain to this day.[33]

Like King John, we all have our little ways.[34] Often enough, more often than we perhaps like, there are thoughts and impulses that force their way into our consciousness; often enough, more often than we perhaps like, there are actions and behavior that impose themselves upon us. This is true of all of us. Most of these little ways can safely be ignored, passed off as simply slips or accidents. But at times and for some people they become crippling. These are our psychoneuroses. Philosophers have recognized that if we are to talk of free will then we must acknowledge that there are what can be called second order desires, desires about our own desires. The point about our psychoneurotic thoughts and impulses is that these are for the most part things that we do not desire. We do not want them yet they impose themselves upon us. It is my thought, my impulse, my action, yet it is not mine and not wanted.[35]

Because these thoughts are not wanted, we ignore them: they are not ours, we say. Psychology in particular ignored them. This was not merely because it had difficulty dealing with the higher or central processes. They were not even included in the "in principle" sketches of psychological theory. Slips were slips, and did not need to be accounted for. Even Maudsley, for all his success in treating the mentally ill, simply ignores these little ways. But they are in fact part of our mental life, part of human behavior. They too, on the very principles traditional psychologists were using, ought to be thought of as having causes. But when slips become incapacitating, they need to be recognized. His training as a physician sensitized Freud to these cases. His training as a scientist made him search for causes. His humanity led him to seek a way to free people from these slips, these little ways that impose themselves upon us.

It is not possible simply to forbid these thoughts, impulses, and actions. Freud in fact tried this route. Following Breuer he tried using hypnosis. The patient was put under hypnosis and the physician directed the patient to in effect remember earlier experiences that seemed to lie behind the symptoms. Upon remembering them the patient would cathartically re-experience them. The symptom would disappear. In effect, the use of hypnotic suggestion amounted to the physician instructing the patient to stop having those little ways. The little ways did indeed stop. Unfortunately, it was only for a while, or only to be replaced by another little way.

The aim is to make the patient free, that is, free in the sense of being in charge of his or her own thoughts and impulses. The method of forbidding does not work. And Freud came to understand why it does not work: it fails to uncover the causes. We all smile when we hear tales of William Ewart Gladstone, while he was Queen Victoria's Prime Minister, taking prostitutes from the East End of London to Downing Street and giving them scripture-based lessons in the expectation of reforming them. He had little effect. Forbidding prostitution is not effective, and neither is making suggestions or giving instructions. One must get to the causes, and only if one seizes control of them will one eliminate the problem. It is the same with our little ways: it is necessary to seize control of the causes, and only then will one be able to free oneself of the problem.

It was with this aim in view that Freud went from hypnosis to the method of free association and dream analysis.[36] The method of free association proceeds as psychologists had traditionally proceeded, by recording the associations that occurred when a certain stimulus was produced. Traditionally, however, the stimulus was controlled – the primary concern was sensory processes. Moreover, the response was also controlled. Details are not important: the point is that the method involved constrained associations.[37] Freud used the same method but with no constraints.[38] The patient was purposely instructed simply to report the ideas that came to mind, and by looking at these ideas one could come to an understanding of the associations that had become established in the patient's mind.[39]

The injunction of the Delphic Oracle was to "Know Thyself." This was the aim of Freud's method. It was to discover the patterns of causation that were at work in the patient. And it was not simply a matter of the physician coming to know these patterns. It was rather the patient, him- or herself, coming to know these patterns. Nor was the aim simply intellectual. The aim rather was to give the patient the knowledge that he or she needed to become a person who is free, in control of him- or herself. If you know yourself, that is, know yourself in a practical way, then it is you who will be in charge.

Freud's basic argument was that his method did put the person in control of him- or herself. In Freud's later terminology, it is the ego that is the center of consciousness, the surveyor of reality that provides the knowledge of how best the instinctual urges might be satisfied. The instinctual urges themselves he refers to as the id. It is here that one finds the mental energy that moves us to act. Much of the id is beyond consciousness, and some of the urges of the id lie unsatisfied, repressed by the ego at an early stage of life because they are found by the ego to be unacceptable: so dangerous are they that they must be repressed. But they will have their way, one way or another. It is these repressed instinctual urges that are the roots of psychoneurotic ideas and impulses. The ego strenuously attempts to deny the existence of these urges, but in vain: if they cannot be satisfied directly, then they will be satisfied indirectly. These dangerous impulses have to do with the child's relations with his or her parents. In therapy, the patient-therapist relationship mimics in many respects the parent-child relationship. This is the phenomenon known as transference.[40] The similarities enable the associative mechanisms to work, and the patient begins to recall the experiences and the impulses that he or she has been forbidding him- or herself to remember. The patient begins to recognize the causes of those ideas and impulses that are found to come quite involuntarily into one's consciousness: one begins to understand the real causes, deep in the past, of one's little ways. He or she also becomes aware of the forces that are leading him or her to resist acknowledging these events even as events let alone causes. The analyst may make suggestions as to the relationships that are present – his or her experience will provide many plausible hypotheses. But there is only one test as to which are the correct hypotheses. It is not simply that the patient finds them acceptable. It is that in coming to know them the patient acquires self-understanding, the knowledge of him- or herself that is required to put him or her in control, that is, in control of him- or herself, that is, in *conscious* control of him- or herself. The most frequent outcome is one in which "*Repression* is replaced by a *condemning judgement* carried out along the best lines." A second sort of outcome is sublimation, the re-direction of the impulse to some culturally approved end. On this outcome, it becomes possible for "the unconscious instincts revealed by [analysis] to be employed for the useful purposes which they would have found earlier if development had not been interrupted." Then there is the third possible outcome, the actual satisfaction of the libidinal impulse. As Freud noted, "A certain portion of the repressed libidinal impulses has a claim to direct satisfaction and ought to find it in life."[41] Whichever outcome the ego allows, the libidinal energy receives a release which the ego approves. No longer must there be a release which intrudes in unwelcome fashion on the territory of the ego: the ego is now in control. As Freud put it, "Psycho-analysis is an instrument to enable the ego to achieve a progressive conquest of the id."[42] Where *id* was, there *ego* shall be.

It is in this sense that one must understand Freud's remark that the test of truth for any hypothesis about the causes of the patient's psychoneurotic behavior must be that it "tallies" with his or her thoughts and behavior. Freud puts it this way: "[the patient's] conflicts will only be successfully solved and his [or her] resistances overcome if the anticipatory ideas he [or she] is given tally with what is real in him [or her]."[43]

Adolf Grünbaum, in his work on *The Foundations of Psychoanalysis*,[44] has argued carefully the thesis of Bergmann and Brunswik that psychoanalytic theory fits the notion of science defended by the Vienna Circle. He defends the scientific nature of the theory on the one hand against those such as Habermas and Ricoeur who want to place Freud's thought in the anti-scientific stream deriving from German Romantic philosophy which insists upon the idea that the study of human behavior requires a method radically different in kind from the method that science uses to study stones and trees. And then, on the other hand, he also defends the scientific status of psychoanalysis against the claims of Popper and others that it cannot be scientific because it is not falsifiable. On Grünbaum's reading, Freudian theory is falsifiable and the method that Freud attempts to use to justify his claims is of a piece with the methods of physics and biology.

At the same time, however, Grünbaum also argues that the specific psychoanalytic method provides no foundation for the theoretical claims. It is science but not good science: it is science without foundations. Indeed, his suggestion is that not only does the theory lack foundations but that there are counterexamples to its claims. It may be falsifiable, but it is also falsified. The theory is in this respect like astrology. Since Freud bases his claims for the theory on the fact that it has had success in the therapeutic context, Grünbaum concentrates on this argument. This is the claim that the theory is supported because the hypotheses located by the theory in fact "tally," to use Freud's term, with what the patient discovers within him- or herself. Grünbaum (p. 138) quotes Freud on this point, about how hypotheses must tally with the experience of the analysand, but argues that Freud provides no grounds for accepting the claim that the hypotheses do so tally. On the contrary, since there are many cases in which psychoneurotic symptoms undergo spontaneous remission (p. 160), there are no grounds to think that the hypotheses finally accepted by the analysand arc anything more than mere suggestions of the analyst.

But, does this really touch the claim made in Freud's "tally argument"? This argument is to the effect that the psychoanalytic hypotheses are necessary to effect a cure. What, however, is a cure? A cure, as we have seen, is not the mere absence of the symptom. It is rather a matter of the patient coming to be in control over his or her ideas and impulses, becoming free from the imposition of unwanted things on his or her consciousness or behavior. A "cure" in this sense could never be anymore than partial, a fact that Freud recognized. But in the context of Grünbaum's argument, the point is that spontaneous remission by itself does not count as a cure. Breuer's use of hypnosis could free the patient of a symptom. It aimed at helping the person recall the event or events that had caused the symptom, and cathartically relive the experience to eliminate the forces that were otherwise finding their outlet as it were in the symptom. But this method by-passed the forces that normally prevented the recalling of the crucial event or events. It bypassed, in other words, the resistances, the forces that were blocking the recall. But these forces, too, are part of the problem. Since the method of hypnosis did not deal with these factors, it could not effect a cure, it could not free the patient, and put him or her in control. Nor does the fact that other therapeutic methods also have success in eliminating psychoneurotic symptoms (p. 161) tell against Freud's claim. On the one hand, it is to be expected on psychoanalytic principles that such will occur: just as a sympathetic listener will do a world of wonders, so can aversion therapy. However, this does not mean that the patient is cured in the sense of being genuinely free; it does not mean that the ego is now in control. On the other hand, if these therapies really do uncover the causes of the psychoneurotic thoughts, impulses and behavior, then why ought that to tell against the psychoanalytic theories? It tells against those theories only if there is disagreement in the assigning of causes. That different therapies are equally successful does not by itself imply that those therapies disagree as to the nature of the causes, the knowledge of which will enable the ego – the person – to take full, or at least fuller, control of his or her own life.

I conclude that Grünbaum's argument that Freud has not vindicated his theories is not successful. To be sure, not all aspects of psychoanalytic theorizing are reasonable; Bergmann and Brunswik had already made this point. But much of the psychoanalytic theorizing is scientific in terms acceptable to the Vienna Circle, at least within the limits imposed by the difficulty of the material: human beings after all, and to repeat, are very complex creatures. The point here is that not only does it pass the test of being an empirical or testable theory but that it is well founded in the facts. There are data that support the theory. These data come from the cures that have been effected by the methods that emerged from Freud's struggle to help people free themselves from aspects of themselves that they did not want. These data are not merely the remission or disappearance of psychoneurotic symptoms; the data consist in the fact that as a result of psychoanalytic therapy patients do come to be in control of themselves, do, in other words, become free – not, to be sure, fully free, but freer, much freer, than they were. Ask them.

– B –

Freud's theories are, I think we can safely say, both empirical and soundly based. In his insistence that our little ways, our slips of the tongue, our dreams, all have causes that need explaining, his work was of a piece with that of Maudsley, though deeper and more comprehensive. Where he went beyond others such as Maudsley was in discovering a tool to explore the causal structure of those little ways. But Freud also went beyond people like Maudsley in his humanity. Unlike Maudsley, he did not attribute the ills of the son to the fact that the father had masturbated.[45] We have seen the three ways in which repressed impulses might express themselves once they are brought under the conscious control of the patient. They might be consciously repressed, they might be allowed to sublimate into wants with more culturally acceptable objects, or they might simply be satisfied. Freud showed that indeed many of the prohibitions that late nineteenth century society imposed on people were in fact pointless, that there were no problems to be found in allowing many of these impulses to be satisfied, and, even more importantly, that repressing them could in fact be dangerous, both to the individual and to society. In this respect, Freud represented in another way the freeing of human beings from unreasonable shackles.

What Freud was arguing is that, in itself, there is nothing wrong with pleasure, and if it can be obtained without harm to oneself and others then there is no reason not to accept it. The idealists had denied the importance of pleasure. "What Act of Legislature was there that *thou* shouldst be Happy?" Carlyle asked,[46] and rejected utilitarianism, or, more generally, Epicureanism. This he did in the name of the higher self, which was held to impose a variety of higher obligations which might well conflict with utility and require the denial of pleasure. Kant could think of few sins more troubling than masturbation. We can smile at that, and use it to provide our undergraduates with something else at which to smirk. But people at one time did in fact take that sort of thing seriously: witness Maudsley. If we are now free from those shackles, then it is due in part to Freud, but not Freud alone. Freud as a humanist was part of the tradition deriving from the Enlightenment, aiming to free humankind from the chains of superstition and to provide through science rather than metaphysics and theology the tools that could be used to improve the human lot. The Vienna Circle was part of that same tradition.

Moritz Schlick, who, while he lived, was the center of the Circle, wrote on ethics. His little book on *The Problems of Ethics* is exemplary.[47] He argued that the primary motivators were the pleasantness and unpleasantness of our feelings.[48] Otto Neurath, too, was another major figure in the Circle who also looked to Epicurus to provide the basic framework for ethics.[49] Like Neurath, Schlick rejected the whole idea that ethical principles somehow find their basis in a self that is outside the world of ordinary experience. Like Neurath, he accepted the basic premise of Epicureanism, that human beings aim at pleasure, and he rejected the romantic ideal expressed by Carlyle that there are duties which demand that we forgo pleasure, duties which demand that we live up to standards in a way that denies us the pleasures of this world.

John Stuart Mill had argued,[50] no doubt with the example of Carlyle in mind, that pleasure or happiness was the test of morality because pleasure was not only one of the ends that people seek but the only end.[51] This, he emphasized, was not to say that people did not seek things other than pleasure. On the contrary, there are many ends that humans have, and to aim simply at pleasure almost certainly ensures that it will not be attained. But those things at which humans do aim are *pleasurable*; as Mill put it, they are sought as "parts" of pleasure. Such things are first sought as means to pleasure, and then they come through association to be in themselves pleasant. And so Mill argues on the basis of these psychological principles that people not only do but must seek pleasure: that is just the way they are.[52] However, since they must seek pleasure, it is unreasonable to propose duties of the sort that Carlyle clearly had in mind that would require them to seek some end contrary to that of pleasure. There may be no Act of the Legislature that makes it obligatory that people seek pleasure, but for all that it is true that they *must* seek pleasure.[53] This fact delimits the range of things that could be our duties. Since people are going to seek to maximize their pleasure, what one is going to count as worthy of pursuit, what one is going to count as one's duty, has to be something that will produce that effect. We need an ethics, then, which is an ethics without renunciation.[54]

This was Mill's argument. It in fact goes back as far as Epicurus himself. Schlick does not quite understand Mill on this point; he takes more seriously than one should G.E. Moore's criticism of the inference from "desired" to "desirable." But in his own argument, Schlick adopts the Epicurean position, that what is sought is sought because it is pleasant, that nothing is sought that is not pleasant, and that the task of ethics is to find those things that can as a matter of fact bring about a maximization of pleasure. Schlick's view was that a liberal state, with a minimum of government, would best serve these interests. Neurath thought it better to wed Marx and Epicurus: he argued that one could best achieve the greatest happiness in a society with a planned economy and that Marxist theory pointed the way to such an economic order.[55] These differences are, from the philosophical point of view, differences in detail, mere matters of fact – though of course from the perspective of political action they make a world of difference.

But what of the heroes of whom Carlyle made so much? John Stuart Mill pointed out the problem with reference to St. Simon Stylites.[56] It was a case that showed what people can do, but, surely, he argued, it was not a case that showed what they ought to do. St. Simon could do what he did atop his pillar because in fact he took joy in the idea that he would, by virtue of his being high up there in the air of Asia Minor, be the first to see the Lord upon his second coming. It was Mill's argument that through a process of association, Simon came to feel pleasure in that thought. Schlick makes much the same point: the hero who sacrifices him- or herself for the cause, Carlyle's hero, who forsakes pleasure for duty, does in fact take joy in knowing that he or she is doing what is required.[57]

The problem is that all this just does not ring true. Carlyle is a better psychologist than Mill or Schlick. There is an important sense in which the hero, whether it is Simon or a member of the Hitler SS killing squads, does not take joy in what he or she is doing: it is duty, not pleasure. Duty is the forsaking of pleasure. Whatever Schlick says, it does involve renunciation. Neither Mill nor Schlick make plausible how it is that human beings can find joy in renunciation.

It is Freud's contribution to psychology to reveal the mechanisms by which this happens. It is also his contribution to the enlightenment project. Hume and Mill both knew Calvinism. Both knew the sorts of self-flagellation that Calvinism could produce when one did not live up to the impossible standards that Christian faith required of one. But the psychological theories, which they developed, simply did not provide any plausible explanatory sketch of how the joyless pursuit of duty is possible, or how it is that one can punish oneself for taking pleasure in simple and harmless things like masturbation. Freud provided us with a theory that makes understandable how people can be this way, how they can cripple themselves with guilt, on the one hand, and how they can become intolerant and vicious political and religious fanatics on the other.

None of this challenges the Epicurean argument that pleasure is the standard of duty since we all, of necessity, seek pleasure. But it does enable us to understand how for some people their little ways can include self-mutilation or the burning of others at the stake. We can now understand how it is that being human includes being nasty. If we read Hume or Mill, what we find is a portrait of human beings all of whom are basically decent, good members of the club. They, and thinkers like them, knew that there were counter-examples, from Calvinists to Inquisitors, or, in our own day, to Nazis. But their psychology lacked the resources to account for the deep and evil side of human beings. For better or for worse, but mostly for better, Freud provided the psychological theory that was required. It was a liberating theory. As Thomas Mann put it in his lecture celebrating Freud's eightieth birthday, "on every page he [i.e., Freud] seems to instruct us that there is no deeper knowledge without experience of disease, and that all heightened healthiness must be achieved by the route of illness"; it is through the route of illness that "we have succeeded in penetrating most deeply into the darkness of human nature."[58]

We have so penetrated into the dark side: that is what the methods of psychoanalysis for the first time permitted. In that respect Freud helped further the enlightenment project that he shared with Schlick and the Vienna Circle. Indeed, it was the project of the Delphic Oracle, "Know thyself." But it provided not only understanding but also relief. Freud showed the way out of self imposed human suffering, whether it be the suffering imposed on oneself by the Calvinist or the suffering imposed on others by the religious or political enthusiast. Psychoanalysis provided the tools through which human beings could become masters of themselves and could locate within themselves a way of taking joy in things without having to suffer or without having to make others suffer.

– C –

Carnap was confident. When he wrote in 1928 his book on *The Logical Structure of the World*,[59] what he was attempting was a picture of reality as it is and as it presents itself to us, without the illusions of metaphysics. The "Preface" is important. "This requirement," he tells us in reference to the requirement enjoined upon science by the Vienna Circle "for justification and conclusive foundation of each thesis will eliminate all speculative and poetic work from philosophy" (p. xvii). This project, the elimination of metaphysics and poetry from philosophy, was the enlightenment project. This is not to say that there is no role for the emotions: of course there is. Carnap puts it this way: "The practical handling of philosophical problems and the discovery of their solutions does not have to be purely intellectual, but will always contain emotional elements and intuitive methods." However, as he then adds: "The *justification* [...] has to take place before the forum of the understanding; here we must not refer to our intuition of emotional needs." The work of the Vienna Circle is part of a broader movement. While the irrational forces of religion and metaphysics are both present and, alas, active, nonetheless, Carnap tells his readers,

> We feel that there is an inner kinship between the attitude on which our philosophical work is founded and the intellectual attitude which presently [i.e., 1928] manifests itself in entirely different walks of life; we feel this orientation in artistic movements, especially in architecture, and in movements which strive for meaningful forms of personal and collective life, of education, and of external organization in general. We feel all around us the same basic orientation, the same style of thinking and doing. (p. xviii)

Carnap goes on:

> It is an orientation which demands clarity everywhere, but which realizes that the fabric of life can never quite be comprehended. (p. xviii)

We all have our little ways. But there is no reason to think that in the broad outlines at least we are doomed to failure in our attempts to use science not only for self-understanding but for relief from our suffering. The orientation of the Vienna Circle

> makes us pay careful attention to detail and at the same time recognizes the great lines which run through the whole. It is an orientation which acknowledges the bonds that tie men together, but at the same time strives for free development of the individual. (p. xviii)

The aims of the Vienna Circle are those of Freud: the freedom of the individual from the bondage of illusion and of the constraints that we impose on ourselves and others through those illusions of religion and metaphysics. Carnap is hopeful: "Our work is carried by the faith that this attitude will win the future" (p. xviii). It was more hope than history would justify.[60]

The issues, however, are not just social, they are also personal. As Carnap explains about the philosophers in the Vienna Circle:

> We too have "emotional needs " in philosophy, but they are filled by clarity of concepts, precision of methods, responsible theses, achievement through cooperation in which each individual plays his part. (p. xvii)

We are moved by our cognitive interests. These interests are ends in themselves. But the satisfaction of these interests is also a means. The criticisms of traditional metaphysics and religion that come through clarity are a means to social justice and harmony.[61]

Hume expressed this important point in his own way: "Reason is and ought only to be the slave of the passions."[62] It *is* the slave of the passions in the sense that the love of truth, which reason attempts to satisfy, is itself a passion. It *ought* to be the slave of the passions for the reason that when it makes pretense of coming to know things and more specifically duties that come from beyond the world of ordinary experience, then the result is *dangerous*.

Nietzsche[63] ridiculed the love of truth as a motive for philosophers.[64] They were in fact moved by such things as the need to secure a university chair. But mostly his argument was, on the one hand, the positivist idea that transcendental metaphysics is illusion and, on the other, the idea that these illusions were disguised wishes, the aim of which was to enchain humankind with ostensibly objective duties.[65] These duties were not, when it came down to justification, rules that enabled people to live together, though they are that. The will to power is the will to command others. One commands others in the enterprise of satisfying one's own instinctual urges. One commands them not personally but through the illusion of objective duties. German Romantic metaphysics provided the rationale once the illusions of religion had lost their force. Somehow, these metaphysicians said, there is beyond the world of ordinary experience an objective self or being that commands us.

Nietzsche's program was of a piece with that of the British empiricists. He found his basic ideas in Friedrich Lange's *History of Materialism*.[66] Lange restated the Humean position that what we know we know by sense and that there is nothing in things that is beyond that way of knowing.[67] Nietzsche accepts by way of Lange Hume's argument that there is no self beyond the empirical self, that there is no reality beyond sensible reality, and that this world including humankind as a part of it can be explored under the guidance of the principle that whatever happens has a natural cause, a cause that can be found in the world of ordinary experience. Nietzsche's *Genealogy of Morals*[68] echoes Hume's *Natural History of Religion*:[69] both are part of the enlightenment enterprise of freeing humankind from illusion. To be sure, there are differences. For both, religion is an illusion. But Hume locates the roots of the religious illusion in fears raised by the terrors that confront us from the natural world: God is the means to help us psychologically confront the dread raised by the unknown forces of nature. Nietzsche, in contrast, begins with a natural history of morals. He contrasts the ethics of self-fulfilment of the ancient world and the ethics of renunciation of the modern world;[70] it is the *ressentiment* of the persons who are not successful under the former that leads to development of the latter.[71] It is in *ressentiment* that one finds the psychological origin of our ordinary concept of justice.[72] With this concept goes the concept of punishment,[73] and with that in turn comes the phenomenon of conscience and guilt – self-punishment[74]: "thus began the gravest and uncanniest illness, from which humanity has not yet recovered, man's suffering *of man, of himself ...* "[75] Out of this illness of bad conscience comes the concept of supernatural forces that will enforce the rules of justice, first the ancestors, and these as transmuted into gods: "in the end the ancestor must necessarily be transfigured into a *god*. Perhaps this is even the origin of gods, an origin therefore out of *fear!*"[76] And the gods come, again through fear, to be magnified into the one God.[77] Where Hume has the origins of the gods in a fear of nature, Nietzsche locates the origins in the fear of oneself: God is the dispenser and enforcer of the rules of justice, the *self-imposed* rules of justice. It is these sorts of psychological forces that Freud was to explore. In Nietzsche, as in Hume, the causal story is speculative. Freud provides a causal account of this sort of illusion that is rooted in the scientific picture of humankind provided by psychoanalysis. Hume, Nietzsche, and Freud are all part of the developing enlightenment project of freeing humankind from illusion and from the unreasonable self-imposed constraints demanded by such illusions.[78] We have to see the program of the Vienna Circle, so well expressed by Carnap, in just this same context of the enlightenment program of making humankind free.

It has become a commonplace to locate the Vienna Circle, Carnap at least, within a neo-Kantian framework.[79] After all, had not Carnap studied with them as well as with Frege? This means that one locates the Vienna Circle in the framework that includes Lange and also Nietzsche: all defend and pursue the enlightenment project. Where Nietzsche goes beyond the Vienna Circle is in going back to Hume and offering not only a critique of religion and morality but also a causal story about how these illusions arise and about the interests they serve.

But for Nietzsche, as for Hume, it is only a story: there is no background method beyond the literary to support the claims about the psychological origins of the power that these illusions have over humankind. The requirement of the Vienna Circle for the clarity that comes from the demand for empirical truth goes only so far. One wants also to control oneself, to so control oneself that no longer is it these illusions that are in charge. In order to seize control one needs more than a story, one needs to "know thyself" in the sense that one has the causal knowledge about one's own self that puts one in control of how one thinks and feels and behaves. The positivist critique will not by itself do that. Neither will the insights of literary critics, not even if they are Nietzsche. What one needs is a real method that enables one to gain control of oneself. It was Freud who gave us this method. This was the central human achievement of the twentieth century: for the first time genuine self-understanding really was possible. It was only with this that the enlightenment project of the Vienna Circle could be realized.

There were not only personal relationships between the Freudians in Vienna and the Circle that Schlick gathered about himself. Deeper than that there was the shared project of furthering the enlightenment. Neurath recognized the significance of Freud in this project. Nothing, however, not even Freud's insights into the dark side of human nature, not even the insights of the Nietzsche and the Vienna Circle into the irrationality of religion and German Romantic philosophy – nothing had prepared anybody for the horrors that were to come. Maybe in the end the human condition is beyond comprehension. That is not something that Freud would have said. Neither would Neurath have said that. It might just the same be true ... unfortunately.

[1] Gustav Bergmann, "Memories of the Vienna Circle: Letter to Otto Neurath [1938]," in Friedrich Stadler, ed., *Scientific Philosophy: Origins and Developments*, Dordrecht, The Netherlands: Kluwer, 1993, pp. 193-208.

[2] Arne Naess, "Logical Empiricism and the Uniqueness of the Schlick Seminar: A Personal Experience with Consequences," in Stadler, ed., *Scientific Philosophy*, pp. 11-25.

[3] Naess was himself going through an intensive psychoanalysis at the time he was attending meetings of the Circle (*ibid.*, p. 14).

[4] He told me the story when I was a doctoral student writing a dissertation under his supervision.

[5] The manifesto of the Vienna Circle has recently been re-published and translated; see H. Hahn, O. Neurath and R. Carnap, "Wissenschaftliche Weltauffassung: Der Wiener Kreis" ("The Scientific Conception of the World: The Vienna Circle"), in O. Neurath, *Empiricism and Sociology*, ed. M. Neurath and R. S. Cohen, Dordrecht, The Netherlands: Kluwer, 1973, pp. 299-318. A careful reading of this document shows that many of the commonly held views about logical positivism are false. For example, the manifesto nowhere commits a logical positivist to a foundationist account of knowledge.

[6] The original plan was for Naess to co-author this monograph, but that proposal was later abandoned; see Naess, "Logical Empiricism and the Uniqueness of the Schlick Seminar," p. 20.

[7] It should be noted that alone among the positivists who came to the United States, Bergmann had an impact on the actual development of psychological theory and research. This was through his association with K.W. Spence at the University of Iowa. On the details of this relationship and its importance, see Laurence D. Smith, *Behaviorism and Logical Positivism*, Stanford: Stanford UP, 1986; for the Bergmann-Spence relation, see p. 208ff.

[8] On all these things, see E.G. Boring, *A History of Experimental Psychology*, second edition, New York: Appleton-Century-Crofts, 1957, Ch. 22.

[9] John Dewey, "The Reflex Arc Concept in Psychology," *Psychological Review* 3 (1896), pp. 357-370.

[10] See Gustav Bergmann, "The Contribution of John B. Watson," *Psychological Review* 63 (1956), pp. 265-276.

[11] C.D. Broad, *The Mind and Its Place in Nature*, London: Routledge and Kegan Paul, 1925, p. 6, p. 623.

[12] John B. Watson, "Image and Affection in Behavior," *Journal of Philosophy* 10 (1913), pp. 421-428. On the one hand he asserts that there are no images, and cites as evidence that claimed fact of "the failure on the part of the most earnest upholders of the doctrine of centrally aroused sensation to obtain any objective experimental evidence of the presences of different type-images. I refer to the researches of Angell and of Fernald" (p. 422). On the other hand, he also proposes that between the stimulus and a delayed response in explicit

behavior there must be a piece of "implicit behavior"; it is this with which the image is identified. "There are no centrally initiated processes," Watson claims (p. 423), and he suggests that "it is this type of implicit behavior that the introspectionist claims as his own and denies to us because its neural seat is cortical and because it goes on without adequate bodily portrayal" (p. 424). So they do not exist but are, rather, implicit responses in the periphery of the nervous system. Angell, by the way, disputed Watson's citing his work as an authority for all this; see James B. Angell, "Professor Watson and the Image," *Journal of Philosophy* 10 (1913), p. 609.

[13] On the distinction between various sorts of behaviorism, see Bergmann, "The Contribution of John B. Watson."

[14] See F. Wilson, "Some Controversies about Method in Nineteenth-Century Psychology," *Studies in History and Philosophy of Biological and Biomedical Science* 30 (1999), pp. 91-127.

[15] See F. Wilson, *Psychological Analysis and the Philosophy of John Stuart Mill*, Toronto: University of Toronto Press, 1990, Ch. 8.

[16] G. Bergmann, "Psychoanalysis and Experimental Psychology" *Mind*, n.s. 52 (1943), pp. 122-140; reprinted in M. Marx, ed., *Psychological Theory*, New York: Macmillan, 1951. Page references are to the latter.

[17] E. Brunswik, *The Conceptual Framework of Psychology*, in O. Neurath, R. Carnap and C. Morris, eds., *International Encyclopedia of Unified Science*, Chicago: University of Chicago Press, 1955. The various monographs collected in this combined edition were all originally published separately. Brunswik's monograph came out in this form in 1938. References are to the combined edition.

[18] Bergmann, "Psychoanalysis and Experimental Psychology," p. 353ff [see endnote 16]; Brunswik, *The Conceptual Framework of Psychology*, p. 713ff.

[19] Ernest Jones, "Rationalism and Psychoanalysis," in his *Essays in Applied Psychoanalysis*, vol. II, New York: International Universities Press, 1964, p. 233.

[20] Bergmann, "Psychoanalysis and Experimental Psychology," p. 355.

[21] Ernest Jones, "Free Will and Determinism," in his *Essays in Applied Psychoanalysis*, vol. II, New York: International Universities Press, 1964, p. 186.

[22] Bergmann, "Psychoanalysis and Experimental Psychology," p. 355.

[23] *Ibid.*, p. 358.

[24] Another member of the Vienna Circle who took psychoanalysis seriously was Herbert Feigl. Though he never presented an extended examination of the theories or methods of Freud, he did state that

> There is little doubt in my mind that psychoanalytic theory (or at least some of its components) has genuine explanatory power, even if any precise identification of the repression, ego, superego, id, etc., with neural processes and structures is still a very long way off. I am not in the least disputing the value of theories whose basic concepts are not in any way micro-specified. What I am arguing is that even *before* such specifications become possible, the meaning of scientific terms can be explicated by postulates and correspondence rules [...] and that this meaning may later be greatly enriched, i.e. much more fully specified, by the addition of *further* postulates and correspondence rules.
>
> After recovery from radical behaviorism and operationism, we need no longer hesitate to distinguish between *evidence* and *reference*, i.e. between manifestations or symptoms on the one hand, and central states on the other, no matter whether or not central states are micro-specified (neurophysiologically identified).

From: H. Feigl, "The 'Mental' and the 'Physical'," in H. Feigl, M. Scriven, and G. Maxwell, eds., *Minnesota Studies in the Philosophy of Science*, vol. II, Minneapolis: University of Minnesota Press, 1958, pp. 370-497, here: pp. 394-95. This opinion was expressed long after the demise of the Circle, but there is little doubt that this was also his view back when the Circle was having its meetings.

[25] On Maudsley, see T.H. Turner, "Maudsley, Henry," *Dictionary of National Biography: Missing Persons*, Oxford: Oxford UP, 1993, p. 453f.

[26] Cf. Henry Maudsley, *Physiology and Pathology of the Mind*, London: Macmillan, 1867; and Henry Maudsley, *Body and Mind*, London: Macmillan, 1873.

[27] See Georges Cuvier, "Letter to J.C. Mertrud," in his *Lectures on Comparative Anatomy*, trans. W. Ross, London: T.N. Longman and O. Rees, 1802, vol. I, pp. xix-xl.

[28] Maudsley, *Physiology and Pathology of the Mind*, p. 24.

[29] Maudsley's part in the methodological debates has been examined in Wilson, "Some Controversies about Method in Nineteenth-Century Psychology" [see endnote 14]. On these issues, see also F. Wilson, "Mill and Comte on the Method of Introspection," *Journal of the History of the Behavioral Sciences* 27 (1991), pp. 107-129.

[30] Cf. Wilson, "Some Controversies about Method in Nineteenth-Century Psychology," p. 125f [see endnote 14].

[31] Cf. S. Freud, "The Technique of Psychoanalysis," Ch. VI of *An Outline of Psychoanalysis*, in his *Historical and Expository Works on Psycho-analysis*, trans. J. Strachey, London: Penguin, 1993, pp. 405-416.

[32] Aristotle, *On Memory*, trans. J.I. Beare, in J. Barnes, ed., *The Complete Works of Aristotle*, vol. I, revised Oxford translation, Princeton: Princeton UP, 1984, pp. 714-721, 451b,17-22.

[33] Cf. F. Wilson, *Psychological Analysis and the Philosophy of John Stuart Mill*, Toronto: University of Toronto Press, 1990, Ch. 1 and Ch. 8.

[34] A.A. Milne, *Now We Are Six*: "King John was not a good man – / He had his little ways" (Toronto: McClelland & Stewart, 1927, p. 2).

[35] See Nietzsche's comment that "[W]ith regard to the superstitions of logicians, I shall never tire of emphasising a small, terse fact, which is unwillingly recognised by these credulous minds – namely, that a thought comes when 'it' wishes, and not when 'I' wish; so that it is a *perversion* of the facts of the case to say that the subject 'I' is the condition of the predicate 'think'" (Friedrich Nietzsche, *Beyond Good and Evil*, trans. Helen Zimmern, fourth edition, London: George Allen and Unwin, 1923, Ch. 1, § 17, p. 24).

[36] See S. Freud, *Five Lectures in Psycho-analysis* [1910], trans. J. Strachey, in *Two Short Accounts of Psycho-analysis*, London: Penguin, 1991; see the First and Second Lectures.

[37] For details on how this fits into the standard scientific methodology of empirical science, see Wilson, *Psychological Analysis and the Philosophy of John Stuart Mill*, Ch. 3 and Ch. 8 [see endnote 15]; and "Some Controversies about Method in Nineteenth-Century Psychology" [see endnote 14].

[38] On the difference between free and constrained or controlled introspective analysis, see E.B. Titchener, "The Schema of Introspection," *American Journal of Psychology* 23 (1912), pp. 485-508, here: p. 490ff; see also his "Prolegomena to a Study of Introspection," *American Journal of Psychology* 23 (1912), pp. 427-448. In the former Titchener refers to G.E. Müller, Zur Analyse der Gedächtnistätigkeit und des Vorstellungsverlaufes, I. Teil, in *Zeitschrift für Psychologie. Ergänzungsband* 5, Leipzig: Verlag von Johan Ambrosius Barth, 1911, p. 73, p. 79, p. 95, p. 98f, p. 120. As J.W. Baird states in his review of Müller's extended study, the "presentation is marred at times by an unfortunate tendency toward

prolixity of statement" (*Psychological Bulletin* 15 (1916), pp. 372-375, here: p. 375).

[39] See Freud, "The Technique of Psycho-analysis" [see endnote 11]: "With the neurotics, then, we make our pact: complete candour on one side and strict discretion on the other" (p. 407).

[40] S. Freud, "Transference," Lecture 27 of his *Introductory Lectures on Psycho-analysis*, [1915-1917], trans. J. Strachey, London: Penguin, 1991, pp. 482-500.

[41] Freud, *Five Lectures on Psycho-analysis*, p. 86 [see endnote 36].

[42] S. Freud, *The Ego and the Id*, trans. J. Riviere, New York: Norton, 1960, p. 46.

[43] S. Freud, "Analytic Therapy," Lecture 28 of his *Introductory Lectures on Psycho-analysis*, pp. 501-517, here: p. 505.

[44] A. Grünbaum, *The Foundations of Psychoanalysis*, Berkeley: University of California Press, 1984.

[45] For the hereditary nature of mental illness, see H. Maudsley, "Illustrations of a Variety of Insanity," *Journal of Mental Science* 14 (1868), pp. 149-162; for masturbation, see his "Insanity and Its Treatment," *Journal of Mental Science* 17 (1871), pp. 311-334, at p. 325.

[46] Thomas Carlyle, *Sartor Resartus* [1853-54], ed. Kerry McSweeny and Peter Sabor, Oxford: Oxford UP, 1987, p. 146.

[47] M. Schlick, *The Problems of Ethics*, trans. D. Rynin, New York: Dover, 1962.

[48] *Ibid.*, Ch. II, sec. 4.

[49] See, for example, O. Neurath, "Personal Life and Class Struggle," in his *Empiricism and Sociology*, ed. M. Neurath and R. S. Cohen, Dordrecht, The Netherlands: D. Reidel, 1973, pp. 247-298, esp. Sec. 5: "Marx and Epicurus."

[50] John Stuart Mill, "Utilitarianism," Ch. 4, in his *Essays on Ethics, Religion and Society*, vol. X of *The Collected Works of John Stuart Mill*, ed. J. Robson, Toronto: University of Toronto Press, 1969.

[51] For various aspects of Mill's proof of the principle of utility, see F. Wilson, "Mill's Proof that Happiness Is the Criterion of Morality," *Journal of Business Ethics* 1 (1982), pp. 59-72; see also F. Wilson, "Mill's 'Proof' of Utility and the Composition of Causes," *Journal of Business Ethics* 2 (1983), pp. 135-158.

[52] Cf. Wilson, *Psychological Analysis and the Philosophy of John Stuart Mill*, Ch. 7 [see endnote 15].

[53] Cf. Wilson, "Mill's Proof that Happiness Is the Criterion of Morality" [see endnote 51].

[54] Schlick, *Problems of Ethics*, p. 199 [see endnote 47].

[55] Cf. Heiner Rutte, "Ethics and the Problem of Value in the Vienna Circle," in T. Uebel, ed., *Rediscovering the Forgotten Vienna Circle*, Dordrecht, The Netherlands: Kluwer, 1991, pp. 143-147; see also F. Stadler, "Otto Neurath – Moritz Schlick: On the Philosophical and Political Antagonisms in the Vienna Circle," *ibid.*, pp. 159-168. Bergmann, in his memoir, indicates some of the relevant differences.

[56] Mill, "Utilitarianism," Ch. 2 [see endnote 50].

[57] Schlick, *Problems of Ethics*, p. 46 [see endnote 47].

[58] Thomas Mann, "Freud and the Future," trans. Helen Tracey Lowe-Porter, in his *Death in Venice, Tonio Kröger, and Other Writings*, ed. F.A. Lubich, New York: Continuum, 1999, pp. 279-296, here: p. 282.

[59] R. Carnap, *The Logical Structure of the World and Pseudoproblems in Philosophy*, trans. Rolf George, Berkeley: University of California Press, 1967; this translates Carnap's *Der Logische Aufbau der Welt*, first published in 1928.

[60] Schlick, too, noted the social meaning of the philosophy of the Vienna Circle, and its opposition to metaphysics; see M. Schlick, "The Vienna School and Traditional Philosophy" [1937], in his *Philosophical Papers*, vol. II, ed. Henk L. Mulder and Barbara F.B. Van de Velde-Schlick, Dordrecht: Reidel, 1979, pp. 491-498. Schlick writes: "The fashionable

philosophic movements have no worse enemy than true philosophy, and none that they fear more. When it rises in a new dawn and sheds its pityless light, the adherents of every kind of ephemeral movement tremble and unite against it, crying out that philosophy is in danger, for they truly believe that the destruction of their own little system signifies the ruin of philosophy itself"; as for its opponents, "the metaphysicians have often accused empiricism of being antiphilosophical. In like fashion, the Vienna school is often reprobated for consisting, not of philosophers, but of enemies of philosophy. The doctrines of this school, it is said, in no way contribute to the development and progress of philosophy, but tend, rather, to dissolve it. It has even been asserted that they are a phenomenon of degeneracy, like so may other manifestations of contemporary culture" (p. 491).

For a placement of Carnap's *Aufbau*, and the Vienna Circle more generally, in a broader cultural context, see Peter Galison, "The Cultural Meaning of *Aufbau*," in F. Stadler, ed., *Scientific Philosophy: Origins and Development*, Dordrecht: Kluwer, 1993, pp. 75-93.

[61] For an account of how conservative-clerical and German Romantic philosophy combined with German nationalism, national-socialism and anti-semitism to fight against the liberal-to-socialist views of the Vienna Circle and its anti-metaphysical empiricist orientation, see F. Stadler, "Aspects of the Social Background and Position of the Vienna Circle at the University of Vienna," in T. Uebel, ed., *Rediscovering the Forgotten Vienna Circle*, pp. 51-77 [see endnote 55]. Given the resistance, documented in this study, of the idealists and other representatives of German Romantic philosophy to the appointment of Schlick, one can understand how the positivists picked Heidegger in particular for well-justified ridicule. But these philosophers made their compromises where the positivists could not. They survived those compromises and now have apparently secured the University against any positivist influence; see Eugene T. Gadol, "Philosophy, Ideology, Common Sense and Murder – The Vienna of the Vienna Circle Past and Present," in Eugene T. Gadol, ed., *Rationality and Science*, Vienna and New York: Springer-Verlag, 1982, pp. 1-35.

[62] D. Hume, *Treatise of Human Nature*, ed. L.A. Selby-Bigge, London: Oxford University Press, 1888, p. 415. For an attempt to become clear on some aspects of what Hume means by this claim, see F. Wilson, *Hume's Defence of Causal Inference*, Toronto: University of Toronto Press, 1997, Ch. 3.

[63] We cannot underestimate the impact of Nietzsche; for a just evaluation, see Thomas Mann, "Nietzsche's Philosophy in the Light of Recent History," in his *Last Essays*, trans. Richard and Clara Winston and Tania and James Stern, London: Secker and Warburg, 1959, pp. 141-177. The impact extended to the Vienna Circle. Herbert Feigl indicates the importance of Nietzsche for Schlick's philosophy in his essay "Moritz Schlick: A Memoir," in Eugene T. Gadol, ed., *Rationality and Science*, pp. 55-82, here: p. 62. Schlick himself invokes the authority of Nietzsche in his essay "On the Meaning of Life," in his *Philosophical Papers*, vol. II, pp. 112-129, at p. 113 and p. 125.

[64] See Nietzsche, *Beyond Good and Evil*, Ch. 1, on the "Prejudices of Philosophers" [see endnote 35]: "It has gradually become clear to me what every great philosophy up till now has consisted of – namely, the confession of its originator, and a species of involuntary and unconscious autobiography; and moreover that the moral (or immoral) purpose in every philosophy has constituted the true vital germ out of which the entire plant has always grown" (§ 6, p. 10f).

[65] Cf. *Beyond Good and Evil*, Ch. 1, § 11, on Kant. Nietzsche rightly points out that the Kantian appeal to categories is no more explanatory than an appeal to dormitive powers. He goes on to indicate how it became fashionable for German philosophers to find faculties for discerning things transcendental. But it was all illusion: "Enough, however – the world grew

older, and the dream vanished" (p. 17). He has already remarked that the "spectacle of the Tartuffery of old Kant, equally stiff and decent, with which he entices us into the dialectic by-ways that lead (more correctly mislead) to his 'categorical imperative' – makes us fastidious ones smile, we who find no small amusement in spying out the subtle tricks of old moralists and ethical preachers" (Ch. 1, § 5, p. 10).

[66] I have used F.A. Lange, *The History of Materialism*, third edition, trans. E.C. Thomas, London: Routledge and Kegan Paul, 1925. The first German edition was published in 1865; volume I of the second edition appeared in 1873, volume II in 1875; the English translation is from this second German edition. Nietzsche's connections with Lange are explored in detail in G. Stack, *Lange and Nietzsche*, Berlin/New York: Walter de Gruyter, 1983.

[67] Compare: "The world of phenomena, to which man belongs as a portion of them, is thoroughly governed by the law of cause; and there is no action of man, not even the supreme heroism of duty, which is not, physiologically and psychologically considered, determined by antecedent development of the individual, or by the shaping of the situation in which he finds himself placed" (Lange, *History of Materialism*, Second Book, p. 230). Lange contrasts his position on causation to those of Hume and Kant (p. 211f). On Hume's view: "The idea of cause cannot be derived from the pure reason, but rather springs from experience. The limits of its application are doubtful, but at all events it cannot be applied to anything that transcends our experience." On Kant's view: "The idea of cause is a primary idea of the pure reason, and as such underlies our whole experience. For this reason, therefore, it has unlimited validity in the sphere of experience, but beyond that has no meaning." On his own view: "The idea of cause is rooted in our organisation, and is, in point of the disposition to it, before all experience. For this very reason it has unlimited validity in the sphere of experience, but beyond it absolutely no meaning." One can see how Lange would be considered a neo-Kantian, given that he shares with Kant the view that the mind is so disposed that it must interpret events as causally related. The difference lies in the fact that the Kantian mind is in the end simply pure reason, where for Lange the mind is the empirical we know in everyday experience. But one can also see the connection to Hume: for Lange as for Hume, all causation is matter of fact regularity: there is no need for laws to be brought somehow under the forms of the categories of pure reason.

Lange contrasts his view with that of the empiricists as depending upon the fact he accepts, where they do not, that "experience is no open door through which external things, as they are, can wander in to us, but a process by which the appearance of things arises within us" (p. 188). The importance of this point is that

> When it has once been demonstrated that the quality of our sense-perceptions is entirely conditioned by the constitution of our [sense] organs, we can no longer dismiss with the predicate "Irrefutable but absurd" even the hypothesis that the whole system also, into which we bring our sense-perceptions – in a word, our whole experience – is conditioned by an intellectual organisation which compels us to feel as we do feel, to think as we do think, while to another organisation the very same objects may appear quite different, and the thing in itself cannot be pictured by any finite being. (p. 158)

Nietzsche comments perceptively on this in *Beyond Good and Evil*:

> To study physiology with a clear conscience, one must insist on the fact that the sense-organs are *not* phenomena in the sense of the idealistic philosophy; as such they certainly could not be causes! Sensualism, therefore, at least as regulative hypothesis, if not as heuristic principle. What? And others say even that the external world is the work of our organs? But then our body, as part of this external world, would be the work of our organs! But then our organs themselves

would be the work of our organs! It seems to me that this is a complete *reductio ad absurdum*, if the conception *causa sui* is something fundamentally absurd. Consequently, the external world is *not* the work of our organs – ?
(Ch. 1, § 15, p. 22)

This brings Nietzsche back closer to Hume than to the neo-Kantianism of Lange.

[68] Friedrich Nietzsche, *On the Genealogy of Morals, Ecce Homo*, ed. Walter Kaufmann, New York: Random House, 1967.

[69] David Hume, *The Natural History of Religion*, ed. H. Root, Stanford: Stanford UP, 1956.

[70] *Genealogy of Morals*, First Essay, § 10 [see endnote 68]: "While every noble morality develops from a triumphant affirmation of itself, slave morality from the outset says No to what is 'outside,' what is 'different,' what is 'not itself'; and *this* No is its creative deed" (p. 36). Schlick makes the same point, though of course in his more sober way: "It is characteristic," he says, of our modern morality that "all of its most important demands end in the repression of personal desires in favor of the desires of fellow men" (*Problems of Ethics*, p. 79 [see endnote 47]). To this he contrasts the ancients' ethics: "The ancient classical ethics is not an ethics of self-limitation, but of self-realization, not of renunciation, but of affirmation" (*ibid.*, p. 80).

[71] Nietzsche, *Genealogy of Morals*, First Essay, § 11.

[72] *Ibid.*, Second Essay, § 11.

[73] John Stuart Mill made this point in "Utilitarianism," Ch. 5. [see endnote 50].

[74] Nietzsche, *Genealogy of Morals*, Second Essay, § 15.

[75] *Ibid.*, Second Essay, § 16, p. 85.

[76] *Ibid.*, Second Essay, § 19, p. 89.

[77] *Ibid.*, Second Essay, § 20.

[78] Nietzsche's "will to power" is simply the demand to be free of unreasonable constraints. Thus, he speaks of "the *instinct for freedom* (in my language: the will to power)" (*Genealogy of Morals*, Second Essay, § 17, p. 87). The will to power is simply what has come to be known as the desire for negative liberty. Nietzsche unfortunately too often clothes his notion of the will to power in rhetoric redolent of the German Romantic philosophy that he despised. He allows his despising of the reason of the German Romantics – the reason that claimed, wrongly, to be able to transcend this world for another – to become a despising of all reason, and an over-valuing of the instincts (cf. Mann, "Nietzsche's Philosophy in the Light of Recent History," p. 161 [see endnote 63]). This leads him at times to falsely contrast all morality, all restraint, with life, with the will to power (see *ibid.*, p. 162). But, of course, even negative liberty, if it to be enjoyed to the fullest possible extent, requires *some* restraint. Otherwise it is simply the war of all against all. The errors are connected. Reason, in its reasonable sense, will tell you what restraints are necessary for the fullest possible self-realization of all. It is these combined errors that lead Nietzsche to the rhetoric of the blond beast who tramples others underfoot that so endeared him to the Nazis. When we read these parts of Nietzsche's writing, then, as Thomas Mann puts it, "the clinical picture of infantile sadism is complete, and our souls writhe in embarrassment" (*ibid.*, p. 165).

[79] See Michael Friedman, "The Re-Evaluation of Logical Positivism," *Journal of Philosophy* 88 (1991), pp. 505-519; "Epistemology in the *Aufbau*," *Synthese* 93 (1992), pp. 15-57; "Carnap's *Aufbau* Reconsidered," *Noûs* 21 (1987), pp. 521-545; and "Geometry, Convention and the Relativized A Priori: Reichenbach, Schlick, and Carnap," in W. Salmon and G. Wolters, eds., *Logic, Language, and the Status of Scientific Theories*, Pittsburgh: University of Pittsburgh Press, 1994, pp. 21-34; and A. Richardson, *Carnap's Construction*

of the World, Cambridge: Cambridge UP, 1998.

The general thrust of these works is to argue that Carnap's project is neo-Kantian *rather than* empiricist. "The aim of the *Aufbau*," we are told, "is not to use logic together with sense data to provide empirical knowledge with an otherwise missing epistemological foundation of justification. Its aim, rather, is to use recent advances in the science of logic [...] together with advances in empirical science (Gestalt psychology, in particular) to fashion a scientifically respectable *replacement* for traditional epistemology" (Friedman, "The Re-Evaluation of Logical Positivism," p. 509). The point is that the replacement could well be one that aims to meet the spirit of empiricist epistemology while rejecting some of the shortcomings that had become evident, e.g., the failure to take account of the relational structures present in the world as we ordinarily experience it – this was a real defect in traditional empiricism, and for this the tradition had been criticized by the idealists; on this point, see F. Wilson, "Bradley's Impact on Empiricism," in J. Bradley, ed., *Philosophy after F.H. Bradley*, Bristol: Thoemmes Press, 1996, pp. 251-282.

A second point is that the positivists, Carnap in particular, rejected the traditional empiricist account of geometry and opted instead for a neo-Kantian position (Friedman, "The Re-Evaluation of Logical Positivism," p. 510ff, and also "Geometry, Convention, and the Relativized A Priori: Reichenbach, Schlick, and Carnap"). Where the empiricist tradition made geometry straight-forwardly empirical, the neo-Kantians, following Lange, located it in the necessary structure of how as a matter of fact we think about the world. The positivists maintained that an adequate account of geometry required that there be a conventional component. This component is *a priori*, but a relativized *a priori*, a convention adopted *pro tem* because it facilitates providing a factually adequate account of the geometry of the world. This introduction of an *a priori* element into geometry, it is claimed, makes the positivists more neo-Kantian than empiricist. But would empiricists such as Mill have disagreed? It is more that they would have welcomed such a view, as a more adequate re-statement of the position that they were trying to defend. Carnap, in his own way, may have been inspired by the neo-Kantian tradition, but his allowing a conventional element into geometry is much less neo-Kantian than it is an improved statement of the empiricist position.

Finally, it is claimed that the positivists took the special sciences as foundationalist for their philosophy, rather than their philosophy providing a foundation for the special sciences. "There is no privileged vantage point from which philosophy can pass epistemic judgment on the special sciences: philosophy is conceived as rather following the special sciences so as to reorient itself in response to their established results" (Friedman, "The Re-Evaluation of Logical Positivism," p. 515). But the positivists *did* conceive of their task as involving the critique of the special sciences. Thus, rather than simply being accepted, what biologists said in their scientific writings was to be scrutinized carefully for metaphysical error so that their views could be placed on a secure philosophical and epistemological footing; see, for example, Schlick's essay "On the Concept of Wholeness" (in *Philosophical Papers*, vol. II). Schlick and the other positivists were following good empiricist tradition in taking solid parts of natural science for granted and defending the body of science from the incursions of metaphysics. Hobbes and Locke saw it as part of their task to provide a foundation for the new science and to defend it against the Aristotelianism that was still deeply entrenched in the universities; on this latter point, see F. Wilson, *The Logic and Methodology of Science in Early Modern Thought*, Toronto: University of Toronto Press, 1999.

If there is neo-Kantianism in the background of the positivists, then it is also true that they mostly overcame it. As Nietzsche could accept the empiricist side of Lange and reject the Kantian dross, so the positivists such as Schlick and Carnap could accept from neo-Kantianism what suited their empiricist program and thus reject the Kantian refuse.

WITTGENSTEIN – POETRY AND LITERATURE

Rudolf Haller
University of Graz

I.

In this paper I intend to present Wittgenstein from two perspectives, which in a certain sense are not in harmony. We may think of the two selected models or types which constitute the same character thus: one is the analytic *philosopher* partly formed by a strange mixture of Frege and Russell with Schopenhauer, Tolstoi, and Dostoevskii. The other is the *artist*, whose aim is the perfection of forms, be they of construction, furniture, poetry, or philosophical texts. The unity of these artificially distinguished characters is a precondition for an interpretation of Wittgenstein's general attitudes and prejudices in regard to art, music and literature, and, in general, form and style. Wittgenstein finds the first application of the analytic method or style in logic, in the language of signs which he had studied with Frege and Russell. We know about these early steps by way of Wittgenstein's notes written in 1913, dictated to George E. Moore during his stay in Norway in April 1914, and especially from his diaries of the First World War dating from August 1914 to January 1917.

II.

In taking up this topic I am well aware that other philosophers have long wrestled with the very same difficult and problematic questions for a long time and have achieved remarkable results. I am especially thinking of Georg Henrik von Wright's essay "Wittgenstein and His Time" and his talk at the symposium in honor of Jaakko Hintikka in Helsinki in 1989, "Wittgenstein and the Twentieth Century."[1] The first part of Wright's study provides an overview of the general background of modernity from the turn of the century to the 1930s: modernity viewed as the legacy of the Age of Enlightenment, the achievement of the French Revolution, the rise of science and industry, and the desire to liberate humankind, whatever this means. One outcome of this process was the modernisation of our ways of life: mobility, urbanisation, and the total change from an agricultural to an industrial society along with democratisation. We can observe these developments in many countries, especially in the USA and in many parts of Europe, and in a few other countries,

---

Writing the Austrian Traditions: Relations between Philosophy and Literature.
Ed. Wolfgang Huemer and Marc-Oliver Schuster. Edmonton, Alberta:
Wirth-Institute for Austrian and Central European Studies, 2003. pp. 37-47.

like Japan, who are now in competition with old Europe and the USA. As might be expected, and as Marx, Engels, Lenin, and other authors had predicted and demonstrated in their works, these changes were paralleled by other social, political, and economic revolutions. Wright rightly underlines that "in origin it was an optimistic mood," which impregnated the leading ideas and the hope for steady progress in the liberation of humanity. And these general expectations reflected also one of the main ideas of the nineteenth century: the *idea of evolution* not only in nature, as we find it in Darwin and Mach, but also if we think of Hegel, Comte, or Spencer in the history of ideas and societies – as, for instance, von Hayek has pointed out in his masterpiece *The Counterrevolution of Science*.[2]

While the optimistic idea of steady progress was boosted for some time by the rapid growth of science and industry, it cannot be ignored that during the very same period an equally strong counter-movement arose. Against the rationalistic system of Hegel there was Kierkegaard's religious critique, and later the much more forceful attack on the leading ideologies of the nineteenth century advanced by Nietzsche. All of the metaphysical comfort of great philosophy had to be destroyed, relieved from the search and need for metaphysical substitutes. Not only Christian morality was questioned: the entire ethos of the modern time was something to be overturned. But Nietzsche's work was not merely destructive; he was not simply the *Alles-Zermalmer*, he was not playing with incitement, but was concerned much more basically with a new kind of honest morality.

Another movement countering the superficial optimism of the "progressists" came from Russia with the writings of Dostoevskii and Tolstoi. Like Nietzsche, who placed Dostoevskii on the same level as Schopenhauer, de Vigny, Leopardi, and Pascal,[3] Wittgenstein had an enthusiasm for Dostoevskii's "romantic pessimism." Although the writing as well as the life of Tolstoi had a deep impact on Wittgenstein, this did not diminish the high esteem in which he held Dostoevskii and especially the *Karamasov*.[4] But, even if it were true that Wittgenstein preferred Dostoevskii, and I think it is, his own way of life and his decision at the end of the war to free himself of his inheritance and wealth were deeply influenced and motivated by Tolstoian ideas. Biographical publications and documents produced by Wittgenstein's friends and pupils have provided a wealth of data and interpretation both in respect of his life and his philosophical remarks. We may think of the biographies by McGuinness and Monk, the recollections of his friends and students, and the prodigious literature based on these accounts.

If we direct our interest to Wittgenstein's relation to and understanding of literature, we have to distinguish between different kinds of literature (poetic, philosophical, scientific, or religious texts, etc.). What I intend to do is to try to understand a little better the fact that Wittgenstein was not only a philosopher – one of the two or three most important philosophers of the twentieth century – but that he was many-sided in a deep sense. Even in philosophy he was not merely a creative logician: he was also a revolutionary defender of ordinary language and its use in philosophy; he was the first of a long line able to escape the enduring scholastic school as well as the habit of compiling compendia; but he also nevertheless accepted the power and value of tradition. What I am interested in is not so much Wittgenstein's philosophical texts and their interpretation, but his understanding of literary works of the past and especially of his own time.

After the period of the *Logisch-philosophische Abhandlung*, which after all was neither a *"Abhandlung"* nor a *"Tractatus"* in the usual style, he decided to write *remarks*. Some of them are so concentrated and perfect in form and content that they could be mistaken for aphorisms. Actually he himself was aware of this danger, which is similar to that of unintentionally turning a straightforward sentence into a rhyme. For Wittgenstein, style was not only an aesthetic category; it was first and foremost a moral one. "Writing in the right style," he says, "is setting the carriage straight on the rails."[5] Unsurprisingly, from time to time he criticises his own style, e.g.: "My style is like bad musical composition."[6] Style has to do with one's self; it is a way of reacting to the world and to ourselves. And this, very often, has to do with religion. I personally think that one of the marks of Wittgenstein's character was undeniably his strong religiosity (which he separated from his philosophy as far as possible) and steady search for God's protection. If we read the so-called *Secret Diaries*, we find again and again the cry to God for help, even in the form of a prayer, as on April 7, 1916: "Gott helfe mir. Ich bin ein armer unglücklicher Mensch. Gott erhöre mich und schenke mir den Frieden! Amen."[7] ("Help me God. I am a miserable, wretched human being. Hear me, God, and grant me peace! Amen.")

We, who have read and studied the *Tractatus* (completed at the end of the First World War in 1918) and the *Philosophical Investigations* (the first part of which was finished at the end of the Second World War in 1945, which is also the date of his preface to his second book), normally see his work as the most important contribution, first, to the philosophy of Logical Empiricism in the 1920s and 1930s, and then to the broader wave of analytic philosophy arising after World War II.

It is well known that for a time after the First World War Wittgenstein contemplated becoming a monk. However, Russell was right: it was "an idea, not an intention."[8] But even an idea may point to an important fact, namely that Wittgenstein's genuine perspective was beyond modernity also in regard to religious beliefs. In 1919 Russell states that "[I] was astonished when I found that he has become a complete mystic," and he refers to Wittgenstein's interest in Kierkegaard, Angelus Silesius, and Tolstoi's writing on the Gospels. Many of the later remarks in his diaries written in the thirties signify Wittgenstein's steady concern with religion. Since he does not understand the real Christian belief ("Den eigentlichen *Christenglauben* – nicht den *Glauben* – verstehe ich noch gar nicht"),[9] he is struggling constantly with his inescapable desire to reach certainty: "Die Leiden des Geistes loswerden, das heißt die Religion los werden."[10] ("To get rid of the pain of mind means to get rid of religion.")

Almost all remarks are in one way or another connected to the problem of language and the problem of our life – and both problems relate to the question of faith: "Gott laß mich fromm sein aber *nicht* überspannt"[11] ("God, let me be devout, but *not* overstrained"), asks Wittgenstein in his private notes. He is warning himself again and again, knowing the snares of language: "Aber was ist am Gebrauch der Zeichen Tiefes? Da erinnere ich mich, erstens [...], daran, daß die Probleme, die durch ein Mißdeuten der Formen unserer Sprache entstehen immer den Charakter des Profunden haben"[12] ("But what profundity is there in the use of signs? I remember, first, [...] that the problems arising from a misinterpretation of the forms of our language always have the character of profundity.") Repeatedly we are reminded that all of our conduct is linked with language or, better: language games. A good example is found in Wittgenstein's remark of February 4, 1937:

> I can well deny the Christian solution of the problem of life (redemption, resurrection, judgement, heaven, hell), but by this the problem of our life is not at all solved, for I am not good and not happy... And how can I know, what picture of the order of the world I would have in mind as the only acceptable one if I lived in a different way, in a completely different way. I cannot judge... If one lives in another way, one speaks in another way. With a new life one learns new language games.[13]

Thus we can learn new uses of language if we change our life and the principles of life, and this is also proof that we have changed the ways we think and feel. In the same year Wittgenstein offers another remark concerning the dogmas of our thinking and the power of literature – in this case religious literature – to influence people:

> The effect of making men think in accordance with dogmas, perhaps in the form of certain graphic propositions will be very peculiar: I am not thinking of these dogmas as determining men's opinions but rather as completely controlling the *expression* of all opinions. People will live under an absolute, palpable tyranny, though without being able to say they are not free. I think the Catholic Church does something rather like this. For dogma is expressed in the form of an assertion, and is unshakable, but at the same time any practical opinion *can* be made to harmonize with it.[14]

III.

After his death, nearly fifty years ago, there is an almost general view (especially in publications in English) that Wittgenstein – who had, apart from one article, not published anything but the *Tractatus Logico-Philosophicus* – was perhaps the most important philosopher of the twentieth century. That he belonged to the history of English philosophy seemed obvious. Started with his philosophical studies before the First World War in England with Russell, his training as a philosopher was English. And with a few exceptions – perhaps with several soldiers during the war (Ludwig Hänsel, Michael Drobil) and the members of his family – he did not belong to any circle in Vienna. I do not think he had much contact with artists and writers in Vienna. When he met Loos, whom he already knew personally in 1914, together with von Ficker, during the early 1920s, he was disgusted: he found him *"versmokt."*

But this did not alter his high regard for Loos's revolutionary decision to liberate modern architecture from unnecessary decoration. The house that Wittgenstein designed for his sister, Gretl Stonborough, in Kundmanngasse in Vienna, originally designed by Paul Engelmann, was a task which in some way should have helped to overcome the fact and catastrophe that he had to quit his job as a teacher. On the other hand, it did give Wittgenstein the chance to practice and to prove his aesthetic sense and his abilities as an engineer. Together with Engdmann, whom he won as a friend during his time in Olmütz, he put all of his talent into the construction and details of this house, which reflects the ideas and constructions of Adolf Loos. That, on the other hand, he both did not at all like Loos's engagement in an almost political movement for new architecture *and* found him somewhat strange was, I think, *not* an obstacle to the inclusion of Loos's name in the list of people who had a decisive influence on his own thinking. At certain moments Wittgenstein was convinced that there was truth in his idea that he "really only think[s] reproductively." It is worthwhile quoting this confession from 1931:

> I don't believe I have ever *invented* a line of thinking, I have always taken one over from someone else. I have simply straightaway seized on it with enthusiasm for my work of clarification. That is how Boltzmann, Hertz, Schopenhauer, Frege, Russell, Kraus, Loos, Weininger, Spengler, Sraffa have influenced me [...] What I invent are new *similes*.[15]

Although I do not want to dwell on this list, I think that we have to take it seriously and that it in fact comprises the most important figures in Wittgenstein's intellectual life. It is noteworthy that this list, written almost three years after his return to England in 1931, includes only one Englishman – Russell – but four Germans: Heinrich Hertz, Arthur Schopenhauer, Gottlob Frege, and Oswald Spengler. Evidently not all philosophers, these Germans were, at different times, of central importance to the evolution of Wittgenstein's work. The list also reflects the temporal order of these influences, since of the five Austrians, he mentions Boltzmann first, followed by Kraus, Loos, and Weininger (whom he met before the twenties), and finally Sraffa (whom he met immediately after his return to England; actually Sraffa's name is emphasised especially in Wittgenstein's preface to his second main work, the *Philosophical Investigations*).

Unfortunately there does not exist a similar list of poets and writers who may have contributed to his understanding, even if they did possibly have a special role in his "work of classification" – his *Klärungswerk* as he has called it. But on the basis of different sources, I think he could have made similar lists for literature. Most of the following names would no doubt have been mentioned: of the writers and poets from Germany, first and foremost, is Goethe, who has a special place in Wittgenstein's life, and then Friedrich Schiller, Gotthold Ephraim Lessing, Heinrich von Kleist, Matthias Claudius, Eduard Mörike, Ludwig Uhland, Albert von Chamisso, Wilhelm Busch, and certainly Georg Christoph Lichtenberg; from Switzerland, Gottfried Keller, and from Austria, Franz Grillparzer, Johann Nestroy, Nikolaus Lenau, and Rainer Maria Rilke. But others should also be mentioned, for instance, Ferdinand Kürnberger and Ludwig Anzengruber, Russian writers (especially Dostoevskii and Tolstoi), and the famous Indian Rabindranath Tagore.

Wittgenstein was for some time a regular reader of *Der Brenner*, edited by Ludwig von Ficker, and even before the First World War a temporary subscriber to the journal *Die Fackel*, edited by Karl Kraus. The first journal was indeed a more or less Catholic literary journal. Nevertheless, or perhaps just because of this fact, one could find there poems by Georg Trakl and Rainer Maria Rilke. That even Karl Kraus praised this journal as "the only honest periodical in Austria," and hence the only honest periodical in Germany,[16] persuaded Wittgenstein to donate to this journal 100,000 Kronen (at that time quite an enormous amount of money), of which Trakl and Rilke were to receive 20,000 Kronen each; 10,000 Kronen went to the journal *Der Brenner*, and the balance was distributed among fourteen other people.

It was through these transactions that Wittgenstein received Georg Trakl's poems, which he evaluated as brilliant, in spite of the fact that he could not understand them.[17] Actually, in November 1914, Wittgenstein wanted to visit Trakl, who was at the time ill and in a Krakow hospital. But Trakl, who had previously attempted suicide, died after a final attempt two days before Wittgenstein's ship "Goplana" arrived in Krakow. In his diary Wittgenstein notes: "Ich bin gespannt, ob ich Trakl treffen werde. Ich hoffe sehr." ("I am curious whether I shall meet Trakl. I very much hope so.") Receiving the sad news in the hospital, he writes: "Dies traf mich sehr stark. Wie traurig, wie traurig." ("This affected me very strongly. How sad, how sad.") In a letter to Ludwig von Ficker he repeats what he thought of Trakl's poems: "Ich verstehe sie nicht; aber ihr *Ton* beglückt mich. Es ist der Ton der wahrhaft genialen Menschen."[18] ("I do not understand them; but their *tone* makes me happy. It is the tone of truly ingenious people.")

We know for a fact that Wittgenstein was well acquainted with at least these two journals, *Die Fackel* and *Der Brenner*, which means that at a certain time he had a general picture of the kinds of lyric and prose writings available and an idea of what modern literature, at least German modern literature, was about. If, however, we turn our attention to the oft-mentioned examples of the kinds of literature Wittgenstein actually liked and read, we will mainly have to look the past; most of his citations and remarks point in that direction. There is no doubt Wittgenstein had quite a good and perhaps even excellent knowledge of classical literature. Whenever possible he read a text in its original language; he even worked on his Latin in order to read the *Vulgata* in the appropriate language.

IV.

Wright, in his aforementioned papers, calls our attention to three authors, all of whom have dedicated their work to the question: what kind of relation or correspondence is there – or can there be found – between Wittgenstein and his philosophy on the one hand and modernity on the other. The three authors are Allan Janik,[19] co-author with Stephen Toulmin of *Wittgenstein's Vienna*; Janos Christof

Nyíri, the Hungarian philosopher who ascribes to Wittgenstein not only a conservative style but also a conservative anthropology;[20] and S. Stephan Hilmy, with his studies on the later Wittgenstein.[21] I will not discuss any of these except for a very brief observation on Nyíri's view of Wittgenstein's conservatism and a remark on Hilmy's attempt to stress – or overestimate – the difference between the early and the later Wittgenstein.

No one reading Wittgenstein's writings, and especially the remarks to be found in his notes and letters concerning his relation to his time, can fail to observe that a number of these remarks can be read and understood as expressions of a traditionalist or, in Nyíri's view, conservative way of thinking. Nyíri claims that neo-conservative thinkers directly influenced these remarks and, especially, Wittgenstein's later philosophy.[22] Perhaps the best examples cited by Nyíri are the writings of Paul Ernst; Wittgenstein admired this writer and poet, and even wanted to mention Ernst in the preface of a book. "The book" Wittgenstein was alluding to is probably the one he hoped to finish and for which he wrote the preface in November 1930. Nevertheless it seems to me completely wrong to mix up, on the one side, the change of one's life and lifestyle (as motivated by religious and ethical reasons), and, on the other, Wittgenstein's conservative taste and interest in music and poetry with a general neo-conservative political movement. A few characteristic traits of some kind do not make up an ideal; we have to take into account the overall circumstances from which these traits arise. For instance, Mahler's symphonies exemplify a remarkably different type compared to classical symphonies. Wittgenstein believed that Mahler's music was "worthless," but despite this negative judgment, he recognized that "if conditions nowadays are really so different from what they once were that one cannot even compare the *genre* one's work belongs to with that of earlier works, then one can not compare them in respect to the *value* of either."[23] And Wittgenstein adds that he, too, makes this mistake now and then.

It is in this sense that Wright justly criticizes Nyíri's identification of Wittgenstein's criticism of modern civilisation with conservatism; Wright is also justified in correcting Janik's proposal to discern in Wittgenstein's life a strict separation between his philosophy and his personal beliefs. After all, what would it mean to separate philosophizing from personal beliefs? Can we even think of this as anything other than a form of insincerity? No, what Wittgenstein does not say, we, on our part, should not imagine that he had said or thought it, except when there is sufficient evidence. In any case, I do not think that Janik actually suggested what Wright rightly does criticize. What Janik might have found in the later writings of Wittgenstein – and perhaps this is the point he wanted to stress – was the remarkable advice Wittgenstein had for himself and his readers, to be unbiased and not take sides in philosophy: philosophy leaves everything as it is. I shall return to this point later.

With regard to Hilmy's thesis that the philosophy of the later Wittgenstein is in essence a strong departure from his earlier philosophy, I share Wright's doubts; he correctly emphasizes the unity of Wittgenstein's philosophy and his lifelong battle for the proper understanding of philosophy and its task. However, my criticism of Hilmy is not limited to disagreeing with his perception of two different

Wittgensteins, which one may call Wittgenstein I and Wittgenstein II. I am contesting Hilmy's picture of the later Wittgenstein as such. This does not mean that I am not in agreement with many or most of the results of Hilmy's research concerning the earlier sources of Wittgenstein's *Investigations*, which, to a remarkable degree, can be found in the unpublished so-called *Big Typescript* (*TS* 213). I think, for instance, that Hilmy provided good evidence that this typescript has a "far stronger claim to the title 'Preliminary Study for the *Philosophical Investigations*' than *The Brown Books* has."[24]

With his general tendency to exaggerate the difference between the Wittgenstein of the *Tractatus* and his later philosophy, Hilmy does not merely repeat a mistake that marked the early reception of Wittgenstein's work. The trouble is that Hilmy's analysis rests on the erroneous belief that the later Wittgenstein was in total disagreement with his writings of the earlier *Tractatus* period, and equally in total conflict with the logical empiricists. One remembers one of the preface-versions of the "book" Wittgenstein wrote and wanted to publish in the early thirties. In the early version from 1930, he emphasized the huge difference in spirit between the main current of European and American civilisation, "whose expression is the industry, architecture, music, fascism and socialism of our time" and his own anti-modernistic attitude. During the period in which he wrote these versions of the preface, he was deeply influenced by Spengler. While Spengler saw the decline of the West as the fate of Europe, Wittgenstein, unlike Spengler, included also the United States in the decline, although, in agreement with Spengler, he excluded Russia. This general aversion to the political, social, and cultural situation in Europe was not at all unique and was particularly common in Austria. Robert Musil, for instance, notes in his diary that "Europe has never been at such a low ebb as now."[25] And, reflecting on why this is the case, Musil attempts initially to think of man as an "*Ungestalt*," something that accommodates to a given form, but does not shape or construct it. In the same context Musil says: "The human being does not fix the shape of his own life [...]. The causal chains of human development and those of the particular life-form are different."[26]

Wittgenstein may have had similar thoughts about *Lebensform* as early as Musil did – namely at the time of the publication of the *Tractatus*, although I have not find any trace of them. In the 1920s Wittgenstein assessed the mood of the people around him as he had during the final years of the First World War: "We are asleep... *Our life is like a dream.*"[27] And disgusted by his impression of some Austrians in Lower Austria, he said that the people were not human at all but loathsome worms. Thus, already in 1922, he mentions "the idea of a possible flight to Russia," to, as we might guess, the Russia of Tolstoi and Dostoevskii, the Russia beyond Western civilisation.[28] Even when in 1935 Wittgenstein actually went to Russia it was – besides other aims and considerations – in the hope of escaping the strange demands life, namely normal life, makes. And he knew that if "your life does not fit into life's mould," you have to change it so that "it does fit into the mould" – the German word Wittgenstein used was *Form*. To fit into a mould, or life-form, seems to be an image for a complicated process, and we do not know general criteria for fitting into a lifeform because there always remain more options and possibilities beyond the ones which have actually come true or been realized. One might think that the difference between the happy man and the unhappy man does reflect the fitting or non-fitting. But this is not something we can achieve by our will. Wittgenstein never gave up the thought that the world is independent of the will: "Even if everything we wished were to happen, this would only be, so to speak, a favour of fate," he says in the *Tractatus* (6.374). Since there are only logical necessities, no other connection of this kind can be made. The rules we follow in our life are in an essential sense arbitrary. They "are arbitrary in the sense that they are not responsible to some sort of reality – they are not similar to natural laws; nor are they responsible to some meaning the word already has."[29]

V.

Concerning the unity of his work – if this claim has any justification – I assume and take it as a fact that Austrian literature and Austrian philosophy have taken on a shape of their own. But I am aware it would be an exaggeration to state that its literature should be as rigorously distinguished from German literature as Austrian philosophy is from philosophy in Germany. And that has nothing to do with the fact that Kant's and the German idealists' philosophy did not have the same effect in Austria as in Germany. On the contrary, the philosophies of Bolzano and Brentano represent the two lines of the Austrian tradition responsible for the fact that Austrian philosophy has been taken seriously in the last 150 years.

I want to emphasize that: there is, as far as I can see, no indication that Wittgenstein was prejudiced against German literature, but he must have seen a general difference, which in 1929 he formulated as follows: "I think good Austrian work (Grillparzer, Lenau, Bruckner, Labor) is particularly hard to understand. There is a sense in which it is *subtler* than anything else and the truth it expresses never leans towards plausibility."[30]

The problem at the center of Wittgenstein's work was not so much the mind but language: language, he stated, is a labyrinth. You come from one side, and you know where you are ("und du kennst dich aus"); you come from another side to the same spot, and you are lost ("und kennst dich nicht mehr aus"). This is why he directed his interests towards Austrian writers and critics, to Ferdinand Kürnberger and Johann Nestroy: from these two writers he borrowed his mottoes for the *Tractatus Logico-Philosophicus* as well as for the *Philosophical Investigations*. Wittgenstein was also deeply impressed by a play of another Austrian poet and playwright, Ludwig Anzengruber, which engendered in him a religious feeling he never could forget. He later told his friends that this experience occurred when he was twenty-one; he saw the play *Der Kreuzelschreiber* (published 1873), in which "one of the characters expressed the thought that no matter what happened in the world, nothing bad could happen to *him* – *he* was independent of fate and circumstances."[31] "Es kann Dir nix g'schehn! – Du g'hörst zu dem all'n und dös alles g'hört zu Dir! Es kann Dir nix g'schehn!"[32] ("Nothing can happen to you! – You are part of all this, and all this is part of you! Nothing can happen to you!"): this passage in the play impressed Wittgenstein immensely, and he referred to it repeatedly when explaining his religious feelings.

In spite of the fact that in some respects Wittgenstein was a leading modern philosopher and writer, he still remained, from another perspective, critical of modernity: his favorite period in the history of culture ended, as he himself confessed, with the time of Schumann. Thus we may ask ourselves: Why Wittgenstein failed to notice or actually ignored even those artists and writers who, during his lifetime, shared his general background and some of his ethical and moral points of view? Why did he think that *"his* house," although he had been asked to cooperate in its design by the architect Paul Engelmann, did not meet his requirements? Was the house not an example of modern architecture?

We do not find anything in his writings that we could compare to modern literature, nor do we find examples of modern literature in his reading list. Even in the case of Trakl, with whom he had some emotional relationship, does not point to a case of literature which could have served Wittgenstein as a true sample and which he himself did accept. The simplicity he could and did admire in the poems of Mörike was one of the examples of finding the simplest answer in the muddle of philosophical questions. Whereas Wittgenstein had always been interested in contemporary music, and in Gustav Mahler in particular, the works of the poets of that time did not seem to interest him as strongly. But as it is rather unlikely that he did not at least try to feel the spirit of poetry of his time, that is early twentieth century poetry, one can only assume that it must have remained strange to Wittgenstein.

---

[1] Reprinted in: *The Tree of Knowledge and Other Essays*, ed. Georg Henrik von Wright, Leiden: E.J. Brill, 1993.
[2] Friedrich A. von Hayek, *The Counterrevolution of Science*, Glenco, IL: The Free Press, 1952.
[3] Friedrich Nietzsche, *Die Unschuld des Werdens. Der Nachlaß. Bd. I*, ed. Alfred Bäumler, Leipzig: A. Kröner, 1931, p. 391f.
[4] See Ludwig Wittgenstein, *Cambridge Letters*, ed. Brian McGuinness and Georg Henrik von Wright, Oxford: Blackwell, 1995, p. 140. Concerning Tolstoi's influence on Wittgenstein, see Brian McGuinness, *Wittgenstein: A Life*, Berkeley: University of California Press, 1988, p. 156f.
[5] Ludwig Wittgenstein, *Culture and Value*, ed. Georg Henrik von Wright, Oxford: Blackwell, 1980, p. 39e.
[6] *Ibid.*, p. 39e.
[7] Ludwig Wittgenstein, *Geheime Tagebücher 1914-16*, Vienna: Turia and Kant, 1991, p. 68.

[8] Ludwig Wittgenstein, *Cambridge Letters*, ed. Brian McGuinness and Georg Henrik von Wright (Letter of Russell to Lady Ottoline, Dec. 20, 1919), p. 140.
[9] Ludwig Wittgenstein, *Denkbewegungen. Tagebücher 1930-1932, 1936-1937 (MS 183)*, Part 1, ed. Ilse Somavilla, Innsbruck: Haymon, 1997, p. 86 (Feb. 20, 1937).
[10] *Ibid.*, p. 86 (Feb. 20, 1937).
[11] *Ibid.*, p. 75.
[12] *Ibid.*, p. 74.
[13] *Ibid.*, p. 75.
[14] Wittgenstein, *Culture and Value*, p. 28e [see endnote 5].
[15] *Ibid.*, p. 19e.
[16] Quoted in McGuinness, *Wittgenstein: A Life*, p. 205 [see endnote 4].
[17] As Wittgenstein confessed in his diary (Nov. 24, 1914).
[18] Ludwig Wittgenstein, *Briefe an Ludwig v. Ficker*, ed. Georg Henrik von Wright, Salzburg: Otto Müller, p. 22.
[19] Allan Janik, *Essays on Wittgenstein and Weininger* (= Studien zur Österreichischen Philosphie IX), Amsterdam: Rodopi, 1985. Allan Janik, "Why Is Wittgenstein Important?" in: *Wittgenstein - Towards a Re-Evaluation*, ed. Rudolf Haller and Johannes Brandl (Proceedings of the Fourteenth International Wittgenstein Symposium), Vienna: Hölder-Pichler-Tempsky, 1990, vol. 2, pp. 240-246.
[20] Janos Christof Nyíri, ed., *Austrian Philosophy: Studies and Texts*, Munich, 1981; J.C. Nyíri, *Gefühl und Gefüge: Studien zum Entstehen der Philosophie Wittgensteins* (= Studien zur Österreichischen Philosophie XI), Amsterdam: Rodopi 1986; J.C. Nyíri, *Am Rande Europas: Studien zur österreichisch-ungarischen Philosophiegeschichte*. Ch. IV: "Konservative Anthropologie: Der Sohn Wittgenstein," Vienna: Böhlau, 1988, pp. 91-155.
[21] S. Stephan Hilmy, *The Later Wittgenstein: The Emergence of a New Philosophical Method*, Oxford: Basil Blackwell, 1987.
[22] Nyíri, *Am Rande Europas*, p. 113.
[23] Wittgenstein, *Culture and Value*, p. 67e (remark from 1948) [see endnote 5].
[24] See Hilmy, *The Later Wittgenstein*, p. 37.
[25] Robert Musil, *Diaries 1899-1941*, ed. Mark Mirsky, New York: Basic Books, 1999, p. 266.
[26] *Ibid.*, p. 541.
[27] Paul Engelmann, *Letters from Ludwig Wittgenstein. With a Memoir*, Oxford: Basil Blackwell, 1967, p. 7 (Letter from April 9, 1917).
[28] Paul Engelmann, *Letters from Ludwig Wittgenstein*, p. 52 (Letter from Sept. 14, 1922).
[29] Alice Ambrose, ed., *Wittgenstein's Lectures: Cambridge 1932-35*, Oxford: Basil Blackwell, 1979, p. 4.
[30] Wittgenstein, *Culture and Value*, p. 3e.
[31] Norman Malcolm, *Ludwig Wittgenstein: A Memoir*. Second edition, Oxford: Oxford UP, 1984, p. 58.
[32] Ludwig Anzengruber, *Ausgewählte Werke*, Vienna: Kremer & Scheriau, 1966, p. 172.

REALITY & THE LANGUAGE OF FICTION

John Gibson
University of Toronto

> And as imagination bodies forth
> The forms of things unknown, the poet's pen
> Turns them to shapes and gives to airy nothing
> A local habitation and a name.
>
> Shakespeare, *A Midsummer Night's Dream*

I.

In this paper I will suggest that one can use Wittgenstein to shed light on a puzzle literary language raises for the philosophy of language. Specifically, I will show that his notion of linguistic criteria allows us to understand how literature, speaking as it does about fictions and fictions alone, might nevertheless be able to say something of profound cognitive consequence about reality. Explaining how talk about fictions can be revelatory of reality is, of course, not interesting merely as a puzzle for the philosophy of language. It is upon the belief that it is possible to hang our faith in the humanistic value of the narrative arts, and so much is at stake when we find ourselves called on to address this puzzle. Now most of us do believe, in *some* sense at least, that the language of literary fiction can offer us genuine insights into how things stand in our world. But explaining this with any degree of philosophical respectability has proven to be a tremendously troubling task, and this is where Wittgenstein can help us. With the exception of two authors, Bernard Harrison and David Schalkwyk,[1] I am unaware of any philosopher who has even touched on the possibilities Wittgenstein's notion of criteria opens up for those of us interested in the puzzle of literary language, and in this paper I will map out a precise strategy for importing it into the current debate.

Writing the Austrian Traditions: Relations between Philosophy and Literature.
Ed. Wolfgang Huemer and Marc-Oliver Schuster. Edmonton, Alberta:
Wirth-Institute for Austrian and Central European Studies, 2003. pp. 49-65.

II.

The precise form of the problem that Wittgenstein allows us to solve is well-known and requires very little setting up. It concerns a tension that exists between two basic intuitions we have about the nature of works of literary fiction. One intuition concerns the social and cognitive value of literature, and it tells us that literature offers us a window on our world. We might call this the "humanist intuition" and characterize it as the thought that literature presents the reader with an intimate and intellectually significant engagement with social and cultural reality. It is the idea, one familiar to all of us in some respect, that literature is the textual form to which we turn when we want to read the story of our shared form of life, our moral and emotional, social and sexual – and so on for whatever corners of our culture we think literature brings to view – *ways of being human*. The other intuition concerns how we understand the fiction that goes into a work of literary fiction. For it strikes us as equally intuitive to say that the imaginative basis of literary creation presents to the reader not his world but *other* worlds, what we commonly call fictional worlds. If we think that literature tells us about our world, we have to make this square with the obvious fact that we understand, and certainly read, literature as if it is exempt from the task of worldly exegesis. Literary fiction trades in aesthetic creation rather than factual representation. It speaks about people created on paper, who inhabit worlds made only of words. And from this it seems quite natural to conclude that literature is therefore essentially and intentionally silent about the way our world is, choosing instead to speak about worlds none of which are quite our own. The tension, then, is a matter of how we might reconcile these two intuitions, these basic visions we have of literature as somehow at once both thoroughly our-worldly and other-worldly.

Of these two intuitions, the humanist's has lost out in current philosophy of fiction. The reason for this, of course, is not that anyone believes that we have come to realize that literary fiction is after all irrelevant to life. It is because in many minds humanism is associated with a crude and antiquated tendency in the history of aesthetics. In attempting this reconciliation, humanists have often been guilty of two sins, namely that of forging the connection to our world by taking literature to be a mimetic rendering of reality – and thus relying on the now much disfavored representational view of literary fiction – and then going on to treat as the ultimate object of literary appreciation not the literary work of art itself but this world of which the text is thought to be just a mirror. There is an odd expression Derrida has popularized, "*il n'y a pas de hors-texte.*" If tamed slightly into stating that, at least from the literary perspective, nothing outside the text *matters*, Derrida's curious proclamation brings to light a widely accepted claim. The extra-textual is thought to be the extra-literary, beyond the reach of anyone who wants to illuminate the nature of what we experience when we look between the covers of a novel. To try to step from literature to the extra-textual is to take a step away from the very object of literary theory. And the humanist is typically taken to be the theorist who has failed to learn this basic lesson, the dolt, in a word, who keeps trying to turn the *hors-texte* into the object of literary investigation.

It takes very little argumentation to bring to view the reason many philosophers believe that the humanist necessarily cannot correct his intuition, that in attempting to forge the connection between literature and life he will always end up losing the literary text. The sceptic who doubts that the humanist can offer this reconciliation has a very simple argument at his disposal. The sceptic argues that the humanist must accept the following constraint: he must prove that the value he wants to attribute to a literary text is an actual property of the text itself. If he does not meet this constraint, the sceptic reasonably points out that the humanist will fail to identify a proper literary value, and thus he will default on his promise to tell us something about the nature of literature. But if the humanist accepts this constraint – and he clearly must if he wants to shed light on what we come into contact with in our experience of a work of literary fiction – there seems to be no possibility of giving a linguistic ground to the humanist's claim that literary language can tell us something about the way our world is. As Peter Lamarque argues:

> The particulars presented in a novel are *fictional*, and how can any view, however objective, of *fictional* particulars, give us truth? Ex hypothesi, it is not a view of the real world.[2]

Implicit in the above reasoning is a claim that has the status of a truism in most corners of the philosophy of fiction: literary language eschews worldly reference and representation. It thus appears to cast aside the very tools by which we can use language to create a picture of how things stand in our world. We take, habitually, the notion of reference to describe how a string of words can be understood as being *about* something (by referring to it or otherwise offering a linguistic representation of it). But literature sends its words out to fictional rather than actual addresses, referring to and so "about" the contours of purely imaginary worlds.

We might recall Plato's famous anti-literary fulmination in the *Republic* here. His insight, a reasonable one itself, is that there is something genuinely odd in the very idea of literary language: literature speaks our language as it were – it borrows our words and grammar, our idioms and cultural references – but it does very strange things with these words. In the language of narrative fiction the rails of reference run not from word to world but from word to chimeras, creatures of an author's imagination. And from this it might well appear that literature talks quite literally about nothing, that it is a mere *flatus vocis*. Very few would agree with the conclusion Plato draws from this – that literature should be banned because it invites the innocent among us to mistake fictions for reality – but his claim that the fictional element in literary language implies that it speaks of worlds other than our own would strike much contemporary philosophy as neither odd nor antiquated. For when we find a use of language that neither refers to nor represents reality, it appears to us, just as to Plato, that we have lost all linguistic justification for claiming that this use of language could be trying to tell us something about reality.

The language of literary fiction shares in the sense of our language, of course; an occurrence of the word "pain" in a literary text still means "pain." But it does not *use* our language to talk about *our* world. Rather, it uses it to talk about imagined worlds (or possible worlds, or make-believe worlds, depending on the precise theory to which one is committed). There is, as it is often described, a referential barrier that runs between our world and fictional worlds, a representational divide we appear unable to bridge. Thus if the humanist must show the connection to reality to be in some sense *internal* to a work of literary fiction, and if all we find when we look inside a literary text are words, all of which reach out to fictions rather than reality, the sceptic claims that the humanist intuition must be senseless. Indeed, the humanist's conception of literary language appears to be built upon a paradox, a desire to understand literature in terms of precisely what literature turns out to be contrasted with: a vision of the way our world is.

III.

Yet why, *precisely*, do we feel that the humanist must embrace a paradox if he still wants to claim that literature speaks about our world? The sceptic responds by simply repeating his argument: he tells us that he has already answered this question. And at first we do feel the tug of necessity here; we do feel that there is just no other option open to the humanist. But with a few moments of reflection we can see that the sceptic's anti-humanism does not simply fall in fine *a priori* fashion from his reflections on the absence of worldly representation and reference in literature as, say, idealism does from Berkeley's famous *esse est percipi*. In the latter case, the position is implied by the very words used to state the argument: it just says so much. The same is not true of our sceptic's claim. Saying that literature refuses to represent reality does not in any straightforward sense just amount to the claim that there is *no* point of contact between world and literature. There is an implicit assumption we need to unearth, something that explains why we feel the force of entailment here – we need to ask what gives us this sense that the sceptic's argument reveals the impossibility of the humanistic conception of literary language.

As with most cases in which we feel the presence of paradox without quite seeing its source, there is a larger picture in place, exerting its force on us from behind the scenes. This is what is happening here: there is another commitment, some more basic picture we are beholden to, by virtue of which the sceptic's arguments appear so reasonable. We know that the sceptic hangs his anti-humanism on his arguments against the presence of worldly representation and reference in literature. So the question becomes: what makes us think that humanism is senseless just because of their absence?

What we feel, in feeling the pull of the sceptic's arguments, is the presence of a certain picture of how language and reality are basically hooked up. We feel that there is a divide between language and reality, and that bridging the gap requires the semantic tools the sceptic has taken from the humanist. The sceptic's argument that these semantic tools are unavailable to the humanist has much force because of the role these tools play in this picture. They are *the* tools for bringing language to bear on reality, and naturally we feel that the humanist is lost when they are taken from him. Without them we appear to be left with mere language, words with no worldly point of contact. Our readiness to accept the sceptic's argument is explained in terms of how we hear his arguments. And we do so standing on this more basic picture of the word-world relation, that of *a gap between language and reality* that can only be bridged by the semantic tools that the sceptic has turned against the humanist.

The idea of the divide is at best metaphorical, though two thousand years of debates between idealists and realists have provided many occasions to invoke the picture of a separation in kind between the conventional and the natural, language and reality. It is the idea of the gap between world and word that we must bridge if our words are to connect us to reality, the picture – however one precisely wants to describe it – that informs many of philosophy of language's basic dualisms, that of the divide between (to play on the famous Sellarsian distinction) the logical space of nature and the logical space of language, between the things we talk about and the things in themselves, between the natural and the conventional, word and world.

This picture can be illustrated in a great number of ways, but for our purposes we might say that it tells us that language and world are separated by a window. When language speaks about reality, it looks out of the window and describes what it sees. It attempts to mirror or, as it is more commonly put, "represent" what is on the other side of the window. When we explain the relationship between a linguistic representation and its object, we invoke the common distinctions between a referring expression and its referent, a word and the bit of world to which it corresponds, or reality and our sentential renderings of it. We look through the window and use our words (however we want to explain this) to mirror, like landscape sketchers, what we see. The idea of wedding word and world becomes a question of representational accomplishment, of whether what we say when we look out of the window, is a fair portrait of how things stand on the other side.

A picture of this sort explains why the sceptic casts doubt on humanism with such ease. How can we, if we have a picture of this sort in place, see literature as ever connecting us to the world? When reference to reality and representation of world drop out, we lose the idea that a use of language can describe the actual, and with this picture in place we cannot even envision an alternative mode of contact: humanism is made utterly senseless. For the question obviously becomes: since literature does not look out of this window when it speaks – since it does not even attempt to mirror the actual, or to refer to and represent the real – how could it possibly have *anything* to say that is genuinely informative of extra-textual reality? We just cannot imagine what a point of contact would look like if we speak of literature within this framework of the word-world relation.

IV.

The view of language that the sceptic exploits is this picture in which the relationship between word and world is cast in terms of an initial opposition; this picture that tells us that they remain divided from one another until we succeed in uniting them by way of representation. As intuitive and entrenched as this picture of the word-world relation may be, it is not compulsory. It has been widely attacked by philosophers working in the tradition in which, as Blackburn puts it, "Wittgenstein is admired as the high priest."[3] This tradition distinguishes itself from representationalist and other divide-endorsing pictures by refusing to cast the relation between world and word in terms of a basic opposition. Hilary Putnam, in what is perhaps the most succinct statement available of this alternative, writes:

> What I am saying, then, is that elements of what we call "language" or "mind" penetrate so deeply into what we call "reality" that the very project of representing ourselves as being mappers of something "language independent" is fatally compromised from the very start.[4]

The interesting thing about this alternative picture (and more generally the philosophical tradition that underlies it) is that it can be best seen as an inversion of a very traditional question. It asks us to approach the understanding of the word-world relation by beginning not with the standard question *how does word inform us of world*? but rather by turning this question around and asking *how does world inform word*? In the first case the discussion begins by asking how language might get beyond itself and touch reality, and thus the roots of the idea of the divide are in place in the very way we formulate the question. In the second case we begin by asking how it might be possible to see language as in some (yet unspecified) sense having world *within* it. This distinction moves us away from wondering how a purely contingent and arbitrary creature of convention such as a natural language might be an accurate mirror of independent reality. And in its place it asks us to explore the possibility that language is informed by the world in the very building of its systems of speech; indeed that world is woven into the fabric of our language. We try to find a level at which reality is blown so directly into language that we are entitled to claim that world "is fused into the foundation of our language game."[5] And this allows us to see, I will argue, to reject the idea of a gap between the world and language that is presupposed in the reasoning that makes literary language look like an oddity and humanism an impossibility.

There is a fear that, if we speak of our connection to the world by first stating that language is our sole point of contact, we will ultimately end up trapped by language, unable to escape it and find our way to reality. The first step in the argument I will present – Wittgenstein's argument that we cannot get between "language and its object" – is also the same step that is often thought to lead directly to linguistic idealism. The fear, more specifically, is that if we begin by claiming that we are linguistic creatures through and through, fully determined in what claims we can make about reality by the conceptual categories and vocabularies we inherit from our language, we will then slide hopelessly into a sort of prison of pure convention, locked in language as it were. One of the reasons we are inclined to think this way is that, still clinging to the picture of the divide, we think that opting for language is just a way of opting for the linguistic side of the divide to the exclusion of the side of reality. But, we might notice, this leaves us in the curious position of seeing our language, our perspective, our form of life, as alienating just because they are *ours*. We come to see language and culture as an obstruction to our connection to reality rather than an expression of it. And this, as the Wittgenstein-inspired position I will elaborate tells us, is precisely what we must try to avoid.

The following quotes from Wittgenstein's *Philosophical Investigations* (*PI* henceforth) offer a good point of entrance into our discussion:

Grammar tells what kind of object anything is. (*PI* § 373)

Essence is expressed by grammar. (*PI* § 371)

What Wittgenstein is attacking here is the idea of a second voice – that of reality as it "really" is apart from how it is expressed in our language – that can add a claim to the effect that "you are right to say thus" when we speak about the world. And Wittgenstein means this not in the linguistic idealist's sense that we have nothing but *mere* words, that nothing but *mere* linguistic convention plays any role in validating what we say, without any participation of the extra-linguistic (as though it is not the fact that there is a chair in the corner of my room that entitles me to claim so much but some linguistic oddity, not a "worldly" fact but only a "wordy" fact, whatever this might be). He means it in the sense that "grammatical" rules – the constitutive rules of language – specify what we can meaningfully claim to be the case, and thus we look there to see what we can sensibly say of reality. There is no sense to the idea that the justification of what we say lies fully outside language, as though in speech we send our words out into the world and wait to see whether reality will receive them. It lies within our language, within the perspective with which we confront reality. Grammar, in the broad sense in which Wittgenstein uses the term, provides the conditions for claiming anything to be (as Aristotle often said) a *this,* the very condition for discerning a thing as this or that sort of thing, for speaking about anything as being something at all. The "essence" of what we speak about – conceived not as a metaphysical presence but as this linguistic expression of "what kind of object anything is" – is found within our frame of reference, our language. What the Wittgenstein of the *Tractatus* found in logic, the later Wittgenstein finds in grammar, the rules of everyday natural language. Whereas he once thought that the structure of an ideal logical language would reflect the structure of the real – logic was for the early Wittgenstein "the great mirror" of reality – he later came to embrace the grammar of natural language for establishing this connection between word and world.

When we ask questions about the nature of the things we speak about, we cannot think of this as implying a comparison between the "real" object and the way language frames the object; it cannot be thought of as guided, even in principle, by an idea of establishing an adequate match or representational relation between the expression of world in language and the way the world really is. The reason for this should be clear: it makes no sense to think that we can step outside our linguistic frame to query how our "picture" compares to the reality it "depicts." But this is not because what is outside our frame is simply unavailable to us – if we mean by this that *reality lies there only we cannot see beyond our representations of it*. For what we fail to notice if we think this way is that talk of representation and "mirroring" is illicit at this point, or at any rate uninvited by anything we have said thus far. We begin by accepting that "language tells us what kind of object anything is." But we do *not* take "language" here to imply "rather than reality," as though there is a choice between the two and our opting for language intimates the absence of any participation of reality in determining the linguistic specification of "what kind of object anything is."

Wittgenstein wants us to see that we can understand how words might refer to or represent world only if we ask the much more basic question of *what sorts of prior connection between word and world are presupposed in the very possibility that sentences can represent and refer*? He asks us to see that understanding the basic association between word and world requires an account of how language draws various items in the world – various bits of reality – into its grammar, which it can then use as instruments or standards of representation. As he argues in his famous example, the Paris meter-stick

> is *one* thing of which one can say neither that it is one metre long, nor that it is not one metre long [...] But this is, of course, not to ascribe any extraordinary property to it, but only to mark its peculiar role in the language-game of measuring with a metre-rule. – Let us imagine samples of colour being preserved in Paris like the standard metre. We define: "sepia" means the colour of the standard sepia which is there kept hermetically sealed. Then it will make no sense to say of this sample either that it is of this colour or that it is not. – We can put it like this: This sample is an instrument of the language used in ascriptions of colour. In this language-game it is not something that is represented, but is a means of representation [...] It is a paradigm in our language-game, something with which a comparison is made. And this may be an important observation, but it is none the less an observation concerning our language-game – our method of representation. (*PI* § 50)

We find in this example an elegant metaphor for the relationship between grammar and representational and referential uses of language. The metre-stick in the above example is "not represented but is an instrument of representation" because we give it status in our language as the standard (what grammar calls "essence") of being a metre long, for representing objects in the world as *counting* as a metre. Of course the full story of how language comes to use world as a standard of representation will be more complex than this. In the case of simple objects such as chairs and rocks, the story may be the fairly familiar one of coming to name an object and agreeing on the name we have given it – more complicated, but perhaps not too interestingly so, than what we find in the example of the metre-stick. In the case of our more complex terms such as "personhood," "goodness," "love," and so on, the story will likely boil down to social history. Jealousy, to give a simple example, develops grammatically as our culture develops institutionally. We develop institutions based on the pledge of fidelity (such as in marriage); and once we have examples of people betraying these institutions, we can use the behavior of the wounded (Dido of Virgil's *Aeneas*, for example) as a standard by which we can, so to say, go on to represent the word "jealously."

The point is, we are able to represent and refer to the world in speech because we use the world as a standard of representation and reference when speaking about the sundry objects we experience. And so when we want to illuminate the nature of the objects we talk about – what we are saying about the way the world is when we say that this is that sort of thing – we do not try to take a stab at the nature of the thing as it "really" is apart from how we say that it is. We come to our understanding of the reality of the things we talk about by reflecting on the story of how these bits of the world have been brought into and given shape by our way of life. We come to understand the way our world is, in short, by reflecting not on represented objects but on our standards of representation.

Thus we are not to think that the act of using sentences to refer to or represent the world carries the entire burden of our linguistic connection to reality. We use the world to fix the use of the words in our language, and thus we make the leap to representational and referential speech because language already aligns us with reality – and we should hear this as running very much contrary to the notion that representation explains the basic, initial if you like, union of language and reality. Language absorbs world, building it into the fabric of its grammar. And we account for this not by claiming that language can perform some mysterious metaphysical act. We rather show that the story of the source of our standards of representation is a tale of cultural activity, a matter of how a living practice develops standards of representation by building words upon world.

These aspects of our natural world and human history that we draw into language as standards of representation become what Wittgenstein calls linguistic *criteria*. Our descriptions of reality are made possible by the fact that we possess these shared linguistic criteria. They explain how it is that we are able to speak in a common tongue of anything as being *this* sort of thing, how it is that we are able to "word the world together."[6] They do not "make it the case" that the world is really as we say it is or "establish the truth" of what language calls reality. They provide the conditions of any sort of talk, talk of truth included. Criteria determine the boundaries of meaning and sense, of what we can intelligibly claim to be the case. They are the specifications of the rules of the game, as it were, the standards that account for our alignment with others in communication. They do not function in Wittgenstein's philosophy as a replacement for representation and correspondence talk. The possession of shared criteria expresses the condition, the bedrock, of the possibility of any talk at all.

There is a temptation to think of social theories of meaning of the sort Wittgenstein offers as yet one more chapter in the book of anti-realism, as though saying that criteria are a product of social engagement with one another and our world leads to what it is now fashionable to call "constructivism." The fear is that offering a social rather than metaphysical ground to our criterial connection to reality will invariably lead us to see these criteria as so contingent and arbitrary that we end up finding ourselves with no justification for speaking of these criteria as connecting us to something real at all. In *On Certainty* Wittgenstein offers an argument that allows us to overcome this fear, one which shows us that an insight into our criteria is indeed an insight into something "thickly" real. Like many of Wittgenstein's most interesting arguments, it expresses a profound point with the simplest of insights. It begins by drawing us precariously near anti-realism, and the beauty of the argument lies in how it allows us to keep our balance just before falling over. Consider the following quotes:

> I did not get my picture of the world by satisfying myself of its correctness; nor do I have it because I am satisfied of its correctness. No: it is the inherited background against which I distinguish the true and the false. (*OC* § 94)

And:

> If the true is what is grounded, the ground is not true, nor yet false. (*OC* § 205)

At first glance this may strike us as nothing more than a revised argument for idealism, for the claim being made is that the ground language offers us for speaking about the world – our linguistic criteria – cannot be said to be true. But notice also that the ground cannot be said to be false. And this is curious. I cannot claim truth or falsity for it, so what can I say about it at all? Does not this imply that there is just *nothing* to say, that – as Rorty prods for much the same reasons – there is no longer any reason to talk about a connection between language and reality? Indeed, is it not right to say what linguistic sceptics have always said, that we cannot *know* that language offers us an alignment with the way the world is?

The answer to this question, like most honest answers, is yes and no. I certainly cannot *know* that the criteria of language *truly* reveal how the world is, for there is no truth to be mentioned here that would support my claim that I know it. Criteria express the conditions of truth and falsity, and thus they are not open to assessment for truth and falsity themselves. This much Wittgenstein makes clear and this much the linguistic sceptic has right (and this is why he is so often hard to silence: we cannot just say that he is wrong, that his sceptical hypothesis is simply *false*). When she says "you do not *know* that language gets the world right" I *must* answer "no, I do not *know* that." But notice that, unlike the linguistic sceptic, my saying that I do not know this is not a concession that a truth-value is missing where there should be one. It is not a concession that there is some adjudicating fact that is unfortunately unavailable to us. The sceptic takes our inability to claim knowledge here to qualify what sort of *belief* we can have about the worldly reach of criteria. But what

Wittgenstein is saying is that *there is no belief at this level.* Whereas the sceptic takes this mandatory "I do not know" to show up an epistemic defeat, a failure of knowledge, Wittgenstein responds by saying there is no defeat because the battle is not epistemic: it is not a failure of knowledge because knowledge-claims do not apply here. This is an unusual first step in an argument that promises to unite language and reality, but if we follow the idea it will lead us somewhere very interesting.

The specific problem with the linguistic sceptic is that he demands grounds for the very grounds we have for speaking. Now the grounds the sceptic argues we lack are indeed absent: there is nothing that could voice an assurance that language *truly* expresses reality as it is. But this is not because linguistic criteria are *groundless*, if we mean by this that we have somehow managed to see they are free-floating and that where we once thought that there was a kind of metaphysical anchor we now see that there is nothing at all. What is wrong with saying "groundless" is precisely that we are speaking about the *grounds* of language – to use "groundless" here is to fail to understand what we are talking about: bedrock, beneath which we cannot go. To ask to have our linguistic criteria, our language, vouched for is to ask for grounds for our criteria. But this, of course, amounts to asking for criteria with which we can evaluate the truth of *our* criteria, grounds for our very grounds of meaningful speech. And by this logic we then must ask for an evaluation of these newly acquired criteria and grounds – what grounds them? – and so on until we find ourselves with a very nasty infinite regress. The sceptic's question ceases to be meaningful at this point, requiring as it does that he speak without the support of criteria in fashioning her repudiation of our criteria. Whose criteria does he use to carry out this repudiation, to state his sceptical hypothesis? They cannot be the criteria of our language, for these are what he is questioning. He asks, "How do I know that things are as we say they are, that this is really a chair, the sun, a human, etc.?" What else should we say? What else could we coherently call these things? And on what do we stand when we picture an alternative?

The sceptic's question does not place a wedge between what we say and the way the world is so much as it dissolves the possibility of meaningful speech altogether. In this respect the sceptical impulse is not unlike a certain Scholastic penchant for asking how much time elapsed before God created time. Language refuses to be an ally here. In trying to repudiate the alignment with reality we find in criteria the sceptic speaks from the dark, asking an impossible question rather than one which makes us doubt that our criteria reach all the way into our world. The sceptic does not reveal a gap between language and world in this sense, then: the vocabulary he employs in stating his sceptical hypothesis is drained of its force and empty. He attempts to take up a cognitive perspective towards the possibility of having any sort of cognitive perspective at all, and in so doing he loses language – he is in effect silenced by his own words.

Wittgenstein's response comes at a price, but one that brings reality down to earth and thus to the our-worldly level in the process. We lose the idea that we can have our linguistic alignment with reality vouched for, shown to be true all the way down as it were. We might call this the metaphysical craving, and its satisfaction is denied us. The sceptic, for his part, does make us realize this. Since we cannot respond to his "how do you know" with "of course we know," he makes us realize that we cannot step outside our form of life and speak meaningfully about its linguistic success. But Wittgenstein wants to say that if we lose the ability to claim truth for our alignment with reality, we also lose the ability to doubt it in the way the sceptic envisions.

This is the reward for what might appear to be a huge sacrifice. What forces us to accept that language aligns us with reality is not a right we win from any metaphysical or ontological insight: "What has to be accepted, the given, is – so one could say – *forms of life*" (*PI* 226e), and we cannot step outside the conditions of meaningful speech to try to see what grounds it. We cannot speak of a match between criteria and the way the world is, nor of adequate representation. *But this is because there is no gap that can be meaningfully mentioned at this level.* It is not a hypothesis that our criteria match the facts. It is not a deduction or inference that allows us to make this claim. It is a "grammatical truth," a claim forced on us by the very words we use to communicate with one another. We can say that an insight into criteria is an insight into reality not because criteria show us how word *truly* matches up with world, but because there is, we might say, no dividing distinction to be made between the two at this level. This picture brings the idea of the word-world relation down to earth by making their alignment a fact of life, evidenced by the simple but profoundly revealing point that we succeed in making ourselves understood to one another. The union of word and world is grounded and given expression in the fabric of our living human practices, made visible not through any feat of metaphysical inquiry but by seeing what is already plainly before us: a shared form of life.

V.

The humanist's sceptic, like the traditional semantic sceptic, plays on our fear that a view into language, cut off from any actual thing we might use language to talk about, is a view of words divorced from reality. What we have done is to replace this picture of language that makes literature look to be isolated from reality because of its failure of worldly representation with one in which language is seen as expressing world within itself, not as connecting to an independent reality by mapping it but by building it into its "grammar," its criteria, in such a way that there is no longer any sense to the idea of language as empty of world just on account of its failure to represent or refer to it. What Wittgenstein allows us to see is that the connection between language and reality is prior (in understanding, as Aristotle might say) to the level at which the humanist's sceptic gives his arguments. But Wittgenstein also offers us a way to structure the humanist intuition, as we should be beginning to see. What we have now is a vocabulary that allows us to meet the sceptic's challenge directly, namely to show that we can identify something quite densely real immediately within the literary work, internal to it rather than *hors-texte*.

What I am going to call the "basic humanist claim," the ground-level claim Wittgenstein makes possible for the humanist, can be characterized as follows. We want to say that for some aspect of a work of literature that arouses our worldly interest, we can claim of it that "*this* is ϕ" in such a way that there is no wedge to be placed between the fiction's presentation of ϕ and what ϕ is. We take the demonstrative as functioning to pick out not a represented worldly object (the sceptic has taken this from us) nor a pure creature of fiction (which the sceptic says it must pick out) but ϕ *just as it is*. For those aspects of cultural life that fuel the furnaces of literary creation, we want to say that they are *seen*, just as they are, in the text: that *this* is jealousy, *this* is anger, *this* is suffering, and so on. And we want to be able to say this in such a way that the force of the demonstrative is one of identifying directly within the text something more properly called "life" than the merely lifelike, *veritas* rather than verisimilitude, world rather than a fictional mimesis of it.

Let us give some structure to this discussion with a concrete critical example. In re-reading *Othello* I see that I have missed something; it is one of those instances of finding a new layer of complexity in a work read a number of times before. Although I very well know that Othello is the subject of Iago's angry discussion with Roderigo in the first act, I notice for the first time that never once is Othello mentioned by name. The first time Othello is explicitly referred to it is not by his proper name but by his ethnicity: he is "The Moor" (I.*i*.40). Iago is Othello's *ancient* and confidant – they know each other intimately – and if not for his anger we would certainly expect him to call Othello by his proper name, and this I now see is subtly suggestive. A few lines later Roderigo adds color to our picture of this nameless Moor by calling him "thick-lips" (I.*i*.66); and I begin to see a progression – in that vague way we become attuned to something taking shape when we read a literary work – that culminates in the first important scene of the tragedy. Iago decides to deliver his initial blow by telling Brabantio that his daughter has secretly married Othello. Again, Othello's name is never used, and the words Iago uses reveal why:

> Your heart is burst, you have lost half your soul; Even now, now, very now, an old Black ram is tupping your white ewe; arise, arise, Awake the snorting citizens with the bell, Or else the devil will make a grandsire of you. (I.*i*.87-90)

> Zounds, sir, you are one of those that will not service God, if the Devil bid you. Because we come to do you service, you think we are ruffians, you'll have your daughter covered with a Barbary horse; you'll have your nephews neigh to you; you'll have coursers for cousins, and gennets for germans. (I.*i*.110-13)

> I am one, sir, that come to tell you, your daughter, and the Moor, are now making the beast with two backs. (I.*i*.115)

Iago's tactic in the above passages is to appeal to the crudest part of Brabantio: his gut-level sense of blood and purity, his racial instinct. Iago offers an image, cunningly crafted to pierce Brabantio's paternal instinct, of his daughter with an African animal, being "tupped" by a black ram who will bring not proper grandchildren but cross-breeds into his family line.[7] There is neither a marriage nor a man depicted in Iago's words, just the image of a "white ewe" copulating with a black beast. One would have to be quite naïve to call Iago's tactic here something other than racist. What is striking, and certainly brilliant, about the passage is how perfectly it captures racism, how, we might say, *essentially* racist it is. We see the gradual construction of a dehumanized picture of Othello. It begins with a reduction of his identity to what separates him from everyone else, his ethnicity; and from here on all of the attendant expressions of racism are brought to life: the notion of the perversion of mixed blood, the idea that an act of love with a racial outsider amounts to sex with a sub-human, an animal, and so is a violation of one's body and family.

In order to eliminate a few possibilities that humanists have traditionally and mistakenly used when trying to forge a connection between literature and life, let me say a few words about how one ought *not* try to make *Othello* speak about our world. To begin with, by "this is racism" I do not mean to pick out some *mimetic* function of the work, say, the fact that Iago is acting as a real racist would. Trivially he is, or else we would not be inclined to call his tactic racist. But I mean something deeper than that the racism we see there *looks* like or imitates real racism. I want to say that it *is* racism. Nor - to dismiss another possibility - is my claim to be taken as saying that the text refers to or represents some extra-textual state of affairs. How would we explain this? Do we say that it represents a universal of some sort, that by "this is racism" I mean to say that the text is a representation of some strange metaphysical entity, perhaps Racism As Such? This is one of the faults of many older forms of humanism - their (bloated) metaphysicalism - that we should try to avoid. It is an unwanted idea, and in any case most current literary theory has, I think, finally shown us that the only legitimate application of notions of reference and representation to a work of literature is that of *fictional* reference and representation, to record how a novel describes an imaginatively created world. Lastly, I am not saying with my "this is racism" that the text or the scenes we have reviewed amount to the claim that racism is thus and such sort of thing, as though my "*this*" functions to pick out a proposition of some sort that is implied by the text. As far as I can see, the text does not state either directly or indirectly a truth-valued proposition about the nature of racism. Again, the sceptic is right here: what the text describes and makes assertions and claims about, is the (fictional) world of its narrative line.

Wittgenstein allows us to avoid these errors of traditional humanism without silencing *Othello* on the way our world is. To let the cat out of the bag, the sort of humanistic explanation Wittgenstein opens up for us is the following: when I claim of *Othello* that "this is racism," my "this" has, I suggest, the force of registering that the text speaks on what Wittgenstein would call the *criterial* level of what racism is, bringing before us language as it is involved with reality at "bedrock" rather than in acts of reference and representation. With slight but instructive bombast, we can say that when Iago sets to turning Brabantio against Othello, he becomes our word for racism - so complete is Iago's expression of racism that we see exposed in his words the criteria for this fixture of our form of life.

This is not to attribute any extraordinary powers to Shakespeare, except that power over words we know that writers of his endowment possess. To account for this we need only to point out that, as we have already seen, Shakespeare's Iago, though a creature of fiction, is nonetheless a fiction that draws together at such a level of clarity and order everything we call "racism" that no wedge can be placed between the text's expression of it and what this fixture of our culture most basically *is*. The "is" here, of course, is not the existential "is" of the actual or the empirical. It is the "is" of what Wittgenstein calls "essence," our language's specification of what the world *is* for us. Just as language "expresses essence," (*PI* § 371) we are claiming that the language of *Othello* expresses racism. Just as criteria tell us "what kind of object anything is" (*PI* § 373), we are claiming that literary language in general can be a specific mouthpiece of "what kind of object anything is." My "this is racism," then, does not record either the referential or representational successes of *Othello*, for there is no success to be spoken of here. It records the success of its expression of racism, not as a simple expression of *Sinn*, but of the fundamental connection to our world that underlies what the sceptic took to be just a "mere" word.

In *Inconvenient Fictions*, Bernard Harrison expresses the distinction as I want to recommend it:

> Literary language, the language of narrative fiction and poetry is, root and branch, constitutive language. As such it is non-referential and it makes no statements [...]. It is a language occupied solely with itself, *in a sense*. The mistake promoted by the Positivistic vision of language is to suppose that this sense can be absolute. Language is everywhere hopelessly infected with the extra-linguistic: the relationship between its signs runs ineluctably by way of the world. So there is, just as the critical humanist has always maintained, a strong connection between language and reality; only it does not run by way of reference and truth. Rather, it permeates the thickness of the language we speak.[8]

Our humanist argues that he has provided a picture of language that permits us to make a similar claim, that literature can bring before us reality as it lies within our language rather than reality as we come into contact with it in referential and representational speech. For if literature represents nothing real, we now can see it as bringing into full view our *standards* of representation, our linguistic criteria "for what the world 'is', without themselves being removed from that world."[9] When we say of what we find in a work of literature that *this* is racism, *this* is jealousy, *this* is suffering, we are testifying to the fact that literature has the power to open up language and expose this reality as it is woven into the fabric of our language – that it has the power to beat, if you will, the world out of our words. In this respect, when we find ourselves in the presence of the literary we come into contact with something very much like what Harrison calls "constitutive" language, for we see language showing us its structure and admitting the reality upon which it is built.

We thus find that we do not need worldly reference and representation to account for literary language's ability to speak out our world. Indeed we do not need to look outside the literary work to explain the humanist connection at all, for there is nothing outside of the text that matters to the humanist. We do not need to attempt to unite the literary with anything *hors-texte*. We can look deeper into what is already within our language. Wittgenstein shows the humanist that if he looks deep enough, he will find there our world as well, not as a represented object but as reality as it "permeates the thickness" of the language both we and the literary work of art speak. If this is the case, the humanist, far from being incoherent, is right to insist that literary fiction can offer crucial cognitive insights into the way our world is.

[1] See Bernard Harrison (1993) and David Schalkwyk (1995).
[2] Peter Lamarque, 1996, p. 105.
[3] Simon Blackburn, 1998, p. 231.
[4] Hilary Putnam, 1990, p. 28.
[5] Ludwig Wittgenstein, 1980, § 558. Referring to a disposition of water, Wittgenstein says: "This fact is fused into the foundation of our language-game."
[6] Stanley Cavell, 1979, p. 316.
[7] Should it be worth mentioning, I am not, in emphasizing the text's references to Othello's blackness, asking that we understand the matter as though it is in some way of a piece with race and blackness as it is addressed and understood in (for example) twentieth-century American literature. Iago's strategy here is to dehumanize Othello by making him an outsider, an "other" as it is fashionable to say; and Othello's race is clearly the brush with which Iago paints this picture, regardless of what race and blackness might signify for Iago, Shakespearean audiences, or the structure of the first act. Critics of *Othello*, at least since Coleridge (whose argument against reading Othello as a "veritable Negro" is arguably itself a classic of racist reasoning), generally agree on this interpretation. The Shakespeare scholar Harold Bloom puts the point well, if grandiloquently, when he writes of Iago: "the passed-over officer becomes the poet of street brawls, stabbings in the dark, disinformation, and above all else, the uncreation of Othello, the sparagmos of the great captain-general so that he can be returned to the original abyss, the chaos that Iago equates with the Moor's African origins" (1998, p. 438).
[8] Bernard Harrison, 1991, p. 51.
[9] David Schalkwyk, 1995, p. 288.

References

Blackburn, Simon. "Realism and Truth: Wittgenstein, Wright, Rorty and Minimalism." *Mind* 107 (1998): pp. 157-181.
Bloom, Harold. *Shakespeare: The Invention of the Human.* New York: Riverhead Books, 1998.

Cavell, Stanley. *The Claim of Reason: Wittgenstein, Skepticism, Morality, and Tragedy.* Oxford: Clarendon, 1979.

Harrison, Bernard. "Imagined Worlds and the Real One: Plato, Wittgenstein, and Mimesis." *Philosophy and Literature* 17 (1993): pp. 26-46.

–. *Inconvenient Fictions: Literature and the Limits of Theory.* New Haven: Yale UP, 1991.

Lamarque, Peter. *Fictional Points of View.* Ithaca: Cornell UP, 1996.

Putnam, Hilary. *Realism with A Human Face.* Ed. James Conant. Cambridge, MA: Harvard UP, 1990.

Schalkwyk, David. "Fiction as 'Grammatical' Investigation: A Wittgensteinian Account." *The Journal of Aesthetics and Art Criticism* 53 (1995): pp. 287-298.

Wittgenstein, Ludwig. *Culture and Value.* Ed. G.H. von Wright, trans. P. Winch. Chicago: University of Chicago Press, 1980

–. *On Certainty.* Ed. G.E.M. Anscombe and G.H. von Wright, trans. Denis Paul and G.E.M. Anscombe. London: Harper & Row, 1972.

–. *Philosophical Investigations.* Second edition. Ed. G.E.M. Anscombe and R. Rhees, trans. G.E.M. Anscombe. Oxford: Basil Blackwell, 1997.

THE "SILENCE" OF WITTGENSTEIN AND KRAUS

Newton Garver
State University of New York at Buffalo

I. Preliminaries

Wittgenstein's remark at the end of the *Tractatus*, commending silence for everything other than scientific statements, is perhaps his best-known remark. No doubt it is so well known partly because it comes at the end of the work and partly because it is so resonant, especially in the German original:

> Wovon man nicht sprechen kann, darüber muß man schweigen.

The remark is fascinating also because it seems to be both momentous and trivial, an effect which may well have resulted from the influence of Kraus. Of course, Wittgenstein's remark at the end of the *Tractatus* is hyperbole, a rhetorical device that is perhaps one of the things he learned from Kraus. But there is also a paradox in its being said at all, for it is not the sort of thing that *can* be said, according to the doctrine of the *Tractatus*. This paradox raises questions about the *Tractatus* as a whole, one of which concerns what sort of work Wittgenstein supposed he had written. Another arises in connection with the famous letter to Ludwig von Ficker,[1] in which Wittgenstein said that the more important of the two parts of the work was everything he had *not* written. A third question arises in connection with Wittgenstein's life-long silence[2] about political matters, even though he lived through very troubled times that had many a direct impact on him, and even though he was very close to a number of people – Russell, Keynes, and Kraus in particular – who commented regularly and prominently on political and social matters. Was Wittgenstein's political silence a continuing application of the concluding line of the *Tractatus*, perhaps long after he had repudiated its main philosophical doctrines? Or was the Tractarian silence something that Wittgenstein refined rather than repudiated?

In this paper I will first discuss Tractarian silence and what becomes of it in Wittgenstein's later work, then consider how Kraus's work fits into this framework of thought and what line of thought Wittgenstein might have taken from him, and finally come to the matter of what each did and did not say about Hitler, concluding with an appreciation of the roots of Wittgenstein's silence in his "work of clarification."

Writing the Austrian Traditions: Relations between Philosophy and Literature.
Ed. Wolfgang Huemer and Marc-Oliver Schuster. Edmonton, Alberta:
Wirth-Institute for Austrian and Central European Studies, 2003. pp. 67-79.

II. *The Silence of Wittgenstein*

The silence at the end of the *Tractatus* is not isolated or arbitrary. On the contrary, it is the logical culmination of one main line of argument in the book, the line of argument that has the distinction between *showing* and *saying* as its core. The key thing about this silence is not the absence of noise but the absence of *saying* anything. It may be that most of our noise and certainly most of our utterances are attempts to say something; but we can certainly make noise without saying anything. Some of what we do when we do not really *say* anything, and some of the noise we make when we do not really *say* anything, may be important, even of critical importance. Wittgenstein's point may be put by saying that being meaningful in the sense of having importance does not entail being meaningful in the sense of having sense.

Just as saying does not just consist of utterance, so also silence does not merely consist of the absence of noise. What can be *said* has sense, which means both that it can in principle be either true or false and that it can in principle be completely and uniquely clarified by logical analysis. Anything that cannot be true or cannot be false is senseless – and therefore cannot be *said*, even though it be not only uttered but even shouted. Contradictions cannot be true and therefore say nothing (or everything). Tautologies cannot be false and therefore say nothing. Contradictions and tautologies are both senseless. It does not matter if we shout them from the rooftops, as perhaps Kraus may have been inclined to do. Shouting does not constitute saying something. Therefore even shouting can be a form of silence, when we construe silence as not saying anything.

Just as Wittgenstein did not speak until he was four, we might also say that he again practiced silence in the decade from 1918 to 1928. During this decade he engaged in little philosophical discussion. The silence was never complete. In prison camp in Monte Cassino he read and discussed Kant and Frege with Ludwig Hänsel.[3] When released, he met with Russell to discuss the *Tractatus*. While teaching elementary school in Lower Austria, he met a few times for philosophical discussions with Frank Ramsey. No doubt these discussions were serious. But they were brief interludes in the silence that lasted until he had finished working on the house for his sister, had heard L.E.J. Brouwer's lecture, and had begun meeting with Moritz Schlick. Silence was significant in Wittgenstein's *life* as well as in his early philosophical thought.

It is well known that Wittgenstein often quoted Goethe's line, "Im Anfang war die Tat" (e.g., *OC* § 402).[4] It is less often acknowledged that this motto is a version of Tractarian silence. The point of the silence, after all, is not that there is nothing but speech. Quite the contrary, it is part of the view that the most important things cannot be said – neither the important logical things about the form of reality nor the important ethical things about life. Whatever can be said has one and only one complete analysis. But analysis itself cannot be analyzed, and the beginning and end of analysis must be shown rather than said. The beginning therefore must be a *showing* (a deed) rather than something said (a word). In this sense the beginning and the end must be a kind of silence, and Goethe's line from *Faust* fits not only with Wittgenstein's later philosophical standpoint but also with the Tractarian silence.

"In the beginning was the deed" contrasts of course with the opening words of the Gospel of John, "In the beginning was the word." The contrast is fascinating, with manifold applications. Goethe certainly did not mean to be anti-Christian, and there is little difficulty for a Christian to prefer the synoptic gospels with their emphasis on the *deeds* of Jesus to the Johanine gospel with its emphasis on doctrine. That is one application. A deconstructionist might take Goethe's remark as a rejection of Christian logocentrism – another application. From a Tractarian point of view one could understand the remark as stressing the primacy of showing over saying. This application might also be made by one wishing to stress the continuity of Wittgenstein's later work with the *Tractatus*. On the other hand a commentator like Norman Malcolm or Jaakko Hintikka might try to use this remark to contrast Wittgenstein's early emphasis on propositions (on what can be said) with his later emphasis on doing things (language-games as forms of activity).

Let us look at *PI* § 78 (p. 36e):

> Compare *knowing* and *saying*:
> how many feet high Mont Blanc is —
> how the word "game" is used —
> how a clarinet sounds.
> If you are surprised that one can know something and not be able to say it, you are perhaps thinking of a case like the first. Certainly not of one like the third.

This paragraph makes a point perspicuously. Wittgenstein declines to *say* what the point is, but his examples show us the point. Something further is shown by this section coming at the end of passages that introduce the idea of family resemblances among uses of a word. The point clarifies for us something about the relation between two concepts, and in that sense it is a logical point. Or perhaps better: a "grammatical" one. In the passage where he mentions the ten influences on his thinking (*CV*, p. 19e), Wittgenstein speaks of his work of clarification. *PI* § 78 (quoted above) is without question an instance of such clarification. Unlike the clarification mentioned in the *Tractatus*, however, this passage contains no analysis. The method of clarification is rather that of perspicuous representation (*übersichtliche Darstellung*). Perspicuous representation is a continuation of the earlier emphasis on showing rather than saying (as characteristic of philosophy and logic), and it also examplifies the connection between meaning and use. This method of clarification, which became dominant in his later work, can well be thought of as an elaboration of how to be effective without saying anything – how to use silence. Three points are worth stressing: clarity remains an intrinsic aim, analysis is subordinated to contextual considerations, and silence is something to *use*.

In the remark, in which Wittgenstein notes influences on his later as well as his earlier work (*CV*, pp. 18e-19e), he speaks without qualification of what he is doing as "work of clarification." The clarification serves no further purpose but is an end in itself, as Matthias Kross has correctly argued.[5] Wittgenstein did not change what he was doing but rather how he was going about it.

The most significant change in how he went about it is the replacement of analysis by context as the dominant crux of clarification, as elaborated in the opening sixty-five sections of the *Philosophical Investigations*.[6] Analysis may still be a method of clarification where truth-claims are involved and where they are to be tested through their implications, for this is a context in which Frege's demand for analytical clarity makes sense. Wittgenstein begins the *Philosophical Investigations*, however, with an investigation of the use of expressions which make no truth claim at all, and in these cases understanding requires us to pay attention to the context, in particular to what the person is doing when or through speaking. Hence the basis of linguistic meaning, even when it is to be clarified analytically, is the *uses* of language (language-games) that are woven into the fabric of "this complicated form of life" of ours (*PI*, p. 174e).

That silence is not just an emptiness, but rather something to be used in the context of showing something that cannot be said, may account for Wittgenstein's reported admiration of George Fox, the seventeenth-century charismatic and mystical genius who gathered together the "peculiar" people called Quakers and founded the Religious Society of Friends.[7] Wittgenstein gave Norman Malcolm a copy of the *Journal* of George Fox as a Christmas present in 1948, and Malcolm reports that Wittgenstein read it with admiration.[8]

The significance of the Quaker connection is fourfold. There is first and foremost the matter of silence, prominent in Quaker practice and at the end of the *Tractatus*. There is next the emphasis on the present, prominent in Fox's remark, "There is no time but this present" (adopted by the American Friends Service Committee as a theme for one of its annual meetings some years ago) and finding an echo both in *Tractatus* 6.4311 and in the conversation with Schlick and Waismann, where Wittgenstein insists that "we have already got everything, and we have got it actually *present*; we need not wait for anything" (*WVC*, p. 183). There is thirdly the matter of insisting on alternatives: for Fox and the Quakers it is alternatives to things that government finds necessary, such as bowing, swearing, doffing one's hat, imprisoning miscreants, and warring against enemies; one Quaker historian has called the Alternatives to Violence Project the cutting edge of contemporary Quakerism.[9] Wittgenstein is equally critical of alleged necessities, both in *Tractatus* 6.37, where he says that the only necessity that exists is *logical* necessity, and in his later philosophical practice, where he often responds to claims of necessity by noting possible alternatives and commenting that the alleged necessity is one of a number of ways in which things may proceed. There is finally the matter of style of thinking, eschewing metaphysics on one side and theology on the other. It is a style in which dogmatic starting points are replaced with queries, a Quaker practice documented in Fox's *Journal* and a striking feature of Wittgenstein's later philosophical work that certainly does not find its origin in any of the ten sources of influences he listed in 1931 (*CV*, p. 19e); Wittgenstein's style, his thinking and teaching fit this Quaker pattern, in that on many pages queries outnumber assertions.

An important part of Quaker practice – some think it the most vital testimony to the world – is to seek the "sense of the meeting." This practice emerges from worship, where the predominance of silence and the lack of a presiding officer mean that it is up to each person to feel when the group is of a common mind. Often there is an informal consensus to that effect afterward, and it is said that the meeting was "gathered." In meetings for business it is the job of the clerk not only to help the group become of one mind but also then to record the sense of the common mind. A social scientist might insist that this common mind or consensus is best to be understood as a complex function of the minds of the constituent individuals (following the widely accepted principle of "methodological individualism"), but such reductive individualism is contrary to both the thinking and the experience of Friends. The thinking is that one gives up one's attempt to control the outcome and seeks not what conforms most to one's personal beliefs and interests but rather what is inherent in that which binds the group together. The experience is that of being surprised by what happens. It is true that there could be no groups without individuals, and that individuals must contribute to the formation of the group's mind, but it does not follow that the group does not really have a mind of its own, nor that one must first understand the individual minds in order to understand the group mind.

Wittgenstein wrote extensively on mental matters, or philosophy of psychology, and what he had to say has received extensive comment. Much of the comment, however, is exegesis and defense of Wittgenstein's rejection of inner processes and of traditional behaviorism[10] rather than a consideration of the commonality (or commonability, to use Philip Pettit's word) of mind. It is obvious, however, that many of the elements of thought that Wittgenstein pays close attention to, especially those connected with logic or grammar, are common rather than individual or idiosyncratic. A proposition determines just one point in logical space, but it presupposes the whole of logical space (*TLP* 3.42) – and any other proposition by any other person presupposes exactly the same logical space. Logic is a common element of thought – not something individual, and certainly not solipsistic. The same is true of grammar, in the sense in which Wittgenstein speaks of it in his later work: it provides a framework for "this complicated form of life" (*PI*, p. 174e) we humans share, no matter how wide the divergences in vocabulary, morphology, and syntax. Wittgenstein sought to characterize the features of these common elements of thought as earnestly as any Quaker has sought to articulate the common mind of a Friends meeting.

Two recent books have taken up this theme. Kimberly Cornish, in *The Jew of Linz*,[11] devotes the final part of the book (chapters 8-12) to arguments that attribute to Wittgenstein a "no-ownership" view of the mind, the upshot of which is that consciousness is social rather than individual, a view that he calls "mental socialism." Early evidence for this reading comes from Wittgenstein's remark that "there is no such thing as the soul – the subject, etc. – as it is conceived in contemporary superficial psychology" (*TLP* 5.5421). Cornish – not altogether convincingly – marshals further quotations from Wittgenstein's later work, as well as from medieval sources, Goethe, Schopenhauer, and Geach, to argue that Wittgenstein held the same view of mind through his latest writing.

The other book is *The Common Mind* by Philip Pettit.[12] Although Pettit distinguishes his view from Wittgenstein's, in that his publicity conditions on rule-following are different from those in the Wittgensteinian literature, he does see such publicity conditions as entailing that there is something mental that is common to some group – or at least is available to becoming common (is "commonable"). Pettit makes a powerful case for this view, though without attributing it to Wittgenstein, in the final pages of the book. Though Pettit distinguishes his view from that of Wittgenstein (or Kripke's Wittgenstein), it is nonetheless arguable that, if Cornish is in general right about Wittgenstein, Pettit, especially in the final section of the "Postscript," gives a better account of what Cornish is attributing to Wittgenstein than Cornish does himself.

We might take Wittgenstein's admiration for Fox as further indirect evidence that he responded favorably to a view of mind or thinking that was common or commonable rather than solitary and solipsistic. The practice of silence is, for Quakers, an important part of the discipline of attending to what is common; so, too, for Wittgenstein, though in a different way. For Wittgenstein the important part of what is common is grammar, which is the basis of philosophy.[13] Making grammatical remarks is no doubt as much a language-game as the others Wittgenstein discusses, but it depends on there already being other language-games and therefore could not be a *primitive* language-game. Furthermore its focus is not on the *substance* of what is said (its truth or validity or other cogency) but on the *possibility* (meaning) of what is said. Hence Wittgenstein's insistence that philosophy remain *silent* on matters that concern science and morals:

> It was true to say that our considerations could not be scientific ones. [...] And we may not advance any kind of theory. [...] We must do away with all *explanation*, and description alone must take its place. (*PI* § 109, p. 47e)

Philosophy puts everything before us, and neither explains nor deduces anything. Since everything lies open to view there is nothing to explain. For what is hidden, for example, is of no interest to us.

> One might also give the name "philosophy" to what is possible *before* all new discoveries and inventions. (*PI* § 126, p. 50e)

III. The Silence of Kraus

In 1931 Wittgenstein listed Kraus as one of ten people – and one of several Jews – who influenced him. The context is an interesting and somewhat enigmatic self-assessment, partly in regard to he himself being Jewish:

> Amongst Jews "genius" is found only in the holy man. Even the greatest of Jewish thinkers is no more than talented. (Myself for instance.) (*CV*, p. 18e)

Wittgenstein went on to describe his particular talent and to mention some of those who influenced him most:

> I think there is some truth in my idea that I really only think reproductively. I don't believe that I have ever *invented* a line of thinking. I have always taken one over from someone else. I have simply straightaway seized on it with enthusiasm for my work of clarification. That is how Boltzmann, Hertz, Schopenhauer, Frege, Russell, Kraus, Loos, Weininger, Spengler, Sraffa have influenced me. Can one take the case of Breuer and Freud as an example of Jewish reproductiveness? – What I invent are new *similes*.
> [...]
> What I do think essential is carrying out the work of clarification with COURAGE: otherwise it becomes just a clever game.
> [...]
> It is typical for a Jewish mind to understand someone else's work better than he understands it himself. (*CV*, pp. 18e-19e)

Throughout the list of influences there runs a sharp critique of dominant practices and accepted ways of doing or saying things. One might think of this list when reading Wittgenstein's comment about his own work, "I destroy, I destroy, I destroy!" Kraus was perhaps the most trenchant of the social critics, but Frege's polemics, though more concerned with scholarship and argumentation, are as devastating and unrelenting as anything in Kraus.

In the case of Kraus the criticism is partly political and partly directed against social pomposity in general, but the politics left little imprint on Wittgenstein. The core of Kraus's own work as well as his influence on Wittgenstein concern language. Kraus (1874-1936) was fifteen years senior to Wittgenstein, and he established his unique and influential journal *Die Fackel* before Wittgenstein was ten. It is difficult to characterize Kraus's career, since he worked in so many ways, but a unifying theme to his plays, his poetry, his criticism, and his journalism, was his love and care for an ideal of language and his contempt for the prevailing ways of his time. He was anything but silent. His antiwar play, *The Last Days of Mankind*, ran to 800 pages, and his journal appeared more or less regularly for thirty-seven years. He was loosely socialist, but his main enemy was corruption of the language. His diatribe against Heine concerned Heine's introduction of the *feuilleton* into German papers. The *feuilleton,* which features high-brow intellectual essays on topics of no political importance, is usually written in a florid style that never spares adjectives, adverbs, metaphors, or similes; the *feuilleton* has remained one of the popular features of many German newspapers. One of Kraus's principal targets was Austria's "best" paper, *Die Presse*, which once offered him the job of writing and editing its weekly *feuilleton*.

The triumph of Hitler was not the first or only time that Kraus, in spite of being a prolific writer, was silent in the ordinary sense, and Tractarian silence is a regular feature of his most pungent style of writing. The first public silence of Kraus, the first noticeable interruption in the publication of *Die Fackel*, occurred in 1914, at the outbreak of World War I. Harry Zohn writes:

> The outbreak of World War I forced him [i.e., Kraus] to bear witness to what he regarded as the beginning of the end. [...] Kraus's initial reaction to the new "great times" was silence. The torch was temporarily extinguished, and for several months the torch-bearer was too stunned to participate in the flood of words all around him.[14]

He wrote two extraordinary anti-war works, his 800-page play, *The Last Days of Mankind*, and his biting satirical diatribe, *In These Great Times*. Here are some of the barbs from the latter work:

> In the realm of poverty of imagination where people die of spiritual famine without feeling spiritual hunger, where pens are dipped in blood and swords in ink, that which is not thought must be done, but that which is only thought is unutterable. Expect no words of my own from me. [...] He who encourages deeds with words desecrates words and deeds and is doubly despicable. [...] Let him who has something to say come forward and be silent! (p. 71)

That last line is as fine an invocation to silence as the last line of the *Tractatus*. In both cases silence becomes the instrument of a powerful moral witness.

> Since I am neither a politician nor his half-brother, an esthete, I would not dream of denying the necessity of anything that is happening or of complaining that mankind does not know how to die in beauty. I know full well that cathedrals are rightfully bombarded by people if they are rightfully used by people as military posts. (p. 72f)

In this passage Kraus speaks, but with heavy-handed irony. From Wittgenstein's point of view, such irony is not really *saying* anything. Anyone who understands Kraus realizes that he means just the opposite of what the words seem to say. To put it another way, Kraus *shows* us something by "saying" something he obviously does not mean. To the extent that Kraus restricts his writing and speaking to irony and satire, he is engaged in *showing* rather than *saying* and therefore remains silent in the Tractarian sense.

It is worth noting that the irony here is directed against explanations and justifications of what was happening in the war. When he speaks of the encouragement of deeds with words desecrating both deeds and words, he surely has war propaganda in mind, the ringing words of patriots. There is a strong consensus between Kraus and Wittgenstein about the abuse of language in such justifications: the speaker seems to be saying something that could be true or false, but there are no *facts* that could possibly make such sentences true or false (Kraus's ironic response is equally not an abuse, because it is obviously showing us an absurdity rather making a truth-claim). Kraus was from the beginning antagonistic toward the press, but its role in publishing and popularizing the rationales for violence made him intensify his attack:

> If one reads a newspaper only for information, one does not learn the truth, not even about the paper. The truth is that the newspaper is not a statement of contents but the contents themselves; and more than that, it is an instigator. If it prints lies about horrors, these turn into horrors.

> There is more injustice in the world because there is a press which fabricated it and deplores it! It is not nations that strike one another; rather, it is the international disgrace, the profession which rules the world not despite its irresponsibility but by virtue of it, that deals wounds, tortures prisoners, baits foreigners, and turns gentlemen into rowdies. Its only authority is its unprincipledness, which, in association with a rascally will, can change printer's ink directly into blood. O last unholy wonder of the times! At first everything was a lie, and they always lied so that lies might be told only elsewhere; but now, thrown into the neurasthenia of hatred, everything is true. There are various nations, but there is only one press. The newspaper dispatch is an instrument of war like a grenade, which has no consideration for circumstances either. (p. 77f)

Kraus was equally outraged by the rise to power of Hitler, against whom he had warned in 1922, and his initial reaction was again silence. Here is Zohn again:

> "Mir fällt zu Hitler nichts ein." (I cannot think of anything to say about Hitler.) This is the striking first sentence of Kraus's *Die Dritte Walpurgisnacht* [...], a prose work written in the late spring and summer of 1933 but not published in its entirety during Kraus's lifetime. That sentence [...] may be indicative of resignation and impotence [...], but it is also a hyperbolic, heuristic device for depicting the witches' sabbath of the time. [...] There had been no *Fackel* for ten months when no. 888 appeared in October 1933. Its four pages contained only Kraus's funeral oration on his architect friend Adolf Loos and what was to be the satirist's last poem, with its poignant closing line, "The word expired when that world awoke." Kraus sadly realized the incommensurability of the human spirit with the brutal power structure across the German border, and on the second page of his work he asks this anguished question: "Is that which has been done to the spirit still a concern of the spirit?" The equally anguished answer he gives himself is this: "Force is no object of polemics, madness no object of satire."[15]

We see in this last remark not only anguish but also recognition that a distinctive linguistic activity requires its appropriate context. It is said that after the war Charlie Chaplin admitted that he might not have made *The Great Dictator* if he had known the immensity of the evil. The madness of German fascism destroyed the context in which satire and polemics made sense. Just as Wittgenstein spelled out limits of philosophy and of science, so also Kraus recognized limits of satire.

IV. Political Silence

Arnulf Zweig published an interesting, somewhat tentative, essay on "Wittgenstein's Silence" a few years ago.[16] The silence in question is Wittgenstein's silence, both during and after the war, about the Holocaust. There are two sorts of response to the moral shadow cast by Zweig's essay. One suggests that Wittgenstein's actions may have compensated for his lack of deeds, and the other portrays his silence as stemming from very deep principles and insights.

Kimberly Cornish makes a dramatic inference from established historical data, relying on our imagining what might have been Wittgenstein's two separate lives during his second period in England. Wittgenstein and Hitler were both in the *Realschule* in Linz at the same time for a year; and they were of the same age, having been born within a fortnight of one another; and Hitler does write in *Mein Kampf* of being incensed by an arrogant Jew while at the school. Wittgenstein can therefore, so argues Cornish, be assigned an unknowing and unintentional role in the formation of the beliefs and sentiments that led Hitler to the "final solution." This took no extra time or energy on Wittgenstein's part, and for it he of course deserves neither credit nor blame. But Cornish goes on to assert, with evidence more voluminous albeit less consequential, that Wittgenstein was the Soviet recruiter in Cambridge who got Burgess and others from Cambridge to spy for the Soviet Union in the thirties and forties. What a feat this was! It would have required a great deal of time, travel, concentration, judgment, discretion, and secrecy. One can imagine that Wittgenstein might have realized his earlier relation with Hitler and determined to do something to make up for it – a warrior for a second time, though in a different kind of war with a vastly different role. The definitive characteristic about this role is its secrecy, not a hint of it emerging from any of Wittgenstein's friends.

There is much we do not know about Wittgenstein's life. Reading Kimberly Cornish's book one comes away with a sense that Wittgenstein, that extraordinary man, might well have had several other sides. He did, of course, a prodigious amount of philosophical work, filling notebooks with his thoughts. Anyone who has tried to do such will know that the work he did seems enough to fill a great deal of one's time. In addition there were also the relaxing moments, listening to music or going to "B" movies. But those who have looked closely into his life tell us that there was much more. McGuinness recounts Wittgenstein's front-line experiences in the Great War, and one realizes from Wittgenstein's notebooks of that period that he composed the *Tractatus* while actively engaged at the front.[17] Since the philosophical writing and the military life each seem like full-time activities, the account McGuinness gives makes one realize that Wittgenstein was capable of much more than is an ordinary individual. So, though I remain unconvinced, perhaps Wittgenstein's acts spoke more loudly in the political context of the 1930s and 1940s than any of us realize.

Nonetheless he remained silent about politics in all his works and correspondence. The silence is so striking that it must be construed as deliberate, and therefore as an act of considerable discipline. No doubt this discipline had various sources, but one of its roots is a line of thought he seized on from Kraus: that the great underlying problem of the times, and a key factor in making him feel alienated from the civilization by which he was surrounded,[18] was the abuse and corruption of language. Of course part of the act of seizing upon this line of thought was Wittgenstein's conviction that he understood Kraus's line of thought better than Kraus did!

One key to Wittgenstein's version of the abuse and corruption of language is contained in *Tractatus* 6.37 and 6.375:

> There is only *logical* necessity.
>
> Just as there is only *logical* necessity, so too there is only *logical* impossibility.

If one looks at political speeches, wartime slogans, and party platforms, one encounters a plethora of modal claims that are not matters of logic at all. This phenomenon occurs with both fascists and socialists and (in the American context) with both Republicans and Democrats: President Bush said that Saddam Hussain left him no choice, and President Clinton that Slobodan Milosevic left him no choice – and Presidents Hussain and Milosevic have of course made analogous (but incompatible) modal claims. Even after the fact, historians continue to invoke necessities and impossibilities that lie far outside the domain of logic, in order to explain the events. All these common, almost ritualistic political and historical ways of using language fly in the face of Wittgenstein's characterization of the scope of modality. From the line of thought Wittgenstein articulated, these historical and political statements could not *really* be modal at all, but rather some other sort of use of language masquerading as modal claims. It is the masquerade that constitutes an affront not only to logic but to Wittgenstein's sense of morality.

Wittgenstein, although he changed his views about many things and came to speak more of grammar than of logic in connection with necessity (see *PI* § 246-251, pp. 89e-90e, and § 371-373, p. 116e), continued to regard necessity and impossibility as rooted in the framework of language, rather than in the world.[19] It is this persisting view that lies behind his well-known remark about metaphysics:

> The essential thing about metaphysics: it obliterates the distinction between factual and conceptual investigations. (Z § 458, p. 81)

He might have made a similar remark about political and historical discourse. Such an attitude is clearly indicated by his having become "extremely angry" at Norman Malcolm for Malcolm's having said that a British plot to assassinate Hitler was incompatible with British national character:

> He considered it to be a great stupidity and also an indication that I was not learning anything from the philosophical training he was trying to give me. He said these things very vehemently, and when I refused to admit that my remark was stupid he would not talk to me any more, and soon after we parted. He had been in the habit of coming to my lodging in Chesterton Road to take me on a short walk with him before his bi-weekly lectures. After this incident he stopped that practice.[20]

I take it that Wittgenstein saw the point about metaphysics as central to his whole philosophy, and to the work of clarification about the distinctions necessary for understanding the highways and byways of language, and that it was really stupid of Malcolm not to see that "national character" plays the same sort of role in political and historical discourse that "form" and "essence" play in metaphysics. That is, it disguises a modal claim, where it is easy to see, once the disguise is removed, that the required logical foundation is entirely lacking. Malcolm must at that moment have seemed an integral part of the very civilization from which Wittgenstein felt alienated.

Wittgenstein's outburst may have been nothing but pedagogical despair, with no value judgment implied, as he says in the "Sketch for a Preface." Perhaps by "value judgment" he meant a condemnation, which he would understandably have been unwilling to endorse. But it is difficult to believe that he did not see Malcolm's remark as a moral as well as a logical failure, albeit not a culpable failure. From his earliest discussions with Russell, Wittgenstein saw logico-linguistic clarity as intimately connected with moral purity. Political pronouncements and historical explanations inevitably involve the same sort of blurring of the vital distinction between the conceptual (logical) and the factual that he explicitly attributed to metaphysics. So *of course* he remained silent about the momentous political events of his day. His political silence was a moral act. It was a persistent and conscientious implementation of final words of the *Tractatus*. And it was, ironically, a tribute to Kraus, from whom he had taken the seminal thought that what is rotten and despicable in our civilization stems from abuse of language.

---

[1] Letter 23 (undated), in: C.G. Luckhardt, ed., *Wittgenstein: Sources and Perspectives*, Ithaca: Cornell UP, 1979, p. 94f.

[2] Wittgenstein's silence began when he was very young; according to Ray Monk's biography, *Ludwig Wittgenstein: The Duty of Genius* (London: Jonathan Cape, 1990), he did not begin to speak until he was four.

[3] Brian McGuinness, *Wittgenstein, a Life: Young Ludwig (1889-1921)*. London: Duckworth, 1988, p. 270.

[4] The following abbreviations are used when referring to Wittgenstein's works:

CV = *Culture and Value*. Ed. G.H. von Wright. Trans. Peter Winch. Oxford: Basil Blackwell, 1990.
OC = *On Certainty*. Ed. G.E.M. Anscombe and G.H. von Wright. Trans. D. Paul and G.E.M. Anscombe. Oxford: Basil Blackwell, 1969.
PI = *Philosophical Investigations*. Trans. G.E.M. Anscombe. Oxford: Blackwell, 1968.
TLP = *Tractatus Logico-philosophicus*. Trans. D.F. Pears and B. McGuinness. London: Routledge, 2001.
WVC = *Wittgenstein and the Vienna Circle: Conversations Recorded by Friedrich Waismann*. Ed. Brian McGuinness. Trans. Joachim Schulte and Brian McGuinness. Oxford: Basil Blackwell, 1979.
Z = *Zettel*. Ed. G.E.M. Anscombe and G.H. von Wright. Trans. G.E.M. Anscombe. Oxford: Basil Blackwell, 1981.

[5] Matthias Kross, *Klarheit als Selbstzweck: Wittgenstein über Philosophie, Religion, Ethik und Gewissheit*. Berlin: Akademie Verlag, 1993.

[6] For further details, see Newton Garver, "Context and Analysis," *Journal of Philosophical Research* XXIV (1999): pp. 1-19.

[7] Aspects of Fox's genius are evident in the *Journal*, but appreciating his organizational genius, which allowed the Society of Friends to be among the few seventeenth-century charismatic sects to survive into the twentieth century, requires historical study; see Homer Larry Ingle, *First Among Friends: George Fox and the Creation of Quakerism*. New York: Oxford UP, 1994.

[8] Norman Malcolm, *Ludwig Wittgenstein: A Memoir*. London: Oxford UP, 1958, p. 71f.
[9] Personal communication from Alson Van Wagner.
[10] See, for example, Normal Malcolm, *Memory and Mind*, Ithaca: Cornell UP, 1977; *Thought and Knowledge*, Ithaca: Cornell UP, 1977; and *Nothing is Hidden: Wittgenstein's Criticism of His Early Thought*, Oxford: Blackwell, 1986; Colin McGinn, *Wittgenstein on Meaning: An Interpretation and Evaluation*, Oxford: Blackwell, 1984; and Malcolm Budd, *Wittgenstein's Philosophy of Psychology*, London: Routledge, 1989.
[11] London: Century Books, 1998.
[12] New York: Oxford UP, 1996.
[13] See my "Philosophy as Grammar," in Hans Sluga and David G. Stern, eds., *The Cambridge Companion to Wittgenstein*, Cambridge: Cambridge UP, 1996, pp. 139-170.
[14] Editor's "Introduction" to *In These Great Times: A Karl Kraus Reader*. Ed. Harry Zohn, Montreal: Engendra Press, 1976, p. 14.
[15] *Ibid.*, p. 17f.
[16] Arnulf Zweig, "Wittgenstein's Silence," in *Proceedings of the Nineteenth International Wittgenstein Symposium*, Vienna: Hölder-Pichler-Tempsky, 1997; German version as "Wittgensteins Schweigen," *Bruchlinien: Tendenzen der Holocaustforschung*. Ed. Gertrud Koch, Köln: Böhlau, 1999, 163-180.
[17] Brian McGuinness, *Wittgenstein, A Life: Young Ludwig (1889-1921)*, London: Duckworth, 1988, chapter 7.
[18] See the "Sketch for a Foreword" to *Philosophische Bemerkungen* (*CV*, p. 6e-7e) and following passages (*CV*, 7e-8e), for example: "The spirit of this civilization makes itself manifest in the industry, architecture, and music of our time, in its fascism and socialism, and it is alien and uncongenial to the author" (*CV* 6e).
[19] See, for example, John V. Canfield, *Wittgenstein: Language and World*, Amherst: University of Massachusetts Press, 1981, esp. chapters 9-11.
[20] Malcolm, *Ludwig Wittgenstein*, p. 32f [see endnote 8].

KRAUS ON WEININGER, KRAUS ON WOMEN, KRAUS ON SERBIA

Barry Smith
State University of New York at Buffalo

> Most men profess to respect woman theoretically, in order that much more thoroughly to despise her practically; here this relationship has been reversed. Woman could not be highly valued: but women are not for all that to be excluded, from the start and once and for all, from all respect.[1]

I. Preamble

Otto Weininger was born in Vienna on April 3, 1880. The above passage is taken from the only work he published in his lifetime, a big book entitled *Geschlecht und Charakter: Eine prinzipielle Untersuchung* (roughly: *Sex and Character: An Investigation of the Principles*). This work contains arguments to the effect that:

man alone is rational;

there has never been and could never be a woman genius;

women, like children, imbeciles, and criminals, should have no voice in human affairs;

woman is infinitely porous, infinitely malleable, and infinitely open to external influences;

woman has no soul;

love and understanding are mutually incompatible;

woman is exclusively and continuously a sexual being, man only secondarily and intermittently so;

it is the duty of all women to strive to become men;

every man, even Goethe, even Napoleon, even Kant, is part woman;

women do not exist.

Writing the Austrian Traditions: Relations between Philosophy and Literature. Ed. Wolfgang Huemer and Marc-Oliver Schuster. Edmonton, Alberta: Wirth-Institute for Austrian and Central European Studies, 2003. pp. 81-100.

At the age of twenty-two, Weininger received from the University of Vienna the degree of Doctor of Philosophy *summa cum laude* for a dissertation on the biology, psychology, and sociology of the sexes entitled "Eros and Psyche." On the same day he converted to Protestantism – something highly unusual for a Jew in Catholic Austria. His dissertation grew within the year into the 600 pages of *Geschlecht und Charakter*. Part I, on "The Sexual Manifold," is largely scientific in temper and has some scientific basis in the biology of Weininger's day.[2] Part II, on "The Sexual Types," includes new chapters on the metaphysics of sex, on talent and genius, on the erotic and the aesthetic, and on Jewishness: "The problem of the Jew = the problem of woman = the problem of the slave."

It is an implication of Weininger's work that all human relations, and not only human sexual relations, are immoral, that it is in a certain sense impossible to lead a moral life on this earth. Four months after the publication of the work – not "some years later," as is asserted by Germaine Greer on page 79 of *The Female Eunuch* – Weininger committed suicide. On the 3rd of October 1903 he rented a room in the house on the Schwarzspanierstrasse in which Beethoven had died. The next morning he shot himself in the left side of the chest. His book, which had initially received little attention, immediately became the object of a cult. Weininger's friends and disciples published articles and pamphlets in defense of his ideas. Fragments from his notebooks and diaries were collected and published in a volume bearing the title *Über die letzten Dinge (On the Last Things)*. And *Sex and Character* itself, which eventually went through more than twenty-five editions in German, was almost immediately translated into six other languages, including Hebrew and English. Thinkers of the calibre of Strindberg, Wittgenstein, Joyce – and Kraus – not only took Weininger seriously, but suffered a profound and lasting influence.[3] Strindberg credited Weininger with having solved "the most difficult of all problems" – the problem of woman. "I spelled out the words," Strindberg wrote, "but it was he who put them together." Shortly after Weininger's suicide, Strindberg wrote to Weininger's friend Artur Gerber, as follows:

> Stockholm, 22 October 1903
>
> I understood our dead friend, and I thank you. Some years ago as I stood there, like Weininger, with the hope of going further, I wrote in my diary: Why do I go on? Cato gave himself up to death when he found that he could not hold himself upright above the swamp of sin. It is for this reason also that Dante absolved him from his suicide (Inferno). Now it is I who am sinking, and I will not sink, therefore ... torment! –
>
> I was on my way upwards, but a woman has dragged me back down to the ground ... But still I went on living, because I believed that I had discovered that our association with the earthly spirit woman was a sacrifice, a duty, a test. We are not permitted to live as Gods here on earth; we have to amble about in all this filth, and yet still stay pure, etc. [...]
> Your unknown friend in the distance,
> August Strindberg.[4]

In a letter of July 1903 Strindberg describes *Sex and Character* as a "frightening" book that had "probably solved the hardest of all problems." Strindberg also wrote an obituary of Weininger in which he affirms that all the spiritual and material riches of humanity had been created by males. Woman's love for man he describes as "50% animal heat and 50% hate."[5]

Weininger on the other hand was subject also to attacks. These emanated, above all, from members of the churches, and from the Vienna psychoanalytic movement. In 1904 there appeared in a German medical series a book entitled *Der Fall Otto Weininger* (*The Case of Otto Weininger*) by one Ferdinand Probst. Probst's book is an exercise in posthumous psychopathology. As Kraus wrote: "The psychiatric troublemakers are no longer content to destroy the living. They have started to render expert opinions also on the dead ... "[6]

Sigmund Freud himself described *Geschlecht und Charakter* as a "rotten book, which cannot be taken seriously".[7] Freud also accused Weininger of having stolen some of his own ideas in the writing of *Geschlecht und Charakter* – for another principal thesis of Weininger's work is that all human beings, and indeed all sexually reproducing organisms, are physiologically and psychologically bisexual.

II. Feeling vs. Truth

Weininger is an ethical realist. He believes that there exist ultimate values which in and of themselves demand realization and whose demand for realization outweighs all other considerations. A human being, if he is to lead a moral life, must respect these values in his thoughts and actions, regardless of the consequences to his personal well-being or to the well-being of the society in which he lives. He who fails in this observation is a moral criminal. To the extent that he is conscious of his failure he suffers guilt, and there is, for Weininger, a logical tie between ethical guilt (ethical punishment) and the actions in which it resides. The reality of guilt is a logical mark of the reality of the values Weininger calls ultimate.

Nowadays people rarely talk of "ultimate" values. Rather, the measure of ethical value is taken to be the advantage of society as a whole. The extent to which the isolated individual succeeds in leading a moral life is thus shorn almost completely of its ethical significance.

Weininger's ethical realism will appear as an even more formidable stumbling block to the contemporary reception of his views when we examine the precise nature of the "ultimate values" to which he is committed.[8] The following would be an approximation of a complete list:

[M1] truth, knowledge, honesty, intellectual rigor, consistency, clarity and distinctness of thought;

[M2] the ability to reason, to differentiate, to impose an order upon and to distance oneself from the subject-matter of one's thoughts; to isolate principles and to recognize essences or types; to see the general in the particular; to grasp what is constant in a world of change, to forget nothing;

[M3]   the ability to act in such a way that the principle of one's actions is clearly understood, and therefore also in such a way that one can accept responsibility for those actions; reason and will should coincide; logic and ethics should become identical; the ability to act where action is due, to act in accordance with a will to value; thus one should respect the qualities of resolution, decisiveness, and courage; and one should abjure complacency and pompousness.

To the extent that an action satisfies the above, its value will exhibit permanence; our willingness to accept responsibility for it will be capable of enduring forever. The action will, correspondingly, impose a permanent order upon some segment of the world we experience, of a type which appears most notably in the worlds of philosophy and of artistic creation (and especially in music). The world itself, on the other hand, acquires from the ethical point of view a wholly passive, submissive character, the character of something that is to be shaped according to the moral or aesthetic will of the experiencing subject. The list of values might accordingly be extended:

[M4]   a high value is placed on those actions that impose a permanent form on that which is formless; the will to value is manifested as a will to form.

Finally, the above, purely subjective criteria of the ethical life will be seen to imply a specific constraint upon one's relations with one's fellow human beings (that is to say, upon those of our thoughts and actions which impinge upon our fellows):

[M5]   a human being is to be treated with absolute respect as an equal (potential) source of ethical legitimacy (of truth and of right); he should not be treated in an instrumental way, as a means to one's own ends, however highly valued those ends may be.

I have called the above M-values: we may think of them, for the moment, as the values of the mind. Note that even where M-values have a bearing upon our relations with others, they are wholly individualistic. No ultimate value is placed upon, say, the health of the society in which one lives, not even upon the survival of the human species. Ultimate values can in Weininger's eyes be brought to realization only through the reason and will of a single individual – not, for example, through changes in society brought about by political means. Value is indeed divorced from the nexus of causes and effects. The individual should seek not to concern himself with the affairs and amenities of the world in which he lives. Rather, he should seek to travel light.

It is possible to set forth a complementary list of what might be called W-values by picking out those qualities isolated by Weininger as directly antagonistic to the above. These would include, in no particular order:

[W1] instinct, feeling (as a substitute for or as a beclouding accompaniment of thought); partiality; the inability to distance oneself from the subject-matter of one's thoughts;

[W2] passion, sentiment, sensuality, love (conceived as a bond between individuals somehow leading to an erosion of their respective individualities); togetherness, sociability, solidarity, compassion; comfort, domesticity, well-being, survival;

[W3] spontaneity, impulsiveness, pragmatism, the tendency to be swayed by temporal events instead of dominating them;

[W4] acting in such a way that one works with rather than against nature; being concerned to accept and live within the flow of events rather than to impose an enduring form or order upon the world; living for the moment;

[W5] self-abasement, self-sacrifice, the offering of oneself as a means to the ends of another, or the treatment of another as a means to one's own ends.

W-values are the values of the world. They are values pertaining to what goes on inside the realm of what happens and is the case, values relating to the stream of causes and effects. Where M-values relate to the individual intellect and to its ability to understand and thus also to stand apart from or transcend the objects of its thinking acts, W-values relate primarily to the body and to the nexus of instinctual relations between the body and its surroundings.

III. Man and Value

It is not merely that W-values have no legitimacy as values in Weininger's eyes (so that man has no moral duty to observe them). Weininger believes that any attempt at their promotion, whether on an individual or on a social level, is positively detrimental to the realization of M-values in the universe as a whole. Hence his belief that the W-values are ethically evil, and that they correspond, from the ethical point of view, to the dark, sensualistic side (the weaker side) of human nature. If W-values are conceived as values, then this is because man has been oppressed by woman. To uphold them now may be conceived as a form of atavism. And it is undoubtedly a form of atavism to wish to renounce modern scientific enlightenment in favor of, say, the form of life of the coven or of the tribe.

For Weininger what I have called M- and W-values are, respectively, the values of the absolute man and of the absolute woman. To the extent that someone has it within him to recognize that it is his duty before God (before his conscience, before the universe as a whole) to bring about the realization of value, to that extent he is a man. The absolute woman, as Weininger conceives her, is incapable of experiencing this duty. At best she may suffer the inclination to realize (M-) values not for their own sake, but in order to impress a man.

It should be stressed again that no actually existing human being exhibits in a pure form either the ideal type man or the ideal type woman. We are all to a greater or lesser extent bisexual; we all have within ourselves finite amounts of male and female "plasma," as Weininger conceives it. Moments of masculinity and femininity, of reason and sensuality, and of light and darkness form interdependent, mutually inseparable parts of every human being. Weininger goes so far as to claim that it is possible to determine numerically the distribution of male and female "plasma" in any given individual. A predominance of femininity is marked, for example, by large breasts and hips, by a preoccupation with sexuality and with appearance to the detriment of the life of the mind. High masculinity is characterized by the presence of facial hair and a prominent jaw, and by the capacity to divert one's attention away from purely sexual and personal concerns to other spheres, such as war, politics, athletics, or philosophy. Weininger argues in fact that it is possible to assign degrees of masculinity or femininity even to whole groups of human beings. The Jews, for example, he regarded as the archetypically feminine race, closely followed – in reflection of their lack of interest in the intellectual life – by the English. A perfect marriage, against this background, would be one in which the M- and W-quotients of the marriage partners each add up to 100% when summed together.

IV. On Self-Transcendence

In Part II of *Geschlecht und Charakter*, Weininger moves on to consider human sexuality not in relation to physiological and psychological fact, but rather in relation to pure or metaphysical possibility, to the possibility that human beings should recognize their moral duty, or their guilt, or that they should exercise their freedom as thinking, willing subjects. Pure possibilities of this kind, Weininger insists, are not constrained by facts of psychology or physiology. The latter relate exclusively to regularities actually exhibited in the world of what happens and is the case. Pure possibilities, in contrast, may obtain even in a world in which they are, as a matter of empirical fact, never realized. Weininger now goes on to argue that it is possible, in this metaphysical sense, that the human subject wills that he/she be released from the canker of bisexuality, that he/she be cleansed of what is, in Weininger's eyes, the evil in his/her soul ... and become Man. While this act of will, as pure possibility, is not constrained by empirical reality, its success or failure will depend on the particular mental and physical powers, upon the character of the individual in question. The attempt to realize the ideal type *man* can at best, Weininger believes, succeed only partially and momentarily, and then only in human beings of genius. At worst – for example, in the case of human beings who are, by Weininger's lights, predominantly female – it must tragically fail. Yet not to make the attempt is to abandon oneself to the forces of immorality.

V. Horizontal and Vertical Ethics

I shall suppose in what follows that whatever may be said of Weininger's respective evaluations of the M- and W-values, the distinction, at least, is well-founded. It gives rise to a division between what might loosely be termed vertical and horizontal conceptions of ethics. Vertical conceptions rest on a view of ethical value as residing in a linear, one-directional relation between the individual and some higher authority (God, as something like a father or a fearful judge, in the simplest possible account, though the higher authority may be, for example, the conscience of the subject in question, or some higher self or "moral law within"). Such a vertical relation may be seen also in Freud's account of ego and superego, and it is present also in Kafka, for example in *The Judgment*.[9] Horizontal theories, in contrast, view ethical value as arising out of the existence of reciprocal relations between human beings, interrelations conceived as involving some sacrifice of our respective individualities (the kind of denial of the self which occurs, most evidently, in the relation between the mother and her child, and which is seen by most proponents of a horizontalist ethic as arising from the very fact that individuals live together as members of a common society/tribe/race/class). Horizontalist conceptions of God see Him not as judge or father, but as something like a social worker, a friend, or a cloud of benevolence. The propensity to recognize and to respect vertical values is manifest in the world's major religious traditions in the idea of a last judgment and of God as source of absolute justice. It is manifest in the systems of government and of law that have grown up in civilized societies, in the idea of a divine right of kings, with its conception of the monarch as a direct representative of God on earth.

That societies based exclusively on horizontal values (such as the hippy commune or the Fourierist phalanx) have been notoriously short-lived, is in Weininger's eyes entirely predictable. For it is a precondition of the continuity and survival of larger social groupings that the respect for vertical values should be deeply rooted in its constituent religious and secular institutions, even if this is accompanied by liberal helpings of the rhetoric of love and mutual sacrifice.

VI. The Categorical Imperative

For Weininger, of course, the health or continuity or stability of a society is of as little ethical significance as is the survival of the individual. What is of ethical significance is exclusively the realization of vertical values. This standpoint may seem strange, yet Weininger was able to draw support for his conception from almost the entire tradition of Western philosophy. For the principal philosophers of the West have given overwhelming priority to vertical rather than to horizontal intuitions in their accounts of value – and we should not be tempted to suppose that this uniformity of views is simply the result of the fact that the history of humankind has as yet seen no woman philosopher of the rank of Plato or Aristotle. The uniformity is to be traced, rather, to a purely philosophical idea, which received its earliest formulation some three thousand years ago when the sentence "God created man in His own image" was first conceived: the idea of individual separateness, of loneliness, of freedom from the herd, as an *achievement* of mankind.[10] This idea has colored the thought of the West since Judaic times. It has undergone successive modifications: in the writings of Plato with his conception of the philosopher as a man blessed with god-like spirit; in the medieval conception of man as microcosm;[11] in the monadology of Leibniz; and in the Cartesian *cogito*. It reverts to its primeval form in the writings of Nietzsche.

With Kant, however, as seen through Weininger's eyes, the idea of individual separateness undergoes an almost complete detachment from its Judaeo-Christian origins. Kant, for whom the words "I stand alone! am free! am my own master!" represent the very root of ethics, instituted a new stage in the development of humankind. His work made possible the reversal of the Judaic premise, the propounding of a thesis of total autonomy, to the effect that it is the isolated, individual subject who creates God in his own image. This thesis, present only in seedling form in Kant's own writings, first exploded with full force in the works of the later German idealists, which consist in large part of attempts to draw out its implications. It may appear grotesque to see in Weininger the culmination of a development which began with Kant and Fichte and was carried to successively greater heights by Schopenhauer and Nietzsche. Yet we shall see that, of all the inheritors of the idealist tradition, Weininger was alone in recognizing and embracing certain tendencies intrinsic to the higher morality of the Kantian world view, tendencies which reveal, once they are made explicit, that the entire edifice is fundamentally defective.

Kant's ethical views may be summarized as follows. He insists, first of all, upon the necessity to realize, in one's actions, an intrinsic unity of reason and will. The moral worth of an action lies not in the purpose to be attained by it, but in the principle in accordance with which it is decided upon.[12] Secondly, he insists that our relations with our fellows can be ethical only to the extent that we act so as to treat humanity, as well in our own person as in the person of another, ever as end, and never merely as means.[13] Weininger conceived himself as having merely made precise the implications of this imperative of the Kantian ethic. But there is a further strand in Kant's thought, expressed in his categorical imperative:

> "*Act only on that maxim through which you can at the same time will that it should become a universal law.*" [...] the universal imperative of duty may also run as follows: "*Act as if the maxim of your action were to become through your will a universal law of nature.*"[14]

To fulfil this imperative is to bring about a unity of reason and will.

VII. *Overturning Kant*

It is not easy to see how a universalizing principle of this kind can be brought into harmony with the radically egoistic conclusions that Weininger wishes to draw from the Kantian ethic. According to the more usual interpretations of Kant, this last clause of the categorical imperative is to be understood as imposing a constraint, indeed a considerable constraint, upon those types of action which can be counted as "ethical" within the terms of the earlier clauses. It is seen, in effect, as a fifth column of horizontalism within the Kantian framework.

Weininger, however, turns the usual, comfortable, liberal interpretation of Kant on its head. For him the proposition of universalizability is no more than an afterthought that is, strictly speaking, redundant. For he holds that all of those actions which, of themselves, exemplify the unity of reason and will, and which do not involve the use of another merely as means, are such that the principles in accordance with which they are executed are, of necessity and without further ado, universalizable. If an action is ethical in accordance with the earlier clauses, then this is of itself sufficient to vouchsafe that it is the duty of all human beings to respect the principles that underlie it. This is the case even if, for particular types of human being, the attempt to exercise this duty must tragically fail. Universalizability is thereby conceived not as a prior constraint upon what may count as ethical. Rather, whatever is ethical is to be treated, if necessary via *force majeure*, as universalizable. Because it is ethical to be a man and unethical to be a woman (to abandon oneself to the merely female characteristics in one's biological make-up), it follows that it is the duty of every human being to will that the dark forces of sensuality within his or her breast should be surmounted. Woman must – in the spirit of at least some contemporary feminists – become man. Because the universalizability condition has been conceded so insubstantial a cutting edge, the thesis of total autonomy reaches its simplest possible expression within the Weiningerian ethic: *act on those maxims through which you can will that they serve as laws even in a world emptied of fellow human beings.*

In a world denuded of all consciousnesses outside myself, the W-values of community and compassion crumble into so much dust. The same cannot be said, however, of the M-values of truth, integrity, and resolution. Even in such a world I would still, according to Weininger, be burdened with the duty to exercise a will to value, to think honestly and rigorously, to forget nothing, to accept logic as the judge of all my thinking acts. One is reminded of the moral of Grillparzer's *Weh dem, der lügt* – that every lie, however small, assaults the foundations of the entire human condition.

VIII. Sex and Morality

The next stage in Weininger's development of the Kantian ethic consists in an argument to the effect that – superficial appearances notwithstanding – all of us are already living in a world in which we are in any case cut off from our fellow humans, that ultimate loneliness is not something we are ever able to escape. Here Weininger, with the courage of the monomaniac, is merely pointing out that there is a sense in which the Kantian imperative rules out any contact between human beings which would have positive ethical value. Kant's injunction to treat humanity ever as end, never solely as means, implies first of all, and familiarly, that the innocent contemplation of a pretty face be repudiated as immoral, since this involves the use of the owner of the face merely as the means to one's own personal gratification.

But then all sexual relations, whether they are entered into voluntarily or involuntarily, also necessarily involve the use of another merely as means. This is clear in the case of relations between client and prostitute. However, when reflecting upon sexual relations that are not purely mercenary, there remains the lingering feeling that – even though the desire for sexual gratification may give rise to the treatment of one's partner as mere means – the existence of other bonds between persons in love might somehow cancel out the immorality which would otherwise result. Kant, for example, in a letter to C.G. Schütz of July 10, 1779, states – without a shred of argument – that the immorality which should arise from "the reciprocal use of each other's sexual organs by two people" is cancelled out "if the cohabitation is assumed to be marital, that is lawful, even if only according to the right of nature; the authorization is already contained in the concept [of marriage]." Once we examine the nature of such bonds, however, we see that they rest entirely on the moment of reciprocity: M's willingness to allow W to do his cleaning and cooking is seen as being balanced by the willingness of W to allow M to house, clothe and feed her. But reciprocity cannot cancel out immorality. That two persons are using each other, as reciprocal means, is a double immorality; it is an immorality compounded by collusion. Relations between parent and child, too, involve the use of one person for the gratification of another. The child is brought into the world without his permission having been sought, and molded according to specifications that he is not given the opportunity to approve. Indeed, virtually all relations between human beings, including the simplest forms of trade, and even an act so trivial as riding on a bus, become impossible for the thorough-going Kantian who would lead a strictly moral life. Each involves the use of another solely as means to the agent's own personal ends. It thus appears that the current pejorative use of the word "exploitation" to characterize the relations between, say, an employer and his employees, or between a husband and a wife, has – with its implication that these perfectly commonplace ties are somehow immoral – fundamentally Kantian roots. What those who talk of exploitation have not seen, is that the alternatives canvassed (workers' control of the means of production and the like) serve, from this same Kantian point of view, merely to distribute the immorality among a somewhat larger group of people.

IX. *Woman Has No Ego*

It will by now be clear that the Kantian ethic, in its Weiningerian form, conflicts radically with more familiar conceptions of ethical value. Doing good for one's neighbor, for example, is seen to involve the morally repugnant assumption that the neighbor her/himself would be so unethical as to be willing to collude in our being used as means to her ends. Where the right-minded person is perfectly happy to accept that there is an element of exploitation in the great majority of everyday transactions, and where he of a leftward bent is ready to use the fact of exploitation as an excuse to subvert the whole common life of humankind in order to substitute relations which are, in his eyes, somehow non-exploitative, Weininger draws the conclusion that truly ethical relations between human beings are unattainable, that human relations as such constitute at best a distraction from the ethical life. The problem of loneliness, then, is unresolvable. Our various frantic attempts to solve this problem – travel, sexual conquest, the gathering of worldly possessions – are to be dismissed as so much moral abuse. The only truly moral course is to submit to the duty to accept one's isolation before the world as a whole, to recognize (to will) that there is no problem of loneliness at all. That this is one's duty is not, in the end, susceptible to any proof. The horrifying, tragic fact for man, alone in the universe, is that it has no further sense to submit to this duty.[15] Here we meet bedrock. Only something like the grace of God can help us.

It is the vertical order of the mind which makes possible – even in a wholly solipsistic world – the phenomena of conscience and guilt. These and other related ethical phenomena, as well as what Weininger calls the phenomena of logic (reflection, analysis, introspection), have their foundation in a relation between higher and lower strata of the mind, between what Weininger calls the soul, or intelligible ego, and the merely sensual self. The phenomena of logic and ethics arise where the soul is set in judgment over the empirical ego. And where– as in the case of Weininger's absolute woman – the logical and ethical phenomena are absent, where the mind is just a flow of sensuous data, there the ground for the assumption of a soul or intelligible ego falls away. The perfectly feminine being recognizes neither the logical nor the ethical imperative, and the words "law," "duty," and "duty before oneself" are words and concepts that are alien to her. Thus the conclusion is perfectly justified that she lacks also a supersensual personality. The absolute female has no ego.[16]

X. On Wittgenstein

It is no accident that so much in the above calls to mind the thinking of the early Wittgenstein. Recall, in particular, Wittgenstein's question as to what constitutes the difference between a happy, harmonious life and an unhappy one. This difference cannot be anything physical. Even if everything that we want were to happen, this would only be, so to speak, a grace of fate; for there is no logical connection between will and world which would guarantee it, and we could not in turn will the supposed physical connection. But how, if a man cannot ward off the misery of the world, can he be happy at all? Wittgenstein's answer is: through the life of knowledge, for which we might read: life spent in pursuit of the M-values of truth, honesty, intellectual rigor, and so forth.

Good conscience is that happiness which is vouchsafed by the life of knowledge. The life of knowledge is the life that is happy in spite of the misery of the world. The only life that is happy is the life that can renounce the amenities of the world. Here we return, through Weininger, to Plato's (and the Stoic) conception of the philosopher (of the one who leads a life of knowledge) as being blessed with a godlike spirit. He alone is able to come into contact with the divine order of the world and thereby reproduce that order in his soul. He alone is able to view the world as a whole, *sub specie aeterni*, to liberate himself from the sphere of what happens and is the case.

In the *Notebooks of 1916*, we find only random remarks on matters such as these, interpolated with reflections on logic and formal ontology and with expressions of Wittgenstein's distress at the fact that what he says is not yet clear. Only in the *Tractatus*, completed two years later, do they begin to be consolidated into the framework of a consistent theory. And only there – where we find no more talk of the "life of knowledge" as the highest good – do the no longer simply Weiningerian implications of Wittgenstein's philosophy of the ethical become clear.

XI. Kraus on Woman

Die Fackel served as the platform for Kraus's constant stream of abuse against the moral, social, sexual, political, aesthetic, legal, medical, and above all grammatical failings of his contemporaries. His principal aim was to impede as far as possible – and paradoxically through the medium of journalism – the erosion of thought and culture that he saw as an inevitable consequence of the spread of journalistic cliché. He spent several thousands of pages, in issue after issue of his journal, bewailing the extent to which the press, by continuously feeding its readers with ready-processed feelings and opinions, had denatured their intellectual and emotional lives and destroyed their capacity for moral (and aesthetic) judgment. Journalism and its allies – the information and war-propaganda organs of the state, a medical profession (and some of Kraus's most vituperative attacks were directed against the new pseudo-profession of psychoanalysis) ready to prostitute itself and its jargon to the services of the state – were conceived by Kraus as enemies of language itself. And in the case of *Viennese Society* vs. *the German Language,* Kraus himself served as both judge and defending council. The synchronisation of word and deed he saw as yielding a universal criterion of the ethical. Every misuse of language, however small, assaults the foundations of the entire human condition. And thus if, as Kraus saw it, his contemporaries once fully grasped the meaning of their utterances, if they once truly experienced the reality contained within their words, then their lives and their world would change; the otherwise all-pervading hypocrisy would become impossible. If writers and speakers fully realized what they write and say, if they saw and felt the full impact of the verbal reality that inheres in their words and has only to be uncovered for its effect to be revealed, then they would write and speak differently, and indeed live differently. It is as if we were to say that nobody who had ever fully imagined an execution could fail to plead for the abolition of capital punishment.[17]

As Kraus became more and more convinced of the hopelessness of his task, his critique of the misuse of language gradually became transformed into a form of linguistic theology, skirting the limits of intelligible discourse. Kraus saw the "fall" of German life, as marked by the rise of National Socialism, as a linguistic event, an apocalypse brought about by the black magic of printers ink. The issue of *Die Fackel* of July 1934 consists of a 170-page letter to "the stupid reader, whoever he may be," in which Kraus explains "why *Die Fackel* does not appear."

XII. Kraus and Language

The decay had set in, Kraus believed, because language had been robbed of its rightful and natural position of authority in the abode of thought; for the true writer, in Kraus's eyes, is one who does not seek to interpose his own ego between language and the world. He is not one who has a perfect command of language, but one who is commanded by language, one who recognizes that language must be treated with respect if she is to give of her best – Kraus was fond of pointing out that "language" (*die Sprache*) is of feminine gender. As he himself expressed it:

> Language is the sovereign mistress of thought, and whosoever succeeds in reversing this relation will find that she makes herself useful about the house but will bar him from her womb.

My language is the common prostitute that I turn into a virgin.[18]

Modern writers, and particularly journalists, had increasingly sought to use language as the instrument of their ideas, and their efforts resulted in thoughtless, heartless (artless) pap (compare Heidegger's remarks on the inauthenticity of *Gerede* or chatter.) But not only has language been thus unnaturally forced into a passive, unresponsive role, robbed of its powers of directing the course of thought and of setting a limit to the thinkable; the debauchery of language has also brought a warping and a misdirection of the masculine principles of deliberation, dominance, and control. The modern world is accordingly a world in which (masculine) boorishness has triumphed over (feminine) sensitivity, a world in which the private life of humankind has been muzzled by brute force. It has thereby cut itself off from that concentration of thought and feeling, that harmonious coupling of language and experience, which is the precondition of culture.

XIII. The Personal and the Political

Kraus published in *Die Fackel* some of the writings that appeared in defense of Weininger after the latter's death, including writings of Strindberg. We can now see that he turned Weininger's work on its head. Out of Weininger's vilification of the feminine principle he carved a eulogy of the absolute female which served in turn as the basis for his own attacks on the hypocritical attitudes toward woman and sexuality which pervaded the Viennese society of his day.

Weininger disparaged woman for her sensuality, her monomaniacal obsession with sex and the trappings of sex (beauty, sensuality, clothes, hair), her feeblemindedness, her impressionability, her illogicality, her fickleness, her superficiality, her ability to be easily pleased – and just as easily upset. Kraus glorified woman for these same qualities.[19] Weininger affirmed that the only hope for woman lay in her striving, however vainly, to become man. Kraus found nothing more repugnant, more unnatural, more lacking in charm, than the educated woman. What for Weininger is the soul-destroying capacity of woman to divert the attentions of man away from the truly moral life, Kraus saw as her glorious capacity to nurture and inspire.

Weiningerian individualism, with its vilification of the feminine principle, is transformed, through the filter of Kraus's vision of language, into an individualism that accepts the (restraining) power for good of precisely those qualities that Weininger had so vehemently disparaged. The dualism of masculine light and feminine darkness, a dualism in which the forces of culture (M) and nature (W) are diametrically opposed, is supplanted by an opposition between boorishness and sensitivity, between the mindless public world of incompetent journalists and bureaucrats and the interlocking private worlds of individual men and women. Individual morality and public law, for Kraus as – in a different way – for Weininger, must thereby relate to entirely separate domains. Hence Kraus's glorification of the prostitute, a victim of the confusion of these two domains. Hence his recommendation of the rural life and of the provinces, where character has not yet been laid waste by journalism, where printers ink has not yet discolored the natural life and signifies nothing further than a means which is ready to hand for the communication of "the serious, upright feelings of the private individual."[20] Hence his continuous stream of attacks against the activities of the Austrian public hygiene authorities, who would bring before the courts matters "which properly belong only before the Highest Judge – and probably would not interest even Him."[21] The disgust people felt at the practices uncovered by the hygiene authorities Kraus saw as being rooted in the fact that even the most harmonious affairs in our private lives, when dragged out into the open, seem disgusting to eyes and ears for which they are not intended.[22]

XIV. *Protestant and Catholic Anti-Liberalism*

Kraus, Weininger, and also Wittgenstein were part of a wider counter-liberal undercurrent in turn-of-the-century Austria to which Loos, Engelmann, Hänsel, Hofmannsthal, Ficker, and Ebner also belonged. These are thinkers who in different ways shared a distaste for the modern world and for modern ways of thought, and who therefore did not conceive their work as an attempt to persuade the public of the rightness of certain views. They were well aware that the thoughts expressed would not find general acceptance, but would at best evoke a spark of agreement in those few scattered individuals who had already had those thoughts themselves.

Thus also they were often content to express their thoughts in the form of aphorisms that were only asymptotically intelligible.

It is possible to distinguish within this counter-liberal movement two more or less coherent tendencies of what, with some hesitation, we can call Protestant and Catholic anti-liberalism. The division is not one that can be made to rest simply on the overt religious confessions of their respective adherents. It is more appropriately characterized by appeal to certain family resemblances between the philosophical backgrounds, interests, and beliefs of the individuals involved. Thus the Protestant strain is marked by the prominence of Nordic writers (Kant, Kierkegaard, Ibsen, Strindberg, Hamsun) in the intellectual biographies of its principal adherents. Representatives of the Catholic wing, on the other hand, tended to look to the South of Europe, to the traditions of classical Greece and Italy, to the Baroque, and to the native Austrian heritage of Grillparzer and Stifter.

We have already seen the workings of Protestant anti-liberalism in its most extreme form in the writings of Weininger. Recall that on the day on which he received his doctorate Weininger converted to Protestantism. Catholic anti-liberalism might best be represented by Kraus and by the members of the Brenner Circle. Kraus abandoned the Jewish faith in 1899 and was baptized (in secret) into the Catholic Church in 1911 (he left the Church in 1923), having come to regard atheism as an unnatural state, comparable to an artificially constructed language.

The Protestant and Catholic anti-liberals have this in common: they turned their backs on the existing political order of society. Both stressed the importance of a radical separation of the public and the private, and believed that what was of intrinsic value was rooted in the latter. Where they differed was in their understanding of the locus of the private sphere. Catholic anti-liberals retained a belief in certain pre-liberal values of communal life. They adhered – in theory if not in practice – to the values of the family and of local and neighborly traditions, and they turned against the facelessness of the metropolis. This generated a belief in the importance of a pluralism of authority in society and in the necessity to preserve hierarchical forms. The Protestant anti-liberal, on the other hand, conceived value as residing in the isolated individual (in the vertical relation between the individual ego and his God, or conscience). Protestant anti-liberalism thereby stripped ethical value of its connection with the sphere of what happens and is the case.

Where Protestant anti-liberalism is not recognizably a political doctrine of any form, its Catholic counterpart can be clearly understood as a form of (wistful) conservatism. Catholic anti-liberals sought, in effect, to return to a time when the values of preliberal (or "*altliberal*") Austria as they conceived it were still taken for granted. But they did not, however, act in a simply political fashion: the individuals involved were not, as one now says, agents of reactionary forces in society. Catholic anti-liberals could see perfectly well that the attempt to bring about a restoration of the lost order in society by means of political agitation could only further consolidate the deterioration of those natural ties between individuals that they wished to nurture and sustain. They sought, rather, to exploit those havens of undistorted human life within society where political and ideological interference, the interference of modernity, had not yet made its mark. They sought to preserve those bastions of humanity in the (almost certainly hopeless) fight against the decline of intellectual and moral standards brought about by the growth of the city and by the spread of democracy and journalism.

Thus Protestant and Catholic anti-liberals counterposed to the rationalistic conceptions of humankind derived from the Enlightenment two distinct but equally sceptical images of man. The Protestant anti-liberals, in emphasizing the absolute identity of man (and woman) before the moral law, are capable of generating absurd consequences to the effect that, for example, woman must strive to discover the moral law within her (must strive to become like man), even though, because of the intensity of the forces of darkness which beset her, this attempt will inevitably and tragically fail. The Catholic anti-liberal, in contrast, draw attention to and indeed glorify the differences between human beings, recognizing that a naturally existing complementarity obtains between individuals of different types and that this, so long as it is allowed to express itself naturally, can only have positive ethical value. Catholic anti-liberalism is therefore on the one hand more realistic than its Protestant counterpart: it can allow, for example, that a woman can lead a truly moral life *as a woman*, by practising those womanly virtues which, from a more rigorous point of view, have to be dismissed as of merely superficial importance. On the other hand, it is less optimistic in recognizing intrinsic ethically relevant differences between human beings, in implying that there are human beings who, because of their intrinsic nature, are cut off from the highest forms of moral or intellectual excellence.

XV. *Kraus on Serbia*

Kraus, notoriously, was an enemy not only of journalists and psychoanalysts but also of military authorities and war-mongering politicians. His antimilitarism expressed itself most poignantly in his massive onslaught on Alice Schalek, a female war correspondent who was the incarnation of everything that Kraus opposed. Kraus longed for a golden age when everything could be relied upon to remain in its natural place. He sought harmony and he hated the boorishness of the male, whether as *bureaucrétin*, as bumbling general, or as journalist. Schalek, a female pioneer, a "male-female perversion" (*"mannweibliche Pervertierung"*) who had secured for herself a posting as war correspondent in the front lines of the First World War through energetic persuasion of her employers at the *Neue Freie Presse*. In Kraus's *Last Days of Mankind*, a female journalist modelled on Schalek is one of the few characters who figures repeatedly at different places in the plot; her activities at the front are represented as one of the most extreme horrors of the war.

Schalek is an early incarnation of what, in the era of CNN, has become a commonplace: a journalist who is herself a star and places herself at the very center of events. Kraus presents his version as driving through battlefields as if she is passing through museums, taking her own photographs of the corpses along the way and becoming enthralled at the bodies of the "simple man" in the trenches. She hounds a troop of wounded men marching by with the question "Was für *Empfindungen* haben Sie?" ("How do you *feel*?").

Schalek, like her CNN successors, brings the war into your living room. She brings the human side of war as it actually happens. But this means that no longer is anything in its proper place. Schalek not only has the insidious effect of making war acceptable, but her enthusiastic hopping around in the trenches in the thick of battle means that there is now no haven from the war, and this means that there is now nothing – no noble ideals – worth fighting for.

XVI. Promotional Trips to Hell

From *Die Fackel*:

> I am holding in my hand a document which transcends and seals all the shame of this age and would in itself suffice to assign the currency stew that calls itself mankind a place of honor in a cosmic carrion pit. Even though any clipping from a newspaper has signified a clipping of Creation, in this instance one faces the dead certainty that a generation deemed capable of this sort of thing no longer has any nobler possessions to damage.[23]

Battlefield Round Trips by Automobile!
organized by the *Basel News*
Promotional Trips from Sept. 25 to Oct. 25 at the Reduced Rate of 117 Francs

Unforgettable Impressions
No Passport Formalities!
(...)
Especially recommended as an autumn trip!
(...)

You stay overnight in a luxury hotel – service and gratuities included. [...]
You ride through destroyed villages to the fortress area of Vaux with its enormous cemeteries containing hundreds of thousands of fallen men. [...]
"... A trip to the battlefield area of Verdun conveys to the visitor the quintessence of the horrors of modern warfare. [...]"
You have time after lunch to view battered Verdun, the Ville-Martyre.

Acknowledgments:
With thanks to Berit Brogaard, Wilma Iggers, and Elizabeth Millán-Zaibert for helpful comments.

[1] Weininger, *Geschlecht und Charakter*, 462.
[2] See Janik 1985b.
[3] Ford Maddox Ford and William Carlos Williams were among the early admirers of *Geschlecht und Charakter* in the United States (Sengoopta 2000).
[4] Appendix to Weininger 1920.
[5] Sengoopta, *op. cit.*
[6] *Die Fackel* 169, Nov. 23, 1904, 6-14; cf. Szasz, 144.
[7] Abrahamsen 1946, 55; see Sengoopta 2000. Weininger approached Sigmund Freud with an outline of *Sex and Character* in the autumn of 1901. Freud refused to recommend publication, and advised Weininger to spend "ten years" gathering empirical evidence for his assertions. "The world," Freud said, "wants evidence, not thoughts." Weininger retorted that he would prefer to write ten other books in the next ten years.
[8] See *GuC*, II, chs. 6 and 7, and the essay "Wissenschaft und Kultur" in *UdID*, 142-182.
[9] Compare the discussion of the self as "inner tribunal" in Smith 1981.
[10] Cf. Durzak, 16f.
[11] *GuC*, e.g., 222.
[12] Kant, 65.
[13] Kant, 91.
[14] Kant, 84 (original italics); compare Sengoopta, *op. cit.*, 55ff, where the relation between Man and Woman is compared to the Aristotelian relation between form and matter.
[15] *GuC*, 209ff; Bíro, 73.
[16] *GuC*, 239f.
[17] Stern, 78.
[18] Kraus, 1986, 135 and 293.
[19] See Iggers, Ch. 7; cf. Greer in *The Female Eunuch*, whose view of the characteristic female traits of illogicality and emotionality comes close to that of Kraus. Greer holds that these traits are in fact advantages: "If women had no ego, if they had no separation from the rest of the world, no repression and no regression, how nice that would be!"
[20] Kraus, *Die Fackel*, Nov. 7, 1913, 29.
[21] 1908, 287f.
[22] Cf. Iggers, 164.
[23] Translated in Zohn, 89.

References

Abrahamsen, David. 1946. *The Mind and Death of a Genius*, New York: Columbia UP.
Biró, Paul. 1927. *Die Sittlichkeitsmetaphysik Otto Weiningers: Eine geistesgeschichtliche Studie*. Vienna: Braumüller.

Durzak, Manfred. 1968. "Das Vorbild seiner Jugend: Otto Weininger," ch. 1 of *Hermann Broch: Der Dichter und seine Zeit*. Stuttgart: Kohlhammer.
Engelmann, Paul, et al. 1949. *Dem Andenken an Karl Kraus*. Tel Aviv; repr. Vienna: O. Kerry, 1967.
Engelmann, Paul. 1967. *Letters from Ludwig Wittgenstein. With a Memoir*. Oxford: Blackwell.
Greer, Germaine. 1971. *The Female Eunuch*. St. Albans: Granada.
Hänsel, Ludwig. 1957. *Begegnungen und Auseinandersetzungen mit Denkern und Dichtern der Neuzeit*. Vienna: Österreichischer Bundesverlag.
Iggers, Wilma Abeles. 1967. *Karl Kraus: A Viennese Critic of the Twentieth Century*. The Hague: Nijhoff.
Janik, Allan. 1978. "Wittgenstein and Weininger," in *Wittgenstein and His Impact on Contemporary Thought*. Ed. Elisabeth Leinfellner et al. Vienna: Hölder-Pichler-Tempsky, 25-30.
-. 1979. "Wittgenstein, Ficker and *Der Brenner*," in Luckhardt, ed., 1979, 161-89.
-. 1981. "Therapeutic Nihilism: How Not to Write about Otto Weininger," in Smith, ed., 1981, 263-92.
-. 1985. *Essays on Wittgenstein and Weininger*. Amsterdam: Rodopi.
-. 1985a. "Philosophical Sources of Wittgenstein's Ethics," in Janik 1985, 74-95.
-. 1985b. "Writing About Weininger," in Janik 1985, 96-115.
Johnston, William M. 1972. *The Austrian Mind: An Intellectual and Social History 1848-1938*. Berkeley: University of California Press.
Kafka, Franz. 1953. *Hochzeitsvorbereitungen auf dem Lande und andere Prosa aus dem Nachlaß*. New York: Schocken.
-. 1973. *Sämtliche Erzählungen*, Frankfurt a.M.: Fischer.
Kant, Immanuel. 1972. *The Moral Law: Kant's Groundwork of the Metaphysic of Morals*. Trans. H.J. Paton. London: Hutchinson.
Kohn, Hans. 1926. *Karl Kraus, Arthur Schnitzler, Otto Weininger. Aus dem jüdischen Wien der Jahrhundertwende*, Tübingen: J.C.B. Mohr.
Kraus, Karl. 1908. *Sittlichkeit und Kriminalität*, Vienna: Rosner.
-. 1919. *Die letzten Tage der Menschheit*. Vienna: Verlag Die Fackel.
-. 1922. *Untergang der Welt durch die schwarze Magie*. Vienna: Verlag Die Fackel.
-. 1974. *Briefe an Sidonie Nadherny von Borutin 1913-1936*. 2 vols., Munich:Kösel.
-. 1986. *Aphorismen: Sprüche und Widersprüche, Pro domo et mundo, Nachts* (= *Schriften*, vol. 8). Ed. Christian Wagenknecht. Frankfurt a.M.: Suhrkamp.
Lessing, Theodor. 1930. *Der jüdische Selbsthaß*. Berlin: Jüdischer Verlag, partially repr. as an appendix to the reissue of Weininger 1904.
Luckhardt, C.G., ed. 1979. *Ludwig Wittgenstein: Sources and Perspectives*. Ithaca: Cornell UP.
McGuinness, Brian. 1979. "Wittgenstein's 'intellectual nursery-training' (geistige Kinderstube)," in *Wittgenstein, the Vienna Circle and Critical Rationalism*. Ed. Hal Berghel et al. Vienna: Hölder-Pichler-Tempsky, 33-40.
Mulligan, Kevin. 1981. "Philosophy, Animality and Justice: Kleist, Kafka, Weininger and Wittgenstein," in Smith, ed., 1981, 293-312.

Probst, F. 1904. *Der Fall Otto Weininger. Eine psychiatrische Studie* (= Grenzfragen des Nerven- und Seelenlebens, vol. 31). Wiesbaden: Bergmann.
Sengoopta, Chandak. 2000. *Otto Weininger: Sex, Science, and Self in Imperial Vienna*. Chicago: University of Chicago Press.
Smith, Barry. 1979. "On Tractarian Law," in *Wittgenstein, the Vienna Circle and Critical Rationalism*. Ed. Hal Berghel et al. Vienna: Hölder-Pichler-Tempsky, 456-459.
–. 1981. "Kafka and Brentano: A Study in Descriptive Psychology," in Smith, ed., 113-161; revised version as: "Brentano and Kafka," *Axiomathes* 8 (1997): 83-104.
Smith, Barry, ed. 1981. *Structure and Gestalt: Philosophy and Literature in Austria-Hungary*. Amsterdam: Benjamins.
Stekel, W. 1904. "Der Fall Otto Weininger," *Die Wage* 45.
Stern, J.P. 1966. "Karl Kraus's Vision of Language," *Modern Language Review* 61: 71-84.
Szasz, Thomas Stephen. 1977. *Karl Kraus and the Soul-Doctors: A Pioneer Critic and His Criticism of Psychiatry and Psychoanalysis*. London: Routledge and Kegan Paul.
Weininger, Otto. 1903. *GuC = Geschlecht und Charakter*. Vienna: Braumüller; repr. Munich: Matthes und Seitz, 1980.
–. 1904. *UdlD = Über die letzten Dinge*. Vienna: Braumüller; repr. Munich: Matthes and Seitz, 1980.
–. 1920. *Taschenbuch und Briefe an einen Freund*. Vienna and Leipzig: E.P. Tal.
Wittgenstein, Ludwig. 1921. *Tractatus Logico-Philosophicus*. Sec. ed.; English trans. by D.F. Pears and B.F. McGuinness, London: Routledge and Kegan Paul, 1961.
–. 1964. *Philosophische Bemerkungen*; English trans. by R. Hargreaves and R. White, Oxford: Blackwell, 1975.
–. 1967. "Bemerkungen über Frazers *The Golden Bough*," *Synthese* 17: 233-253; English trans. by J. Beversluis, in Luckhardt, ed., 61-81.
–. 1971. *Prototractatus*. New York: Cornell UP.
–. 1974. *Letters to Russell, Keynes and Moore*. Oxford: Blackwell.
–. 1977. *VB = Vermischte Bemerkungen*, Frankfurt a.M.: Suhrkamp; English version as *Culture and Value*. Sec. ed., Oxford: Blackwell, 1997.
–. 1979. *Notebooks 1914-16*. Sec. ed., Oxford: Blackwell.
Zohn, Harry, ed. 1976. *In These Great Times: A Karl Kraus Reader*, Montreal: Engendra.

DAVID LEWIS ON MEINONGIAN LOGIC OF FICTION

Dale Jacquette
Pennsylvania State University

1. Semantics of Fiction

In "Truth in Fiction," David Lewis raises four objections to a Meinongian semantics of fiction. Lewis does not deny that a Meinongian logic of fiction could be made to work, but identifies disadvantages in Meinongian semantics as a reason for recommending his own possible worlds alternative.[1]

A Meinongian semantics proposes to explain meaning without ontological prejudice.[2] It analyzes the meaning of the sentence "a is F" in the same way and by reference to the same semantic principles, regardless of whether or not a happens to exist. Meinongian semantic domains admit existent and nonexistent objects, including objects ostensibly referred to in fiction, and permit reference and true predication of constitutive properties to existent and nonexistent objects alike. A Meinongian theory thus interprets the sentence "Sherlock Holmes is a detective" as true, on the grounds that what we mean by the putative proper name "Sherlock Holmes" is a nonexistent object described in the fiction of Arthur Conan Doyle that truly has the property of being a detective in the same way and in the same sense as an existent detective.[3]

Lewis proposes an alternative to Meinong's object theory that considers the truth of a sentence in a work of fiction only within an explicit story-context. He explains truth in fiction by (selectively) prefixing (most) problematic sentences with the operator, "In such-and-such fiction..." For example, "Sherlock Holmes is a detective," on Lewis's analysis, becomes, "In the Sherlock Holmes stories, Sherlock Holmes is a detective." This is by no means a trivial transformation that reduces the truth of sentences ostensibly about fictional objects to tautologies, analytic or other *a priori* truths. For it does not follow logically or analytically that Sherlock Holmes in the Sherlock Holmes stories is a detective, since the stories might have described Sherlock Holmes as something other than a detective. The effect of Lewis's proposal is to relocate the truth conditions for a sentence in or about fiction from the immediate content of the sentence to the fictional context in which the sentence appears or to which it applies. The advantage he sees in modal story-contexting is that it avoids the need for nonexistent Meinongian objects.

Writing the Austrian Traditions: Relations between Philosophy and Literature.
Ed. Wolfgang Huemer and Marc-Oliver Schuster. Edmonton, Alberta:
Wirth-Institute for Austrian and Central European Studies, 2003. pp. 101-119.

II. Lewis's Challenge to Meinong

Why not be a Meinongian? What is so bad about nonexistence? Why is it undesirable to refer to nonexistent objects, and why should it be a problem for nonexistent objects to have properties just as existent objects do? How does it help to explain the possession of a property by an object for it to be true that the object exists?

Lewis's modal story-contexting of truth in fiction is in some ways simpler, but in other ways more complex, than the Meinongian theory he criticizes. It is simpler in excluding nonexistent objects. But it entails further complications of its own by requiring a distinction between the semantics for sentences about existent objects as opposed to sentences ostensibly about nonexistent objects. A Meinongian theory by contrast offers a unified, ontically neutral account to explain the meaning of sentences regardless of whatever objects may happen actually to exist or not exist. Lewis's theory is also made more complicated by virtue of positing modal semantic structures of fictional worlds inhabited by objects that do not actually exist.[4] To choose between a Meinongian or Lewis-style semantics of fiction, we must therefore come to terms with conflicting intuitions about potentially incommensurable aesthetic and philosophical values that might cause us to prefer one explanatorily comparable semantic theory over another. If Lewis, as he admits, has no knockdown objections to offer against a Meinongian theory of fiction, then the preferability of Lewis-style modal story-contexting over a Meinongian semantics strongly depends on whether he has successfully uncovered any significant disadvantages in Meinongian semantics as compared with modal story-contexting. Lewis accordingly considers four problems in a Meinongian logic of fiction:

- The problem of distinguishing properties predicated of nonexistent Meinongian objects versus existent entities, and hence of distinguishing the referents of predications involving existent entities versus predications involving nonexistent Meinongian objects.

- The problem of distinguishing a multiplicity of otherwise individually indistinguishable, indefinitely numbered nonexistent Meinongian objects posited in a work of fiction by means of a nonspecific term of plural reference in the absence of adequate identity conditions.

- The problem of restricting the range of quantifiers in comparing the properties of nonexistent Meinongian objects in a work of fiction with those of other nonexistent Meinongian objects in another work of fiction, or with the properties of existent entities.

- The problem of interpreting inferences about the properties of nonexistent Meinongian objects in a work of fiction, especially in conjunction with true propositions about the properties of existent objects that may also be mentioned in the story.

The objections are related and in different ways call attention to the same underlying scepticism about whether properties can reasonably be attributed to the nonexistent objects described in a work of fiction. All four objections, however, can be answered or refuted, thereby blunting Lewis's charge that a Meinongian semantics is at a theoretical disadvantage in comparison with modal story-contexting. A comparison of Meinongian object theory semantics with Lewis-style modal story-contexting, moreover, shows that the two are not incompatible. By itself, without Meinongian object theory, Lewis's proposal is subject to equally powerful countercriticisms. Lewis-style story-contexting needs to be combined with a Meinongian semantics of fiction in order to avoid Lewis's objections to Meinongian object theory and to avoid Meinongian objections to Lewis's story-context-prefixing.

III. Real and Fictional Objects and Properties

Lewis's first objection depends on a peculiar definition of Meinongian semantics. Lewis describes a Meinongian theory of fiction as one that interprets "Holmes wears a silk top hat" and "Nixon wears a silk top hat" as completely on a par, taking descriptions of fictional characters at face value as having the same subject-predicate form. "The only difference," Lewis claims, "would be that the subject terms 'Holmes' and 'Nixon' have referents of radically different sorts: one a fictional character, the other a real-life person of flesh and blood" (p. 261). Lewis rejects this way of contrasting real and fictional objects. He asks:

> For one thing, is there not some perfectly good sense in which Holmes, like Nixon, *is* a real-life person of flesh and blood? There are stories about the exploits of super-heroes from other planets, hobbits, fires and storms, vaporous intelligences, and other non-persons. But what a mistake it would be to class the Holmes stories with these! Unlike Clark Kent *et al.*, Sherlock Holmes is just a person – a person of flesh and blood, a being in the very same category as Nixon. (pp. 261-262)

Yet a Meinongian can and should regard Sherlock Holmes, despite being a fictional character, as a flesh and blood human being as much as Richard Nixon. Lewis does not further explain what he means by a Meinongian semantics. But it is central to Meinong's *Gegenstandstheorie* that nonexistent objects can have the same constitutive properties in the same sense as existent entities, regardless of their ontic status. The existence or nonexistence of an object is something else again. Contrary to the opinion of Shakespeare's brooding Prince Hamlet, to be or not to be is not always the question.

A nonexistent object, in a Meinongian semantics, can be a detective, a winged horse, or anything else that thought might freely intend. Sherlock Holmes for a Meinongian is as much flesh and blood as Richard Nixon. Of course, Sherlock Holmes's flesh and blood is not real, actually existent flesh and blood, any more than, more particularly, say, Sherlock Holmes's left eye is a real actually existent eye, or his violin is a real actually existent violin. The fact that Sherlock Holmes is as much flesh and blood as Richard Nixon is no embarrassment to Meinongian object theory. Lewis distinguishes between the ontic categories of the referents of "Sherlock Holmes" and "Richard Nixon," by saying that Holmes is "a fictional character" whereas Nixon is "a real life person of flesh and blood." This is partly true and partly false. There is indeed a difference in the ontic status of the referents of the proper names "Sherlock Holmes" and "Richard Nixon." It is true to say that Holmes is fictional, and to say that Nixon by contrast is "a real life person." But it is not true to say that Nixon by contrast with Holmes is a "person of flesh and blood." Lewis argues that it would be a mistake to say that Holmes is something other than "a person of flesh and blood, a being in the very same category as Nixon" (p. 262). But a Meinongian logic of fiction is not required to say that Holmes is not made of flesh and blood, and Meinongians will more typically insist that Sherlock Holmes, despite being a fictional nonexistent Meinongian object, is as much flesh and blood as Richard Nixon.

Thus, Lewis's first problem disappears. If we take Lewis's insight a few steps further, however, we might ask about a work of fiction in which the author declares in all sincerity that Holmes is an actually existent entity or real-life being. What are we to say then about the properties and ontic status of Holmes? Existence, unlike the property of being a detective or playing the violin, is not a property that authors can freely bestow on their fictional creations by their narratives.[5] Meinong's object theory accordingly makes an important distinction between nuclear (*konstitutorische*) and extranuclear properties (*ausserkonstitutorische Bestimmungen*).[6] Nuclear or constitutive properties are those such as being red or round, made of flesh and blood, being a detective or playing the violin, that can be had by existent or nonexistent Meinongian objects without prejudging their ontological status. Extranuclear or extraconstitutive properties by contrast are those such as being real, existent, subsistent, complete, necessary, or unreal, nonexistent, nonsubsistent, incomplete or impossible; these properties cannot be truly or falsely predicated of an object without thereby expressing a definite commitment to an object's ontological status. Constitutive ontically neutral properties can be freely truly predicated of objects, as when a novelist or mythmaker dreams up nonexistent fictional objects such as Holmes with the constitutive property of being a detective, smoking a pipe, shooting cocaine, or playing the violin. But extraconstitutive ontically commital properties cannot be freely truly predicated of objects by any act of imagination. A work of fiction, as a result, in which an author maintains that Holmes truly exists, does not truly predicate existence of Holmes. If an author says that Holmes is a detective, on the other hand, then, in a Meinongian semantics, Holmes truly is a detective.

The difference, properly applied, between ontically neutral nuclear or constitutive properties and ontically committal extranuclear or extraconstitutive properties solves many problems in Meinongian semantics. It absorbs the difficulty Lewis mentions, along with strengthened versions such as Russell's problem of the existent round square and Lewis's insufficiently disambiguated problem of the real-life flesh and blood Holmes.[7] We need only distinguish between the properties a Meinongian semantics regards as freely truly attributable to existent or nonexistent objects, and those that are not freely truly attributable, when they have the special function of truly or falsely attributing definite ontic status to an existent or nonexistent object. To the extent that Lewis fails to observe these basic Meinongian distinctions, his first criticism of Meinongian semantics is misdirected.

IV. *Indefinitely Numbered Fictional Objects*

Lewis's second objection to Meinongian interpretations of fiction is logically more interesting. He considers a work of fiction in which an indefinitely numbered "chorus" of fictional relatives is said to attend a fictional character:

> We can truly say that Sir Joseph Porter, K.C.B., is attended by a chorus of his sisters and his cousins and his aunts. To make this true, it seems that the domain of fictional characters must contain not only Sir Joseph himself, but also plenty of fictional sisters and cousins and aunts. But how many – five dozen, perhaps? No, for we cannot truly say that the chorus numbers five dozen exactly. We cannot truly say anything exact about its size. Then do we perhaps have a fictional chorus, but no fictional members of this chorus and hence no number of members? No, for we can truly say some things about the size. We are told that the sisters and cousins, even without the aunts, number in dozens. (p. 262)

A chorus, as judged against certain background information in a given cultural context, according to Lewis, does not contain exactly sixty members, but, as the unnamed story maintains, at least some dozens of sisters and cousins. What might a Meinongian theory of fiction say about predications involving indefinitely numbered nonexistent objects? Does Meinongian semantics run afoul of the difficulties Lewis mentions in this objection?

The property of numerability need not be essentially different from other kinds of constitutive properties such as being red or round, a detective, or a flesh-and-blood person. We similarly do not know the exact height or weight of Sherlock Holmes from the stories, nor how many nonexistent cells or molecules Holmes has in his nonexistent flesh and blood. Nor do we need to know. A fictional object in a Meinongian semantics is incomplete with respect to many, perhaps infinitely many, constitutive properties and property complements. If a chorus in fiction does not need to be all male or all female or any particular distribution of genders, why should it have to have any particular number of members?

A Meinongian in desperation might hold that the example Lewis describes involves an impossible Meinongian object, such as the round square. If to be a chorus consisting of no definite number of members is judged somehow to be a *contradictio in adjecto*, then the chorus that attends Sir Joseph Porter is implicitly impossible. Impossible as well as possible nonexistent Meinongian objects can be freely posited by the author of a work of fiction. But a defender of Meinongian semantics need not go so far in this direction to solve Lewis's problem. There are several choices. A Meinongian can interpret the indefiniteness of the number of chorus members in much the same way as s/he can interpret the incomplete information in a historical report of actual facts no longer subject to verification about the actual number of real members in a real chorus. In both cases, we can assume that there must be a definite number of chorus members, even if we do not know what the number is.

The difference is that in the case of the real chorus there is a definite true answer to the question of how many persons were in the chorus, while in the work of fiction there is no definite true answer. But, again, this is not a problem unique to the indefinite numbering of fictional objects in Meinongian semantics. There is similarly no definite true answer to the question of Holmes's eye color or the precise number of hairs on his head, even though we are probably right to affirm that if Holmes has eyes, then he has some definite eye color, and if he is hirsute, then he has some definite large number of hairs. What, then, is the special difficulty for a Meinongian semantics about an indefinitely numbered fictional chorus?

V. *Quantifier Restrictions in Meinongian Semantics*

The third objection in Lewis's discussion concerns the legitimate scope of quantifiers in Meinongian semantics. Lewis maintains:

> The Meinongian should not suppose that the quantifiers in descriptions of fictional characters range over all the things he thinks there are, both fictional and non-fictional; but he may not find it easy to say just how the ranges of quantification are to be restricted. Consider whether we can truly say that Holmes was more intelligent than anyone else, before or since. It is certainly appropriate to compare him with some fictional characters, such as Mycroft and Watson; but not with others, such as Poirot or "Slapstick" Libby. It may be appropriate to compare him with some non-fictional characters, such as Newton and Darwin; but probably not with others, such as Conan Doyle or Frank Ramsey. "More intelligent than anyone else" meant something like "more intelligent than anyone else in the world of Sherlock Holmes." The inhabitants of this "world" are drawn partly from the fictional side of the Meinongian domain and partly from the non-fictional side, exhausting neither. (p. 262)

The disadvantage that is supposed to accrue to a Meinongian theory of fiction in light of this objection is difficult to understand. I have to strain even to grasp, let alone sympathize with, the problem Lewis seems to have in mind. Why should it be harder in principle to judge whether Holmes was more intelligent than Einstein as opposed to whether Darwin was more intelligent than Einstein? Comparative intelligence is as elusive a concept to define or apply to existent entities as it is in the case of fictional Meinongian objects.

Lewis argues that we can meaningfully compare Holmes's intelligence with Watson's, apparently since they inhabit the same fictional "world." We can do the same for persons who are either mentioned explicitly in particular stories or who, such as Newton and Darwin, belong to the real world historical background against which the Sherlock Holmes stories are written and interpreted. Judging from Lewis's examples, we supposedly cannot compare the properties of fictional objects from different works of fiction, nor achronistically with respect to real world persons who lived after the events of the Sherlock Holmes stories are supposed to have occurred. But why not? What is the logical difficulty in trying to decide whether Hercule Poirot was smarter than Sherlock Holmes, or the opposite, on the basis of how the two fictional detectives handle their respective fictional investigations or how they might most reasonably be projected to handle a hypothetical mystery to be solved, or, for that matter, as a reflection of the accomplishments attributed to them in their respective stories, together with whatever we can infer about the degree and kind of intelligence required for their achievement?

Lewis does not explain his reason for thinking that the two kinds of cases are different. The problem of judging the comparative intelligence of Holmes and Poirot seems no more intractable in principle, just because Holmes and Poirot thus far do not happen to have appeared together in the same story, than it would be if someone were now to include them as interacting in the same work of fiction and would have to decide which of them could plausibly be portrayed as more astute. The fact that no single story has been written in which Holmes and Poirot match wits seems no more an obstacle to comparing their intelligences than trying to do so in the case of existent persons who never interacted in life because they lived many years apart, as in trying to determine whether Julius Caesar was smarter than Napoléon Bonaparte, or the reverse. Of course, arguing – or, rather, stipulating, as Lewis does – that there is an important difference in whether or not an individual occupies the same fictional world as another, or in a world up to a certain point in time of which the author of the fiction or the author's characters could be cognizant, fits neatly into Lewis's alternative modal story-contexting semantics of truth in fiction. But we are not driven to Lewis's approach by this particular criticism of Meinong's object theory.[8]

Lewis's objection about the range of quantifiers in a Meinongian semantics of fictional objects is inconclusive. He considers the sentence, "Sherlock Holmes is more intelligent than *anyone* else, before or since" (p. 262). He recognizes that to interpret this quantified sentence in Meinongian semantics, "The inhabitants of this 'world' are drawn partly from the fictional side of the Meinongian domain and partly from the non-fictional side, exhausting neither" (p. 262). This is perfectly true, but unproblematic. A Meinongian theory of fiction can quantify univocally over all objects generally, both existent and nonexistent. Or, it can restrict quantification more precisely to all or some existent or nonexistent Meinongian objects, both generally and as referred to in all or some definite stories, or in all or some definite historical periods, geographical or cultural milieux. The formal logical devices by means of which such quantification can be achieved are similar to those found in classical logic. They include unrestricted quantification over conditionally restricted subsets of the domain, and restricted quantification. A Meinongian semantics permits all of the desired limitations in quantifiers ranging over the Meinongian model of existent and nonexistent objects. The theory allows fiction makers and interpreters to express complicated properties and comparisons of properties among real and fictional objects.

VI. *Inferences for Meinongian and Existent Objects*

The fourth and final objection in Lewis's critique calls attention to problems in drawing inferences about fictional objects from their properties as described within a work of fiction, especially in conjunction with background assumptions about the real world. Lewis considers a single example:

> Finally, the Meinongian must tell us why truths about fictional characters are cut off, sometimes though not always, from the consequences they ought to imply. We can truly say that Holmes lived at 221B Baker Street. I have been told that the only building at 221B Baker Street, then or now, was a bank. It does not follow, and certainly is not true, that Holmes lived in a bank. (p. 262)

It is true in one sense that the inference from the proposition that Holmes lived at 221B Baker Street, and that the only building that has ever been at 221B Baker Street in the actual world was a bank, so therefore, Holmes lived in a bank, is deductively invalid. Lewis wants to correct the problem by prefixing these propositions with the special modal qualifier, "In such and such a fiction...," which explicitly invalidates the inference. He continues:

> The way of the Meinongian is hard, and in this paper I shall explore a simpler alternative. Let us not take our descriptions of fictional characters at face value, but instead let us regard them as abbreviations for longer sentences beginning with an operator "In such-and-such fiction..." Such a phrase is an intensional operator that may be prefixed to a sentence ϕ to form a new sentence. But then the prefixed operator may be dropped by way of abbreviation, leaving us with what sounds like the original sentence ϕ but differs from it in sense. Thus, if I say that Holmes liked to show off, you will take it that I have asserted an abbreviated version of the true sentence "In the Sherlock Holmes stories, Holmes liked to show off." As for the embedded sentence "Holmes liked to show off," taken by itself with the prefixed operator neither explicitly present nor tacitly understood, we may abandon it to the common fate of subject-predicate sentences with denotationless subject terms: automatic falsity or lack of truth value, according to taste. (p. 262)

My reaction to the fallacy of Holmes living in a bank at 221B Baker Street is rather different from Lewis's. I drive contextualization inward to distinguish an equivocation in the reference to 221B Baker Street in the true fictional predication that has Holmes living there as opposed to the true historical predication of the bank's actual location. As I understand these objects in Meinongian semantics, they are not identical, but are misleadingly equivocally designated by the same term, "221B Baker Street." The problem is widespread in Meinongian semantics. The first step in understanding the difficulty is to recognize how commonplace it is.

Napoléon is the name of a real emperor of France, and of a fictional character in Tolstoy's *War and Peace*. The fact that both are designated by the proper name "Napoléon," by itself, signifies nothing logically, no more than the fact that several persons in the real world can all be named "John Smith." Tolstoy naturally takes advantage of many of the facts he assumes his readers know about the actual Napoléon in creating a fictional Napoléon that bears important points of resemblance to the real emperor. But this need not create undue confusion, regardless of whether or not we try to interpret Tolstoy's fiction in a Meinongian semantics.[9]

Of course, a problem is not solved by remarking on its frequent occurrence. It only leaves more loose ends to bring together. But at least it can be said that Lewis has not uncovered a new, previously unrecognized implication of Meinongian semantics. Meinongians have long advocated the need to distinguish between real and nonexistent objects that may go by the same name and that may even share a significant percentage of their constitutive properties. A disambiguation of equivocal references in and out of fiction is needed in order to avoid the kinds of invalid inferences to which Lewis calls attention. There are at least two different ways of story-contexting a true sentence about a fictional object: Lewis's external or *de dicto* method, and an internal or *de "re"* method. We can distinguish the two methods in this way:

- Lewis-style external *de dicto* story-contextualization

    In the Sherlock Holmes stories, Sherlock Holmes lives in London at 221B Baker Street.

- Meinongian internal *de "re"* story-contextualization

    Sherlock Holmes in the Sherlock Holmes stories lives in London at 221B Baker Street.

It is important to recognize that the *de "re"* external story-contextualization does not necessarily attach directly to an actually existent real world *res* or *res extensa*, but to an object generally irrespective of its ontic status. The difference in the two modes of story-contextualization is most dramatically explicated as a distinction by which Lewis-style external *de dicto* story-context-prefixing qualifies the truth of the entire sentence expressing a predication in fiction, and thereby of the predication of a property to a fictional object. By contrast, internal *de "re"* story-contextualization allows the univocal predication of disambiguated constitutive properties related to the real world or to a fictional world existent or nonexistent objects, including fictional Meinongian objects. The troublesome inference in Lewis's fourth objection is equally blocked by either the external *de dicto* or the internal *de "re"* methods of story-contextualization. We cannot validly infer that Holmes lived in a bank in real life or in the Sherlock Holmes stories from the assumption that Holmes in the Sherlock Holmes stories lived in London at 221B Baker Street, and that 221B Baker Street, London, is in real life a bank. But internal *de "re"* story-contextualization, unlike external *de dicto* story-contextualization, serves only to clarify the exact identity of a relevant fictional object such as Sherlock Holmes, London, or 221B Baker Street, as the one belonging to a certain work of fiction.

What happens if I perversely write a story about Sherlock Holmes in which I deny that Holmes is a detective or that he lived in London at 221B Baker Street, at the same time denouncing all the earlier Sherlock Holmes stories as false? In one sense, I am free to do so. But my impact on the presumptive story context of the Sherlock Holmes stories is likely to be negligible. If I am sufficiently clever and lucky, I might be able to change the content of the Holmes stories context in this way. But it will take much more than merely penning the single sentence I have just written. I may need to develop an entire interesting story or novel-length work that justifies itself as a literary creation on its own merits in addition to reversing some of the properties Sherlock Holmes has acquired in what are recognized as the canonical sources of the Holmes stories.

At the very least, I would need to embed the sentence in a discussion in a philosophical article that over time occasioned enough discussion to have the denials of properties Holmes shares in the other stories become an accepted part of the larger Sherlock Holmes story context. This could happen, but not easily and is not likely. The Sherlock Holmes who is a London detective who lives at 221B Baker Street is relatively safe at least from my efforts to undo his well-established identity. Ironically, the less known a fictional character is, the more insulated it is from character-transforming sequels, spinoffs, parodies, and philosophical thought experiments. In the event that my perverse story should become sufficiently entrenched in the popular consciousness or recognized as necessary to include in canonical Holmes story-contextualizations, there would still be good reason to distinguish Holmes in what had previously been the canonical story-context in which Holmes is a detective living in London at 221B Baker Street from Holmes in my perverse story-context, where he is not a detective and does not live in London at 221B Baker Street. If necessary to avoid confusion in semantic analysis, a theorist could, but hopefully will never need to, go so far as to write:

- Sherlock Holmes in the non-Jacquette Sherlock Holmes stories is a London detective living at 221B Baker Street.

As opposed to:

- Sherlock Holmes in the Jacquette Sherlock Holmes stories is not a detective and does not live in London at 221B Baker Street.

I am not arguing that internal *de "re"* story-contextualization of true sentences in fiction is preferable to Lewis-style external *de dicto* story-contextualization. I only want to observe that the internal *de "re"* method does not inherit the exceptions Lewis acknowledges to his external *de dicto* story-contextualizations. It is easy to see that Lewis's proposal faces special problems when he story-contexts entire sentences and larger units of discourse, instead of particular references to individual fictional characters or objects.

VII. *Lewis's Modal Analysis of Fictional Worlds*

The proposal to attach story context prefixes to some sentences in a work of fiction provides only part of Lewis's modal semantics. The truth of the sentence, "In the Sherlock Holmes stories, Holmes is a detective," requires analysis. The ordinary language prefix functions as a fictional modal operator, saying in effect that it is not categorically true that Holmes is a detective, but only in certain logically possible worlds associated with the Sherlock Holmes stories.

Lewis describes a standard modal structure in which a proper subset of logically possible worlds is distinguished as "somehow determined" by a work of fiction. A sentence with its Lewis-style story-contexting prefix is true in Lewis's modal system if it is true in every such logically possible world. Thus, he explains:

> Our remaining task is to see what may be said about the analysis of the operators "In such-and-such fiction...". I have already noted that truth in a given fiction is closed under implication. Such closure is the earmark of an operator of relative necessity, an intensional operator that may be analyzed as a restricted universal quantifier over possible worlds. So we might proceed as follows: a prefixed sentence "In fiction f, ϕ" is true (or, as we shall also say, ϕ is true in the fiction f) iff ϕ is true at every possible world in a certain set, this set being somehow determined by the fiction f. (p. 264)

The possible worlds approach is interesting and worth developing. But there are also drawbacks in applying modal structures to the logic of fiction. It is important first of all to recognize that modal interpretations are not precluded from Meinongian semantics. There is no reason why a Meinongian logic of fiction could not also be interpreted by means of logically possible worlds. If we think it is true that Sherlock Holmes might have killed Moriarity, then we may find it indispensable to appeal to the modality of this "might" by positing a subset of logically possible worlds in which Holmes has the property of having killed Moriarity. The question remains whether it is necessary to suppose that fictional objects exist in nonactual logically possible worlds, or whether they can have different properties without existing in any logically possible world. The point is that Meinongian logic and a modal theory of logically possible worlds are not exclusive choices. We can and may need to have both. The question is rather whether the logically possible worlds approach favored by Lewis-style *de dicto* modal story-contexting by itself without nonexistent Meinongian objects can provide an adequate semantics of fiction.[10]

There are difficulties first of all about how a fictional world is to be specified. It is one thing to speak loosely of a fictional "world" as that part of a semantic domain designated as containing nonexistent objects associated with the propositions of a work of fiction. It is another matter to invoke an entire logically possible world associated with a work of fiction or within which the propositions of the fiction are true, and the action of the plot, if any, takes place, involving the fictional characters and objects of the story. The modal approach without benefit of Meinongian object theory must posit nonactual logically possible worlds in which Sherlock Holmes exists as a complete entity, with definite eye color, a definite number of hairs on his head, a definite number of blood cells at any given time, and so on. Such exact specification is not required within the modal theory as a practical task, but the possibility is presupposed. We can wave a wand and stipulate that there are such worlds. But the modal interpretation seems unnecessarily complex in its implications when we recall that its primary philosophical justification is to avoid referring and truly predicating constitutive properties to nonexistent objects.[11] Consider that Lewis's (counterpart) modal semantics of fiction is committed to the existence of indefinitely if not infinitely many different logically possible worlds in which, for example, a counterpart Holmes exists and has precisely 2,000,000 hairs on his head on a certain day, and another in which another relevantly similar counterpart Holmes exists and has precisely 2,000,001 hairs, and so on, in every combination with every other minute specification of Holmes's complete set of properties as an existent object in distinct nonactual logically possible worlds. If Lewis has no decisive refutation of Meinongian object theory, and the question of whether or not to go the Meinongian route is mostly one of comparative aesthetic factors like simplicity, economy, fecundity, and the like, then Lewis's modal structures bereft of Meinongian object theory might be at a distinct disadvantage in the choice between competing semantics of fiction.

Another limitation of Lewis's non-Meinongian modal analysis is even more discouraging. There is no reason to suppose that a work of fiction cannot ostensibly refer to and truly predicate properties of fictional objects that cannot exist in any logically possible world. Meinong, as an implication of the free assumption of intended objects, allows the semantic domain of object theory to include not only contingently nonexistent objects, but also metaphysically impossible objects, such as the round square. Meinong need not say contradictorily that the round square is both round and such that it is not the case that it is not round, or square and such that it is not the case that it is not square. But we should not imagine that there can be any logically possible world where the round square exists and truly has the property of being both round and square. Other more subtle examples are also available. Suppose that an author writes a sequel to the Sherlock Holmes stories in which Holmes meets Gottlob Frege, who, according to the story, successfully effects the reduction of mathematics to logic. There may be logically possible worlds in which Holmes meets Frege, but there are surely no logically possible worlds where mathematics turns out to be reducible to logic. Lewis addresses the problem of impossible fictions when he writes:

> I turn finally to vacuous truth in impossible fictions. Let us call a fiction *impossible* iff there is no world where it is told as known fact rather than fiction. That might happen in either of two ways. First, the plot might be impossible. Second, a possible plot might imply that there could be nobody in a position to know or tell of the events in question. If a fiction is impossible in the second way, then to tell it as known fact would be to

know its truth and tell truly something that implies that its truth could not be known; which is impossible. (p. 274)

Since my intuitions about truth in impossible fictions are largely at odds with Lewis's, I can only try to articulate my views and recommend others to test their agreement or disageement against my misgivings. Lewis distinguishes between blatant and latent impossible fictions. As an example of blatant impossibility in fiction, Lewis considers a story like the one above about Frege, concerning the troubles of the man who squares the circle. A latently impossible fiction by contrast is one in which an author through forgetfulness or the like inadvertently falls into inconsistency, as when Conan Doyle in different stories attributes to Watson the property of having been wounded only once both in the shoulder and in the leg.[12]

Where the plot in a work of fiction is blatantly impossible, Lewis claims that anything, every proposition, is (vacuously) true. He states:

> According to [...] my analyses, anything whatever is vacuously true in an impossible fiction. That seems entirely satisfactory if the impossibility is blatant: if we are dealing with a fantasy about the troubles of the man who squared the circle, or with the worst sort of incoherent time-travel story. We should not expect to have a non-trivial concept of truth in blatantly impossible fiction, or perhaps we should expect to have one only under the pretence – not to be taken too seriously – that there are impossible possible worlds as well as the possible possible worlds. (pp. 274-275)

Why should we suppose that according to the story Lewis mentions it is equally true that the man who squared the circle did not square the circle? Or, with reference to the previously mentioned story, why conclude that Frege both reduced mathematics to logic and did not reduce mathematics to logic, that Sherlock Holmes met Frege and that it is not the case that Holmes met Frege, that grass is green and grass is not green? Why suppose that there must occur such inferential explosion in the semantics of fiction, except as a consequence of a questionable allegiance to the paradoxes of strict implication in a classical modal framework? I do not suppose that the authors even of blatantly impossible fictions intend any and every proposition to be logically implied by introducing impossible objects or impossible elements of plot. I am also unprepared to adopt whatever consequences follow from a Lewis-style modal story-contexting *de dicto* approach to the logic of fiction when the acceptability of such a theory as opposed to a Meinongian *de "re"* theory is the problem at issue.

The alternative for an unconventional modal analysis of fiction may then be to expand Lewis's modal structures to include logically impossible as well as logically possible worlds, as some logicians for other reasons have already proposed.[13] Another solution might be to replace the classical propositional logic that Lewis presupposes with a paraconsistent logic.[14] These suggestions represent significant departures from anything Lewis envisions, and their complexity and ontic prodigality would need to be evaluated in comparison with an arguably more straightforward revisionary Meinongian object theory.

Lewis recommends a different type of analysis for fictions that are not so blatantly impossible. He inquires:

> But what should we do with a fiction that is not blatantly impossible, but impossible only because the author has been forgetful? I have spoken of truth in the Sherlock Holmes stories. Strictly speaking, these (taken together) are an impossible fiction. Conan Doyle contradicted himself from one story to another about the location of Watson's old war wound. Still, I do not want to say that just anything is true in the Holmes stories! (p. 275)

I do not understand why Lewis thinks that absolutely anything is true in the blatantly impossible story of the man who squares the circle, but not in the Holmes stories. What explains the difference?

Lewis suggests that we maintain logical consistency in the inconsistent Holmes stories by splitting them up into distinct story-contexts. He is willing to follow such a practice even within a single story for the latently inconsistent fragments of its distinguishable parts. This suggests that it is not so much the blatancy of inconsistency in the squared circle story that makes its impossibility unavoidable, but the fact that a single object is defined as having impossible properties in a single compact story subcontext, rather than as the effect of incompatible properties attributed to the object in separate sentences included in the unfolding of a story. The distinction seems superficial, since an inconsistency distributed over multiple sentences might be every bit as blatant as one that is condensed, from the standpoint of the author's deliberate intentions versus forgetfulness in concocting an inconsistent fiction.

To see that there is no clearcut distinction between blatantly and inadvertently impossible fictions, consider the case of Piggy in William Golding's *Lord of the Flies*. Piggy is described as nearsighted. But the bullies among the stranded children who eventually revert to a state of nature steal his glasses and use them to start fires, which cannot be done with the concave lenses needed to correct for nearsightedness. Is this a blatant or latent impossibility? Should the answer depend on what Golding intended, and how much he can reasonably be assumed to know or not to know about geometrical optics? Must the semantics of fiction first settle the problem of the intentional fallacy of which Monroe C. Beardsley and William K. Wimsatt warned the interpreters of artworks?[15] It appears that we cannot decide the status of the impossibility in these works simply by appealing to the question of whether or not it can be resolved by fragmenting the story. We can separate those parts of the text that contain sentences describing Piggy as nearsighted as belonging to a different substory than those describing his glasses being used to concentrate rather than diffuse sunrays in starting a fire. But this does not resolve the impossibility. Nor does it seem reasonable to attribute to Golding the desire to fictionalize even the laws of physics in the "world" projected by his novel. And Piggy, as the particular character he is portrayed as being, seems to vanish if he is not held together by the properties of being both nearsighted and having the kind of glasses the other boys covet for their fire-starting ability, and by the power their possession confers.[16]

The question is not one of blatancy or latency, but of how inconsistency of any sort in an impossible fiction is to be understood. Shall we posit nonexistent impossible Meinongian objects or offer some variation of Lewis's modal story-contexting interpreted in terms of logically possible or impossible worlds. Meinong's *de "re"* semantics in this light appears significantly simpler in comparison with Lewis's *de dicto* modal story-contexting. Are the aesthetic tradeoffs required by a non-Meinongian modal approach to the semantics of fiction adequately compensated by satisfying the pretheoretical desire at all costs to avoid referring to and truly predicating properties of nonexistent objects? Lewis evidently believes so. But in the absence of a more powerful argument against Meinongian theory, the difficulty and disadvantage seem to belong to Lewis's modal analysis.

VIII. *Toward a Universal Semantics of Fiction and Nonfiction*

It is a remarkable fact that writing and reading as well as talking and writing about fiction proceed so smoothly with so few occasions – primarily those manufactured by logicians and philosophical semanticists – in which it is necessary explicitly to disambiguate story context, internally or externally.

That such disambiguation can always be done in an intuitively correct way is theoretically comforting, even if it bestows no practical advantage on reading or writing or thinking critically about fiction. A novel can be indistinguishable in content, phenomenologically, so to speak, from the reader's standpoint, from a history, as in the fiction of Daniel Defoe, William Thackery, Tobias Smollett, and many other realistic writers. David Hume, in *A Treatise of Human Nature*, makes a similar observation:

> If one person sits down to read a book as a romance and another as a true history, they plainly receive the same ideas, and in the same order, nor does the incredulity of the one, and the belief of the other, hinder them from putting the very same sense upon their author. His words produce the same ideas in both; tho' his testimony has not the same influence on them. The latter has a more lively conception of all the incidents. He enters deeper into the concerns of the persons; represents to himself their actions and characters and friendships and enmities: he even goes so far as to form a notion of their features, and air and person. While the former, who gives no credit to the testimony of the author, has a more faint and languid conception of all of these particulars, and except on account of the style and ingenuity of the composition can receive little entertainment from it.[17]

The fact that fiction functions smoothly without explicit Lewis-style semantic prefixes suggests that philosophically unprejudiced producers and consumers of fiction do not regard the reference and true predication of constitutive properties to nonexistent objects as indistinguishable from that occurring in science or history or extradisciplinary true-or-false factual reporting. This is also why the fine line between fiction and science or history is sometimes easy to blur, and why scientific and historical frauds can be perpetrated. Such facts are more philosophically significant for logic and semantics than is often appreciated. They powerfully suggest, as Meinongians insist, that the reference to and true predication of constitutive properties to existent, abstract, or nonexistent objects function univocally in precisely the same way in fiction as in science or history. The logic of thought, if it is to be metaphysically indifferent and ontically neutral, must be the same for any discourse, regardless of its intention in conveying what happens to be true or what happens to be false. What is it to logic whether or not Sherlock Holmes exists? What is it to logic whether or not phlogiston or the planet Vulcan exist, or, for that matter, whether or not protons and neutrons or the planet Neptune exist?[18]

---

[1] David Lewis, "Truth in Fiction," *American Philosophical Quarterly* 15 (1978): pp. 37-46; repr. in Lewis, "Truth in Fiction," with Postscripts to "Truth in Fiction," in Lewis, *Philosophical Papers* (Oxford: Oxford UP, 1983), Vol. I, pp. 261-280. All parenthetical page references in the text and notes refer to this edition.

[2] Lewis refers to Terence Parsons, "A Prolegomenon to Meinongian Semantics," *The Journal of Philosophy* 71 (1974): pp. 561-580, and Parsons, "A Meinongian Analysis of Fictional Objects," *Grazer Philosophische Studien* 1 (1975): pp. 73-86. See also Parsons, *Nonexistent Objects* (New Haven: Yale UP, 1980), p. 54: "we don't confuse 'Holmes doesn't exist' with 'According to the story, Holmes doesn't exist'." Parsons considers degenerate fictions that seem to involve nothing but extranuclear (nonconstitutive) predications: "*Story*: 'Jay exists. The end.' *Story*: 'An object doesn't exist. The end'" (p. 198). Parsons expresses doubt about whether the examples are genuine stories, and from an aesthetic viewpoint this is perhaps a legitimate concern. But it is hard to see what the passages lack in syntactic or semantic content that would disqualify them as (exceedingly uninteresting) stories.

[3] A more precise and thereby necessarily narrower characterization of the story-telling context, in light of the author's many imitators, and the occurrence of Sherlock Holmes in multiple story-telling contexts, can be written as, "In the stories and novels of Sir Arthur Conan Doyle, Sherlock Holmes is a detective." There is, moreover, no obvious reason to limit story-telling context from above or below, allowing more general inclusion of related writings beyond those the author actually composed or even contemplated, such as "In all of world literature at any time now or in the future, Sherlock Holmes is a detective," and more specific and to that extent potentially uninteresting but nevertheless semantically valuable contexting of propositions to the very sentence of a work of fiction in which the proposition is expressed, as in "In the ninth sentence of Sir Arthur Conan Doyle's *A Study in Scarlet*, Sherlock Holmes is a detective." See Dale Jacquette, "Intentional Semantics and the Logic of Fiction," *The British Journal of Aesthetics* 29 (1989): pp. 168–176; Dale Jacquette, *Meinongian Logic: The Semantics of Existence and Nonexistence* (Berlin and New York: Walter de Gruyter & Co., 1996), pp. 256-264; see also Barry Smith, "Ingarden vs. Meinong on the Logic of Fiction," *Philosophy and Phenomenological Research* 41 (1980): pp. 93-105.

[4] Lewis:
> As a first approximation, we might consider exactly those worlds where the plot of the fiction is enacted, where a course of events takes place that matches the story. What is true in the Sherlock Holmes stories would then be what is true at all of those possible worlds where there are characters who have the attributes,

stand in the relations, and do the deeds that are ascribed in the stories to Holmes, Watson, and the rest. (Whether these characters would then *be* Holmes, Watson, and the rest is a vexed question that we must soon consider.) (p. 264) Lewis provides a more detailed explanation of the modal apparatus for the interpretation of his story-contexting prefixes in his Analyses 0,1,2 [see endnote 9 below].

⁵ An account of the unassumability of existence in Meinongian semantics is given by Richard Routley, *Exploring Meinong's Jungle and Beyond*, interim edition (Canberra: Australian National University, 1981), pp. 47-48, 180-187. A useful discussion of related topics appears in Kit Fine, "The Problem of Non-Existents," *Topoi* 1 (1982): pp. 97-140; see also Kit Fine, "Critical Review of Parsons's *Non-Existent Objects*," *Philosophical Studies* 45 (1984): pp. 95-142.

⁶ Meinong introduced the distinction between *konstitutorische* and *ausserkonstitutorische Bestimmungen* (constitutive and extraconstitutive properties) in *Über Möglichkeit und Wahrscheinlichkeit: Beiträge zur Gegenstandstheorie und Erkenntnistheorie* (Leipzig: Verlag von Johann Ambrosius Barth, 1915), repr. *Alexius Meinong Gesamtausgabe*, eight volumes, ed. Rudolf Haller and Rudolf Kindinger in collaboration with Roderick M. Chisholm (Graz: Akademische Druck- u. Verlagsanstalt, 1969-1978), VI, pp. 176-177. Findlay, in *Meinong's Theory of Objects and Values* (London: Oxford UP, 1963) proposed the English translations "nuclear" and "extranuclear" (p. 176); see Dale Jacquette, "Nuclear and Extranuclear Properties," *The School of Alexius Meinong*, ed. Liliana Albertazzi, Dale Jacquette, and Roberto Poli (Aldershot: Ashgate Publishing Company, 2001).

⁷ Bertrand Russell, "On Denoting," *Mind* 14 (1905); repr. in *Logic and Knowledge: Essays 1901-1950*, ed. Robert C. Marsh (New York: G. Putnam's Sons, 1956), p. 45. Russell, "Review of A. Meinong, *Untersuchungen zur Gegenstandstheorie und Psychologie*," *Mind*, 14 (1905), p. 533. Meinong's reply to Russell's problem of the existent round square appears in *Über die Stellung der Gegenstandstheorie im System der Wissenschaften* (Leipzig: Voightländer, 1906), pp. 16-17; see also Alexius Meinong, *Über Möglichkeit und Wahrscheinlichkeit*, pp. 278-282. I critically discuss Meinong's reply to Russell in Jacquette, "Meinong's Doctrine of the Modal Moment," *Grazer Philosophische Studien* 25-26 (1985-1986): pp. 423-438; "A Meinongian Theory of Definite Description," *Axiomathes* 5 (1994): pp. 345-359; see also Dale Jacquette, *Meinongian Logic*, pp. 80-91 [see endnote 3].

⁸ If we want to be able to say that Sherlock Holmes is taller than Hercule Poirot, given their absolute heights as described in their separate stories but in no single combined story, then isolating these facts in distinct logically possible worlds does not help. There will of course be a logically possible world in which both characters exist, but these will not be part of any Lewis-style modal analysis of the works of fiction in which Holmes and Poirot are featured. The problem is related to Lewis's counterexample sentence 6. A related criticism of Lewis's story-contexting is discussed by Jonathan Kastin, "The Logic of Fictional Descriptions," *Conference* 4 (1993): pp. 16-30; see also Peter Lamarque, "The Puzzle of the Flash Stockman: A Reply to David Lewis's *Philosophical Papers* and 'Truth in Fiction'," *Analysis* 47 (1987): pp. 93-95. A similar puzzle for Meinongian semantics is discussed by Jacek Paśniczek, *The Logic of Intentional Objects: A Meinongian Version of Classical Logic*, Synthese Library Volume 269 (Dordrecht: Kluwer Academic Publishers, 1998), pp. 165-166. Paśniczek's problem, unlike Lewis's, concerns definitely numbered but intensionally indistinguishable fictional objects, as in a story about ten magic rings. I criticize Paśniczek's analysis in the expanded version of this essay, under the title, "Truth and Fiction in David Lewis's Critique of Meinongian Semantics," *Metaphysica: International Journal for Ontology and Metaphysics* 2 (2001): pp. 73-106, and in Jacquette, Review of Jacek Paśniczek, *The Logic of Intentional Objects: A Meinongian Verson of Classical Logic*, in *Journal of Symbolic Logic* 64 (1999): pp. 1847-1849.

[9] Lewis acknowledges the semantic complications entailed by historical fiction:

> I have said that truth in fiction is the joint product of two sources: the explicit content of the fiction, and a background consisting either of the facts about our world (Analysis 1) or of the beliefs overt in the community of origin (Analysis 2). Perhaps there is a third source which also contributes: carry-over from other truth in fiction. There are two cases: intra-fictional and inter-fictional" (pp. 273-274)

Lewis's Analysis 1 and Analysis 2 offer rigorous formulations of modal story-contexting semantics. He explains:

> ANALYSIS 1: *A sentence of the form 'In the fiction f, ϕ' is non-vacuously true iff some world where f is told as known fact and ϕ is true differs less from our actual world, on balance, than does any world where f is told as known fact and ϕ is not true. It is vacuously true iff there are no possible worlds where f is told as known fact.*" (p. 270)

> ANALYSIS 2: *A sentence of the form 'In the fiction f, ϕ' is non-vacuously true iff, whenever w is one of the collective belief worlds of the community of origin of f, then some world where f is told as known fact and ϕ is true differs less from the world w, on balance, than does any world where f is told as known fact and ϕ is not true. It is vacuously true iff there are no possible worlds where f is told as known fact.*" (p. 273)

Terence Parsons, in *Nonexistent Objects*, similarly distinguishes between "native" and "imported" fictional objects (pp. 51-60, 182-189) [see endnote 2]; see Parsons, "A Prolegomenon to Meinongian Semantics," pp. 575-577 [see endnote 2], and Parsons, "A Meinongian Analysis of Fictional Objects," pp. 83-85 [see endnote 2].

[10] See Jacquette, "Modal Meinongian Logic," *Logique et Analyse* 125-126 (1989): pp. 113-130; Jacquette, *Meinongian Logic*, pp. 149-164. [see endnote 3].

[11] Lewis:

> We sometimes speak of *the* world of a fiction. What is true in the Holmes stories is what is true, as we say, "in the world of Sherlock Holmes." That we speak this way should suggest that it is right to consider less than all the worlds where the plot of the stories is enacted, and less even than all the worlds where the stories are told as known fact [...] But it will not do to follow ordinary language to the extent of supposing that we can somehow single out a single one of the worlds where the stories are told as known fact. Is the world of Sherlock Holmes a world where Holmes has an even or odd number of hairs on his head at the moment when he first meets Watson? What is Inspector Lestrade's blood type? It is absurd to suppose that these questions about the world of Sherlock Holmes have answers. The best explanation of that is that the worlds of Sherlock Holmes are plural, and the questions have different answers accordingly. If we may assume that some of the worlds where the stories are told as known fact differ least from our world, then these are the worlds of Sherlock Holmes. What is true of throughout them is true in the stories; what is false throughout them is false in the stories; what is true at some and false at others is neither true nor false in the stories. (p. 270)

[12] Lewis writes, in Postscript B in the reprinted version of "Truth in Fiction":

> An inconsistent fiction is not to be treated directly, else everything comes out true in it indiscriminately. But where we have an inconsistent fiction, there also we

> have several consistent fictions that may be extracted from it. (Perhaps not in the very hardest cases – but I think those cases are *meant* to defy our efforts to figure out what's true in the story.) I spoke of the consistent corrections of the original fiction. But perhaps it will be enough to consider *fragments*: corrections by deletion, with nothing written in to replace the deleted bits.
>
> ("Impossible Fictions," *Philosophical Papers*, Vol. I, p. 277)

[13] See Graham Priest's guest-edited issue of *Notre Dame Journal of Formal Logic* 38 (1997), on "Impossible Worlds," especially contributions by Edwin D. Mares, "Who's Afraid of Impossible Worlds?" (pp. 516-526); Daniel Nolan, "Impossible Worlds: A Modest Approach" (pp. 535-572); and David A. Van der Laan, "The Ontology of Impossible Worlds" (pp. 597-620). See also Jaakko Hintikka, "Impossible Possible Worlds," *Journal of Philosophical Logic* 4 (1975): pp. 475-484. In *The Logic of Inconsistency: A Study in Non-Standard Possible-World Semantics and Ontology* (Totowa: Rowman and Littlefield, 1979), Nicholas Rescher and Robert Brandom distinguish between "inconsistent" and "impossible" worlds; see p. 4: "It is necessary to insist [...] that one should avoid speaking of *inconsistent* worlds as *impossible* worlds. This would be question-begging, for it is a prime aim of the present analysis to show that they can be considered as genuinely possible cases." Rescher and Brandom's logic is paraconsistent, but it is clear that a Meinongian semantics might interpret the modalities of impossible objects like the round square either by means of impossible or inconsistent worlds.

[14] See *inter alia* Stanislaw Jaskowski, "Propositional Calculus for Contradictory Deductive Systems," *Studia Logica* 24 (1969): pp. 143-157; N.C.A. da Costa, "On the Theory of Inconsistent Formal Systems," *Notre Dame Journal of Formal Logic* 15 (1974): pp. 497-510. A valuable collection on paraconsistent logic is the extensive volume edited by Graham Priest, Richard Routley, and Jean Norman, *Paraconsistent Logic: Essays on the Inconsistent* (Munich and Vienna: Philosophia Verlag, 1989); see also Graham Priest, *Beyond the Limits of Thought* (Cambridge: Cambridge UP, 1995).

[15] William K. Wimsatt and Monroe C. Beardsley, "The Intentional Fallacy," *The Sewanee Review* 54 (1946): pp. 3-23.

[16] William Golding, *Lord of the Flies*, introduction by E.M. Forster (New York: Coward-McCann, 1962).

[17] David Hume, *A Treatise of Human Nature* [1739-40], edited by L.A. Selby-Bigge, second edition revised with notes by P.H. Nidditch (Oxford: Clarendon Press, 1978), Book I, Part III, Section VII, pp. 97-98.

[18] I am grateful to The Institute for Arts and Humanistic Studies, The Pennsylvania State University, for a Term Fellowship in 1997-1999, which made possible completion of this among related research projects.

PHENOMENOLOGICAL REDUCTION AND AESTHETIC EXPERIENCE: HUSSERL MEETS HOFMANNSTHAL

Wolfgang Huemer
University of Toronto

In December 1906 Hugo von Hofmannsthal made a conference tour through Germany, reading his paper "The Poet and this Time."[1] On December 6 he was in Göttingen where he visited a distant relative, Malvine Husserl[2] (née Steinschneider), and her husband Edmund Husserl. A few weeks after this meeting, on January 12, 1907, Husserl wrote a letter to Hofmannsthal in which he thanks him for a present, presumably Hofmannsthal's book *Kleine Dramen*.[3] He goes on to compare Hofmannsthal's theory of aesthetic experience to the phenomenological method. Husserl's letter is of philosophical interest because it was written at a time when he was just beginning to develop the phenomenological reduction and, thus, to make his "transcendental turn," that is, when he began to explore phenomenology.

I. Husserl's Letter

Let me first sketch briefly the timeline of Husserl's development of the phenomenological reduction. The first publication in which Husserl introduces the phenomenological reduction is his *Ideas* from 1913. Husserl had begun to develop the phenomenological method much earlier, though. In his *Logical Investigations* from 1900/01 he took a methodological approach that he calls – clearly under a strong Brentanian influence – "descriptive psychology." In the years to follow he began to revise this methodological approach. From the notes from the *Nachlass*, some of which were published in the meantime, we know that Husserl developed the phenomenological reduction in the years 1905-1907. Already in his lectures on time-consciousness from 1905 Husserl presents "statements that foreshadow the phenomenological reduction of his later philosophy" (Sokolowski, 1964, 74), but it is not until the time of his lectures on *The Idea of Phenomenology* between April 26 and May 2, 1907, that he introduces the phenomenological reduction to a broader audience.

Thus, at the time when Husserl wrote his letter to Hofmannsthal, he was in the process of elaborating his phenomenological reduction; interestingly, Husserl begins his letter by excusing its delay with the remark that

> finally syntheses of thoughts that were long sought for offered
> themselves. I was very busy fixing them. Your book *Kleine Dramen*,
> which was always next to me, was an important stimulus, even though I
> could read only a little at a time. (Husserl, 1994, vol. VII, 133)[4]

I think it is fair to assume that the "syntheses of thoughts" Husserl is writing about are related in some way or other to his elaboration of the phenomenological reduction. If that assumption is correct, Husserl states explicitly that Hofmannsthal's work was an important stimulus for his development of the phenomenological reduction.

Husserl goes on to state that Hofmannsthal's purely aesthetic description of inner states is very interesting to him, as a phenomenologist. He explains that in recent years he has been working on the phenomenological method that

> requires us to take a stance that is essentially deviating from the "natural"
> stance towards all objectivity, which is closely related to that stance in
> which your art puts us as a purely aesthetical one with respect to the
> represented objects and the whole environment. The intuition of the pure
> work of art is taking place in a strict cancellation of each existential
> stance of the intellect and each stance of the feeling and the will, which
> presupposes the existential stance. Or better: the work of art puts us in (is
> forcing on us, as it were) a state of pure aesthetic intuition that excludes
> this kind of [*existential*] stance. (Husserl, 1994, vol. VII, 133)

Husserl distinguishes the natural attitude of everyday life, in which we take an existential stance towards the things in our environment from the purely aesthetic and the phenomenological attitude.

Once we have taken the phenomenological attitude, our stance towards our physical environment, towards science and what is believed to constitute reality, changes radically. Everything becomes "questionable, incomprehensible, a riddle" (Husserl, 1994, vol. VII, 134). There is only one way to solve this riddle: by bracketing all questionable assumptions and beliefs, especially our existential beliefs, and taking objects as what they are, or better, as what they become in this attitude: *phenomena*. The task of the phenomenologist is to describe these phenomena in his reflective analysis. Husserl writes in his letter:

> If all perception is questionable, then the phenomenon "perception" is the
> only givenness [*the only thing that is given unquestionably*], and before I
> accept one perception as veridical, I look and research by merely
> observing [*rein schauend*] (merely aesthetically, as it were): what does
> veridicality mean, i.e., what is perception as such and what is the
> perceived objectivity? (Husserl, 1994, vol. VII, 134f)

According to this description of the phenomenological reduction, we have to apply a universal doubt, a methodological scepticism à la Descartes, and observe and describe those phenomena that cannot be doubted. And here again Husserl equates the "phenomenological look" with aesthetic experience.

Toward the end of the letter, however, Husserl stresses that there are some differences between the purely aesthetic stance and the stance of the phenomenologist.

> The phenomenological look is, thus, closely related to the aesthetic look in "pure" art; but, of course, it is not a look in order to enjoy aesthetically, but to research, to discover, to constitute scientific affirmations of a new (philosophical) dimension.
> (Husserl, 1994, vol. VII, 135)

Thus, while the phenomenologist and the artist take the same kind of attitude, they do so for very different reasons. In the purely aesthetic experience one looks for pleasure, while the phenomenological reduction serves philosophical and scientific goals.

This last point of Husserl's letter stands in direct contrast to one of the main theses of the paper, "The Poet and this Time," that Hofmannsthal read on that evening, after his meeting with Husserl. Hofmannsthal discusses the role poets play in a time when life has become increasingly chaotic and people seem to have lost their interest in poetry and read instead many scientific and journalistic texts. Hofmannsthal claims that these people are looking for something other than the information conveyed by the scientists and the journalists: it is their thirst for poetry that makes them read all these technical texts. Even if they are reading the newspapers or scientific texts, they are, according to Hofmannsthal, looking for poetry, often without even knowing it. His point is that all these writers are poets to some degree because they all use the same instrument: the living language. Of course, only the real poets know how to create the magic of poetry. Only they can give the people what they are actually looking for and so satisfy their thirst for poetry.

Thus, according to Hofmannsthal, the philosopher and the poet have the same goal, but only the poet can achieve this goal, while all other writers are doomed to fail. Husserl, on the other hand, seems to hold that the artist and the phenomenologist have two different goals, two completely different agendas, and that both can achieve their goals in their own ways.

II. *Husserl's Three Ways to the Phenomenological Reduction*

Husserl's letter to Hofmannsthal is, as far as I know, the only place where he compares the phenomenological reduction to aesthetic experience of pure art. He does not even use this comparison in the lecture *The Idea of Phenomenology* that he gives only three and a half months later.

Throughout his lifetime, Husserl continued to refine and revise his phenomenological reduction. At different stages of his development he explains the need for this methodological approach in different ways and even distinguishes between different kinds of reduction. Iso Kern has shown in his article "Three Ways to the Transcendental Phenomenological Reduction" that Husserl introduced the phenomenological reduction in three major ways: the Cartesian way, the way via intentional psychology, and the way via ontology. The first way has the most relevance for the present discussion, but it is worthwhile reviewing the other two briefly.

In the *way via intentional psychology* phenomenologists concentrate on mental phenomena and exclude physical phenomena from their research just as physicists concentrate on physical phenomena and exclude mental phenomena. Husserl develops this strategy from the 1920s on.[5]

The *way via ontology* points, roughly speaking, to the fact that every perception of objects must remain "unintelligible" in principle as long as it is analysed in the natural attitude rather than understood in the context of a subjectivity that brings about the intentional relation. "The objects of experience and eventually the whole world come to be grasped in their basic structure [...] as an 'index' or 'guide' to the subjective a priori of constitution" (Bernet/Kern/Marbach, 1993, 70).

The *Cartesian way* is characterized by the attempt to provide an Archimedean point, a secure foundation for all sciences. Outer perception cannot fulfill these high standards, since error is always possible. In consequence, we have to bracket our beliefs in the existence of the physical objects perceived. What cannot be doubted, however, are our occurring mental acts of perception. Thus, the phenomenologist studies these acts of perception as mere mental acts, without paying much attention to the objects towards which they are directed. In his letter to Hofmannsthal, Husserl motivates the phenomenological reduction in this Cartesian way, as we have seen above.

In his later works, mainly in *Crisis,* Husserl criticizes the Cartesian way. He points out that it is characterized by a loss of the external world: when we bracket all our beliefs concerning the existence of objects in our physical environment we seem to lose the physical world and can study only the left-overs, as it were, or, as Husserl calls it, the *phenomenological residuum.*

Moreover, the Cartesian way raises expectations it cannot fulfill. Since we give up our belief in the existence of the outer world for methodological reasons, we might expect that at a later point in the phenomenological enterprise we may return again to this belief after an appropriate justification. In other words, we expect Husserl to make a move that has the same result as Descartes's move in the *Meditations.* Husserl, however, never fulfills these expectations, but rather calls them a *misunderstanding;*[6] in the phenomenological reduction, the world becomes a mere "phenomenon" – and that is what it stays. In addition, the *Cartesian Way* leads to a solipsistic point of view that cannot provide a foundation to explain intersubjectivity. For these reasons, Husserl gradually became dissatisfied with the *Cartesian Way* to the phenomenological reduction and developed other ways to introduce his method. It was not until the nineteen-twenties, however, that Husserl abandoned completely the *Cartesian Way.*

III. The Strength of Husserl's Comparison

We have seen, in the letter to Hofmannsthal, that Husserl characterizes the phenomenological method as a bracketing of all beliefs in the existence of the objects in our environment, which are beliefs that become "questionable, incomprehensible, a riddle" to the phenomenologist (Husserl, 1994, vol. VII, 134). Thus, he is clearly introducing the reduction through the *Cartesian way* – and he will do so again a few weeks later when he introduces the phenomenological reduction in his lectures on *The Idea of Phenomenology*.[7] His later critique of this *Cartesian way* as a method attaining the phenomenological reduction explains why he does not exploit the comparison between phenomenological reduction and aesthetic experience elsewhere: the *Cartesian way* fails because it gives an incomplete and misleading idea of the phenomenological reduction.

Between 1905 and 1907 Husserl struggles considerably to find a way to introduce the phenomenological reduction. Since it is a special kind of experience, it is difficult to explain it to anyone who has not personally experienced the phenomenological reduction. In his lecture *The Idea of Phenomenology*, Husserl says at one point, after describing the phenomenological reduction:

> This discussion is, of course, only a roundabout way [*Umwege und Behelfe*] of helping us to see what is to be seen here. (Husserl, 1999, 35)

In this context we can state that Husserl's letter to Hofmannsthal is at least one more roundabout way of explaining what it is like to perform the phenomenological reduction, even though it is not a very successful one.

IV. What Husserl Should Have Said

Does that mean that the comparison between the phenomenological reduction and Hofmannsthal's aesthetical theory is a dead end, an unimportant subsection in the history of philosophy? It is, in the way Husserl explores it. Yet, there is another, more fascinating analogy between Husserl and Hofmannsthal that the former could have exploited.

Hofmannsthal, as is well known, gained his first literary merits very early in life. At the age of seventeen he started under the pseudonym "Loris" to publish poems that caught the attention of the literary circles of the time. Hofmannsthal's work in general, but especially his early work, is strongly characterized by the ideas of aestheticism. In this early period he wrote the dramas that were published in the collection *Kleine Dramen* and that he gave to Husserl as a present.

A few years later, however, at the age of twenty-five, Hofmannsthal undergoes an important development. He experiences a crisis – or at least he pretends to do so – that is triggered by his emerging scepticism with respect to language. Hofmannsthal expresses this crisis in *The Lord Chandos Letter*, which becomes probably the best known of all his texts. He writes this letter in 1902, nearly four years before he meets Husserl. A fictional text with autobiographical elements, situated in the early seventeenth century, it is a letter from Lord Chandos to the philosopher Francis Bacon.

In the first part of the letter Lord Chandos describes his early literary successes, and emphasizes that the act of writing had come easily to him in his early life. He enumerates all the plans he had had for literary works and states that in his earlier literary endeavors he had been strongly influenced by aestheticism. But this description of his earlier writings and projects is only an introduction to the main point of his letter, which is to explain why he can no longer write as he used to. He states that he is now unable to identify with his early works and cannot continue to work on his earlier projects. Lord Chandos sums up his problems by saying:

> My situation, in short, is this: I have utterly lost my ability to think or speak coherently about anything at all. (Hofmannsthal, 1986, 19)

This inability to speak and think progresses in stages. First, he finds it impossible to use abstract words, and then this disability quickly spreads to all levels of language or, to put it in Wittgensteinian terms, to all other language-games. The words and phrases of everyday conversation seem more and more "undemonstrable to me, so false, so hopelessly full of holes" with the result that he must make a supreme effort to sustain even the most banal and everyday conversation and to hide the fact that he cannot use language in the way he used to (Hofmannsthal, 1986, 21).

It is important to see that Lord Chandos is expressing doubts about language only; he does not question the existence of his physical environment, the "outer world," or parts of it, but only his ability to refer to his environment by means of language:

> Everything fell into fragments for me, the fragments into further fragments, until it seemed impossible to contain anything at all within a single concept. (Hofmannsthal, 1986, 21)

This new state in which the poet finds himself is not only a state of loss – loss of the ability to apply language. There are "blissful and quickening moments" in which he has experiences he before never thought possible (Hofmannsthal, 1986, 22):

> There is something ineffable, you see, something one could probably never define, that makes itself known to me at such times, filling like a vessel some arbitrary feature of my everyday surrounding with a prodigal surge of more exalted life. [...] Each of them [i.e., *everyday objects*], or, for that matter any of a thousand others like them that the eye glides over with understandable indifference can all at once, at some altogether unpredictable instant, assume for me an aspect so sublime and so giving that it beggars all words. Or it may happen that only the idea of some object remote from me is suddenly accorded to the brim with that gentle but irresistible flood of divine feeling. (Hofmannsthal, 1986, 23)[8]

This crisis with respect to language progresses to another state in which the poet has a new state in which he has a whole new range of experiences. He does not experience new kinds of objects, though; it is not that his physical environment has changed – rather, he experiences his familiar environment in a new way.

The *Lord Chandos Letter* was an important step in the development of Hofmannsthal's work. It has often been interpreted as a critique of the pure aestheticism he had held earlier in his earlier years and the beginning of a stronger emphasis on the moral dimension of life. Still a matter for discussion is whether the crisis expressed in the letter was a radical turning point in Hofmannsthal's life, "a crisis that compelled him to reject all that had gone before" (Janik/Toulmin, 1973, 114), or whether, as a result of the disproportionate emphasis on the Chandos crisis, "the overall unity of Hofmannsthal's work has been distorted and overlooked" (Daviau, 1971, 29).[9] For our discussion, however, this question is not relevant. What is important is that, with this letter, there is a whole new dimension to Hofmannsthal's theory, and Husserl could have made a strong comparison between phenomenological reduction and aesthetic experience if he had exploited this new dimension of Hofmannsthal's theory. There are several aspects of this comparison that could have worked for Husserl.

First, in the phenomenological reduction as well as in Hofmannsthal's state of crisis, we lose the ability to comprehend the world around us "with the simplifying glance of habit." We do, however, gain a new way of experiencing our environment in which we "examine at curiously close range all of the things that surface in such [everyday] conversation" (Hofmannsthal, 1986, 21). Once they are in these new states of mind, Husserl and Hofmannsthal can experience their physical environment as they could not have done earlier, when they were still, to use Husserl's expression, in the "natural attitude."

Second, as I have pointed out above, Husserl's actual comparison fails because it emphasizes the *Cartesian way* as a step into the phenomenological reduction. A comparison with the *Lord Chandos Letter* would allow Husserl to discard this way. He could stress that the phenomenological reduction is a change of attitudes in which we open ourselves up to a whole new range of experiences, just as Lord Chandos's changed attitude made it possible for him to have a range of new experiences. Lord Chandos is not sceptical with respect to the existence of the external world, but only with respect to our ability to speak about the external world. Hence, Husserl could have used this comparison to stress the point that in the phenomenological reduction we do not "lose the external world." He could thus have anticipated his own critique of the *Cartesian way*, i.e., of the way he used to introduce the phenomenological reduction in its early stages. In addition, he could have emphasized that we gain a new way of describing these objects and mental experiences that are directed toward them. Thus, a comparison to Hofmannsthal's later aesthetic theory could have helped Husserl express his intentions more clearly than the comparison, which he presents in the letter, to Hofmannsthal's early theory.

This does not mean, however, that the comparison is perfect or that Hofmannsthal's crisis and Husserl's phenomenological reduction are exactly the same kind of experience; in fact, they are quite different in several respects. Husserl thought that the two kinds of experiences serve two completely different purposes, whereas Hofmannsthal expresses his contention in the paper he read at Göttingen, i.e., four years *after* the *Lord Chandos Letter*, that all written language serves to quench the thirst for poetry – a goal that, according to him, only poets can achieve. Another crucial difference lies in the ways in which they introduce their new methods of looking at things: while Hofmannsthal describes his crisis as something that he slid into, something that came upon him without any effort on his part, Husserl presents his phenomenological reduction systematically, as the result of hard work and an active and deliberate attempt to establish a new method of philosophy.[10] In addition, Hofmannsthal states that the experiences that he has in this new state of mind – and that he describes so eloquently in his letter – are ineffable, while Husserl thinks that it is the task of the phenomenologist to describe what he experiences in the state of phenomenological reduction.

V. Conclusion

The comparison between phenomenological method and aesthetic experience that Husserl makes in his letter to Hofmannsthal fails because Husserl refers to the aesthetic theory Hofmannsthal had held before he wrote the *Lord Chandos Letter*, i.e., he compares it to the theory that Hofmannsthal had modified four years before they met. However, Husserl could have made a strong point if he had compared his views to the ones Hofmannsthal actually held when they met. There is an important analogy between Husserl's phenomenological method and Hofmannsthal's aesthetic theory, but Husserl could not see that analogy at the time he wrote the letter.

The question remains why Husserl refers to Hofmannsthal's early aesthetic theory, i.e. to a theory Hofmannsthal gave up four years before Husserl wrote his letter. Why did he not consider the *Lord Chandos Letter* and Hofmannsthal's language-crisis? I think there are several reasons. First, we know from the letter that Husserl had read Hofmannsthal's book *Kleine Dramen*, a collection of plays Hofmannsthal wrote before his *Lord Chandos Letter*. Second, Husserl never was a great reader, so it is quite possible that he did not know about Hofmannsthal's turn. And third, even if Husserl had known about Hofmannsthal's turn, he probably could not have appreciated the advantages of this other comparison at the time since he had not yet recognized the problems of the *Cartesian way* for the phenomenological reduction in early 1907, when he wrote the letter to Hofmannsthal.

---

[1] "Der Dichter und diese Zeit," printed as Hofmannsthal (1907).
[2] See Hirsch (1968, 109).
[3] For these biographical details, see Schuhmann (1977, 100ff) and Hirsch (1968, 108ff).
[4] Since Husserl's letter has not yet been translated, I have translated all passages that are quoted.
[5] He argues for it for the first time in his lecture "Erste Philosophie" (1923/24).
[6] See *Erste Philosophie* (1923/24), Husserliana VIII, 174.
[7] In this lecture, the *Cartesian way* is already combined with the *way via ontology*.
[8] Translation slightly altered.
[9] For an interesting discussion on that topic see also Le Rider (1997, 101ff).
[10] This is mainly a difference of how the two have presented their ideas. Hofmannsthal expresses in a very eloquent way that he has "utterly lost my ability to think or speak coherently about anything at all" (Hofmannsthal, 1986, 19), which raises numerous doubts about whether the letter describes autobiographically an actual crisis Hofmannsthal went through. Husserl, on the other side, writes in a letter that he was driven by demons in his development of the phenomenological reduction. He writes about the decade between the *Logical Investigations* and *Ideas*: "A development has never been more straight, more goal oriented, more predestined, more 'demonic'" (Husserl, 1994, vol IV, 412; my translation),

which suggests that the development of the phenomenological reduction was not only the result of a systematic effort, but also something that Husserl slid into, very much like Hofmannsthal's description of being overcome by the crisis; see also Smith (1995, 102) and Schuhmann (1994, 6f). I want to take this occasion to thank Barry Smith for drawing my attention to this letter and Husserl's "darker side."

References

Bernet, Rudolf, Iso Kern, and Eduard Marbach. 1993. *An Introduction to Husserlian Phenomenology.* Evanston: Northwestern UP.
Daviau, Donald G. 1971. "Hugo von Hofmannsthal and the Chandos Letter." In: *Modern Austrian Literature* 4: 28-44.
Hirsch, Rudolf. 1968. "Edmund Husserl und Hugo von Hofmannsthal. Eine Begegnung und ein Brief." *Sprache und Politik. Festgabe für Dolf Sternberger zum siebzigsten Geburtstag.* Ed. Carl-Joachim Friedrich and Benno Reifenberg. Heidelberg: Verlag Lambert Schneider. 108-115.
Hofmannsthal, Hugo von. 1907. "Der Dichter und diese Zeit." *Gesammelte Werke: Prosa II.* Frankfurt a.M.: Fischer. 222-258.
–. 1986. *The Lord Chandos Letter.* Trans. Russell Stockman. Marlboro: The Marlboro Press.
Husserl, Edmund. 1959. *Erste Philosophie (1923/24). Zweiter Teil: Theorie der phänomenologischen Reduktion* (=*Hua* VII). Ed. Rudolf Boehm. The Hague: Nijhoff.
–. 1970. *Logical Investigations.* Trans. J.N. Findlay. London: Routledge.
–. 1970. *The Crisis of European Sciences and Transcendental Phenomenology: An Introduction to Phenomenological Philosophy.* Trans. David Carr. Evanston: Northwestern UP.
–. 1983. *Ideas Pertaining to a Pure Phenomenology and to a Phenomenological Philosophy. First Book: General Introduction to a Pure Phenomenology.* Trans. F. Kersten. The Hague: Nijhoff.
–. 1994. *Briefwechsel. 10 Vols.* Ed. Karl and Elisabeth Schuhmann. Dordrecht: Kluwer.
–. 1999. *The Idea of Phenomenology.* Trans. Lee Hardy. Dordrecht: Kluwer.
Janik, Allan, and Stephen Toulmin. 1973. *Wittgenstein's Vienna.* New York: Simon and Schuster.
Kern, Iso. 1977. "The Three Ways to the Transcendental Phenomenological Reduction in the Philosophy of Edmund Husserl." *Husserl: Expositions and Appraisals.* Ed. Frederick Elliston and Peter McCormick. Notre Dame: University of Notre Dame Press. 126-149.
Le Rider, Jacques. 1997. *Hugo von Hofmannsthal: Historismus und Moderne in der Literatur der Jahrhundertwende.* Trans. Leopold Federmair. Vienna: Böhlau.

Massimilla, Edoardo. 1998. "L'Arte pura e la sfinge della coscienza: una lettera di Edmund Husserl a Hugo von Hofmannsthal." *Archivio di Storia della Cultura* XI: 193-213.
Schuhmann, Karl. 1977. *Husserl Chronik. Denk- und Lebensweg Edmund Husserls.* The Hague: Nijhoff.
Schuhmann, Elisabeth, and Karl Schuhmann. 1994. "Einführung in die Ausgabe." Husserl (1994), vol. X. 1-70.
Smith, Barry. 1995. "Edmund Husserl, Briefwechsel." *Husserl Studies* 12: 98-104.
Sokolowski, Robert. 1964. *The Formation of Husserl's Notion of Constitution.* The Hague: Nijhoff.

THE "SOFT LAW" OF AUSTRIAN HISTORICAL LOGIC SINCE THE ENLIGHTENMENT IN THE ARTS AND SCIENCES

Mark E. Blum

University of Louisville

A "national historical logic" is a normative manner whereby the culture tracks time and ascribes cause and effect to the events of public and private life. One can call the nation's historical logic the pattern for structuring the "what," "how," and "why" of events. A national historical logic begins in the conception of individuals whose vision speaks to the populace of a time. A national historical logic is not only the formal historiographical creations of those who practice the discipline of history. It is also the historical perspective of novelists, dramatists, journalists, and other professionals who contribute to the historical understanding of the nation's populace. Nationally, the conventions of a historical logic are known both informally in everyday expressions and in the more formal genres that govern the historical aspects of inquiry and expression. The genres of literature, historical writing, and scientific explanation into event-structures are composed intuitively in emulation of what is the sense of "right order" of the authorities in the many spheres of the nation's culture. This intuitive construction is generated by the private as well as public demand for forms of narration that communicate a succession of events comprehensible to all parties. The dissemination of a national historical logic is a combined effort of the many institutional expressions of the nation's culture – the press and other communications media, the schools, and other private and public organs.

National historical logics are artful cognitive products that respond to national political-social experience. A national historical logic is the product of the contingencies of history. It is most often a manner of defending the populace and the state against the trials of time and event. A national historical logic becomes the support of tradition and continuity, although it can become a fecund influence upon the regeneration of cultural life when changed. A nation's historical logic as an impetus for renewal occurs infrequently, mainly due to the difficulty and time required to reorient cultural norms. Indeed, historical-logical norms are most often hardly appreciated in their presence and meaning. Even when recognized, massive institutional response is required for changing a national historical logic. The outcome of this inertia is inadequate response to the emerging issues of a nation. As

---

Writing the Austrian Traditions: Relations between Philosophy and Literature.
Ed. Wolfgang Huemer and Marc-Oliver Schuster. Edmonton, Alberta:
Wirth-Institute for Austrian and Central European Studies, 2003. pp. 131-142.

an artful defense and guide, a national historical logic can, as the Freudian superego, be mistaken in its normative guidance as times change within the nation. A national historical logic changes slowly, if at all, as its premises become embedded in the culture's educational and policy-making norms.

The "nation-state" is central to what its cultural-historical logic becomes. If we can accept the premises of Aristotle and Hegel, the human is a political animal. The *zoon politikon* is the creature of the polis. The polis since the Enlightenment, at least, is the nation. Austria developed its national historical logic under the influence of the structure of the Holy Roman Empire in its weaknesses and strengths. The Habsburg dynasty in particular gave form to the "what," "how," and "why" of the structure of historical events. Indeed, Austrian historical logic will have many elements that are analogous to how a family experiences time. Although I will comment upon Austrian historical logic since the Enlightenment, its structure as I present it began earlier with the emergence of Habsburg authority in Europe. Most prominent in its historical logic is the sense of an evolving form bridging times and places, like a family dynasty, which I will call a *morphological* logic. Historical cause within this morphological form will focus upon *the reciprocality of diverse historical agents*, as within a family milieu (and a multi-national state). In its best sense, Austrian historical logic promotes a vision of stability and equity among diverse voices. Its historical purview of an event is *non-dramatic* as an evolving form has neither radical breaks nor special emphases – every phase of maturation is equally important.

Adalbert Stifter's "das sanfte Gesetz," "the soft law,"[1] articulated in the introduction to his 1852 collection of novellas *Bunte Steine*,[2] is one of the more explicit descriptions of this historical logic as a "right order." While Stifter inherited these norms, his restatement of them with the profound humanism of his narratives is the best introduction to Austrian historical logic. In 1842, Stifter composed one of his many descriptions of natural events that earned him the Emperor's medal for art and science several years later. This particular description of a forest begins one of his tales of human existence, entitled *Der Hochwald*. Stifter's "soft law" of nature and humankind can be seen in the passage, and is an apt introduction for my discussion of Austrian historical logic in the arts and sciences since the Enlightenment:

> On the midnight side (that is, north) of the Austrian land a forest stretches its dawning streaks westwards for thirty miles, beginning at the source of the river Thaia and strives forward until that borderknot where the Bohemian land collides with Austria and Bavaria. There, as often with crystallized pinnacles, a multitude of immense saddles and ridges sprang against each other and pushed up a rough massif, which now manifests its forest shadow over three lands and sends down undulating rolling land and rushing streams to each on all its sides. The forest bends, like its kind often does, along the course of the line of mountains, and it goes then toward the midnight side many days journey further. The place of this forest swing, now comparable to a secluded sea inlet, is in the self-correction it betook, is what we intend to narrate.[3]

Stifter articulates an Austrian narrative norm of sensitivity to the durational Gestalt of a changing state-of-affairs inherited from his predecessors in the arts and the sciences (Gestalt as a conceptual approach to human perception is credited to the Austrian psychologist, sociologist, and poet Christian von Ehrenfels). Stifter's forest is depicted as a living, changing, even self-correcting being that nonetheless maintains a form, albeit accommodative toward its contingent milieus, over time. Such a logic of change over time is what I will term a morphological understanding of history. All change is towards the fulfillment of a form, albeit a form whose growth may continue without foreseeable end.

There is another unique aspect of this Gestalt recognition in Stifter and the Austrians that warrants Stifter's term "the soft law": the form is not a unity imposed upon particulars, rather it is a unity composed out of the aggregate of particulars. The form itself changes as the particulars meet immediate empirical challenges accommodatively, rather than the zero sum game of either/or (Oskar Morgenstern and John von Neumann, arguably stemming from lands with a deep Austrian heritage, have provided valuable insight into this aspect of game-theory). The forest does not pit its direction and being against an opposing force, such as the inhospitable ground of the massif or the "Grenzknoten" (a metaphor for "problem") of the conjoining of the three lands. Rather, the trees are determined to find a way to grow that simultaneously preserves the parental form even as it borders on the inhospitable.

The method in this morphological accommodation to external challenge is an avoidance of, indeed scepticism, toward inflexible ideas. The forest bends tree by tree when necessary. The Austrian historian Oswald Redlich has noted that Austrian historiography shuns "Übergeschichte," where metacognitive categories reshape known facts.[4] Rather, Austrian historiography is described by the majority of Austrian historians as "streng, exakt, objektiv" (Fellner, 1985, 93). History is the intersubjective movement of individuals toward each other and their environ, and the account focuses upon each particular relationship in depth and detail – like a Freudian case-study. The Austrian historian Ludo Moritz Hartmann emphasized in this tradition that whatever is individual belongs to a form generated by the intersubjective whole composed in that time by all individuals (Fellner, 1985, 168-69, 173). Austrian historiography is not conceptually impaired in the absense of the broad explanatory principles of the German historicist tradition from Herder through Hegel to Marx, from Ranke to Dilthey to Meinecke; rather, the conceptual organizer of events is the very form itself comprised by the historical facts, cohered as a total Gestalt by those facts. Stifter describes this Gestalt composed of the aggregate of many particulars in his "soft law," as he argues for the integration of the many smaller laws that characterize the singularity of each event in humankind or nature participating in the summative form (*Vorrede/Bunte Steine* in *Stifters Werke*, 2: 15-17). If a unifying principle for the totality is to be sought, it is the "walten," the proportionate "sway" of intersubjective integration from particular to particular ("Letter to Aurelius Buddeus [August, 1847]," in *Stifters Werke*, 1: 72). Is this good physics? Ernst Mach, the Austrian physicist, argued for what he called a physics, where rather than seeking the one explanatory law that generated all entailed phenomena, the physicist restricted himself/herself to a rigorous description of the empirical facts and relationships of immediate phenomena.[5]

The Austrian philosopher Franz Brentano spoke of the aggregative form generated by many as the "one in the many." He refered to this in his text on aesthetics, as he discussed the reciprocal causality of the many aspects and dimensions of any work of art.[6] Brentano's parenting of modern phenomenology, the rigorous observation of how a thing or state-of-affairs presents itself, enabled him to see the differing Gestalts of the "one in the many." Brentano, as he spoke of the principle of "the one in the many" understandably felt he had to address the seemingly self-evident proposition of science that there is a "one."[7] His modest embarrassment in his discussion stemmed almost certainly from the weight of German thought that there is a "one" behind all entailed particulars. Indeed, that is the counter-example to Austrian-German thought, the normative historical logic of the northern German lands since the Enlightenment, which is "the many in the one."

Franz Stuckert, in an essay on the North German writer and poet Theodor Storm, articulates quite clearly the converse historiographical idea of the German, the "many in the one." Stuckert points out how an overarching principle subsumes all particular examples in Storm's poetry into a "übergeordnete Einheit."[8] A Zeitgeist of that time and place, as it were, is created that all phenomena of that time share. He offers the following poem as illustration:

> Es ist so still; die Heide liegt
> Im warmen Mittagssonnenstrahle,
> Ein rosenroter Schimmer fliegt
> Um ihre alten Gräbermale;
> Die Kräuter blühn; der Heideduft
> Steigt in die blaue Sommerluft.
> (1966, 72)

The stillness is the time all have. There is an overarching principle that, when changing, confers total change to everything subject to it. The "alten Gräbermale" is a trace of this dialectical movement. The next poem Stuckert quotes relates to how the presence and absence of wind that marks certain seasons so radically affects the particulars of reality:

> Am grauen Strand, am grauen Meer
> Und seitab liegt die Stadt;
> Der Nebel drückt die Dächer schwer,
> Und durch die Stille braust das Meer
> Eintönig um die Stadt.
>
> Es rauscht kein Wald, es schlägt im Mai
> Kein Vogel ohne Unterlass;
> Die Wandergans mit hartem Schrei
> Nur fliegt in Herbstesnacht vorbei,
> Am Strande weht das Gras.
> (1966, 74)

Stuckert shows in Storm's vision of seasonal change the dialectical time of the German, the sharp contrasts of thesis and antithesis, so different from the gradual evolution of Austrian time.

The Austrian does not depict sharp changes of reality in a quantum change of Zeitgeist; rather the entire past contributes to what becomes in the present. Franz Brentano, for example, speaks in his reflections on time and history of the importance of those who have come before, lending their gains to the present inquirer:

> The investigations of conic sections begun in ancient times by Archimedes and Apollonius were at first of purely theoretical, mathematical interest. Centuries later Kepler made their work applicable to astronomy, but again only because of a theoretical interest. Yet as a result the investigations became of practical use, inasmuch as the progress made in astronomy did a great deal to forward navigation. The seaman who avoids a shipwreck by observing with precision the geographical latitude and longitude owes the fact that he is alive to theories which originated solely from a yearning for knowledge twenty centuries earlier.[9]

In an essay on his conception of genius, Brentano writes in the same vein: "In science, the greatest discoverer is only differentiated from the imitator and apprentice by (a non-specific) degree" (*Grundzüge der Ästhetik*, 92). In short, he testifies to the morphology of knowledge over time through the efforts of an intergenerational extended family; the development of knowledge is seen as a constant problem-solving through reflective appreciation of what has been as one goes forward. Sigmund Freud developed a therapy for the mentally ill and the slightly neurotic founded upon this appreciation of the *duration* of the past in the present. As an inquirer, Freud followed Brentano's advice to the letter, albeit one that was sustained by the Austrian normative style of inquiry even without Brentano's emphasis upon exhaustive exploration of the single phenomenon to unfold its complex origins.

The root causes of the differences between the German and the Austrian historical logic are to be found in the separate histories of the seat of the Holy Roman Imperial throne for half a millenium and the German kingdoms, principalities, bishoprics, and free cities. There was a cleft between German and Austrian political history, before and after the Enlightenment, a cleft that had an influence on how citizens of each nation perceived the nature of their historical experience. The half-millenium of the Habsburg dynasty gave a paternalistic pattern to Austrian political life. The strength of this "family-oriented" norm was in the highly interpersonal tone of political life. A dynasty never dies, although one measures life within it by the generations that are born and die. It is a constant, yet changing form, whose character is fulfilled again and again. A dynasty is a protean form, porous in its expression as differing persons manifest it. A morphological historical vision includes birth, maturation, and death, yet continuance of the form as seeds of the old are reborn as the new. Franz Grillparzer gives evidence of his awareness of the pivotal role of the life and death of the rulers as the standard for duration and change in political life in his drama *Kaiser Ottokars Glück und Ende*. Merenberg sends his son Seyfried to the Archbishop of Mainz, an elector of the Emperor-to-be, with a letter that will warn the Archbishop of the poor character of Ottokar. If the letter does not arrive on time, Merenberg reflects, Germans will be under the influence of the wrong man for a lifetime: "One day too late is thirty years too early!"[10]

The dynastic administration of the people through bureaucracies became known in the Enlightenment as *cameralism*, a governance by chambers designed in their separate purviews to embrace the many aspects of the nation's life. Austrian cameralism, especially in the age of Maria Theresa and her son Joseph, gave evidence of the goodwill of the parental authorities. As a family, each member was perceived as a distinct life with individual interests. The notion of the "the one in the many" differentiated Austrian cameralism from the Prussian or Saxon form in this respect. Joseph von Sonnenfels, the Austrian cameralist, speaks of the "aggregate will" of the diverse population of the Austrian state that is the whole. Even the ruler has no more rights than those equated with their stewardship of this "aggregate will."[11] The German cameralists, on the other hand, stressed the state as having its own reasons in the interest of the people, but not in the sense of being its aggregate will. Samuel Pufendorf's cameralist ideas were the touchstone of this vision of the "many in the one."[12]

Louise Sommer points out the most significant difference between the German and Austrian cameralists is the former's penchant for abstract principle governing the particular, while the Austrian sees the state and its political/economic life from the point of view of the diversity of empirical practice (1920/1967, 6, 12). Austrian cameralism at its best was a benign outreach by bureaucratic officials into the daily lives of its charges, in a face-to-face encounter that governance at a distance could not so equitably match. As conditions changed, Austrian cameralism treated the shifting values of agriculture, trade, and manufacture with proactive oversight that constantly engaged the populace in intersubjective dealings with government officials. Sonnenfels was proud of this interpersonal concern, evidenced by an article he wrote in 1784 discussing the proper style of conduct for the Austrian bureaucratic official.[13] The German cameralism was more distant and directed by statute law, more *laissez-faire*, but thereby more impersonal (Sommer, 1920/67, 12).[14] The dichotomy of the Austrian interpersonal concerns and the German legal-rights-based concerns was also reflected in criminal law. Sonnenfels used his influence to "soften" criminal justice and its punishments. Albion Small writes of this "softness" in relation to the written law:

> A favorite idea of his was that in criminal cases the penalty of ascertained guilt should be determined by the vote of the majority of judges; the question of guilt or innocence however, as well as of the mitigating or aggravating circumstances, should be settled only by a unanimous vote. In practice this proposition would in most cases simply lead to the release of the accused. (Small, 1909, 484)

Reinhard Merkel has pointed out that this "soft" attitude toward a rigorous application of civil or criminal law persisted in Austrian society, differentiating it from the German.[15] Paragraph 48 of the 1803 legal code and paragraph 54 of the 1852 legal code, called "ausserordentliches Milderungsrecht," were designed to regulate the parameters of exceptional circumstances and the accordingly softened penalities (Merkel, 1994, 90). Increasingly, this "mildness" became a self-evident norm in Austrian justice. In 1911 a German jurist referred to the "anarchical condition of Austrian legal practice" in this regard (Merkel, 1994, 91).

The profound contributions in interpersonal understanding that arose in the forms of practice in Austrian psychiatry, law, drama, literature, and the fine arts in nineteenth- and early twentieth-century *fin-de-siècle* culture can be linked to this stress on the intersubjective nature of human reality and its ancillary ethic of reaching cooperative, empathic, common practices that was the hallmark of the Enlightened absolutism of Maria Theresa and Joseph II. The single-minded individuality, indeed ruthlessness of Faust had no place in Austrian culture then or afterwards.

The problem of "family-oriented," empathic, cooperative norms in governance lay in the inevitable weakening of a self-directed, assertive political will among the members of the society who were not governors. Kant's recognition that one cannot be "given" freedom perhaps stemmed from his observation of the discontent of many freed serfs in Joseph II's Austria, as well as the discomfort of religious minorities with the new public schools of Joseph II. The Austrian will to assertive independence was "co-opted" one might say by the "soft law." The self-concept of individual Austrians never freed itself from the presence of others for whom one must care or whose care one must recognize. The strengths of this interpersonal world were in its cultivation of an accurate recognition in the arts and the sciences of interdependence and its facilitating forms of empathy. From the Enlightenment Momus of Gottfried Prehauser through Kafka's Momus in *The Castle*, the barbed humor penetrating private aims and a too self-absorbed project will bring the Austrian individual back to the gravity of an interdependent world. The weakness of this embeddedness among others was in a discomfort with the final responsibility and aloneness of selfhood that bred for the German the Faustian paradigm. The Austrian political horizon will never leave its past behind to start fresh, no more than the prodigal son could ever fully distance himself from his parents. The Austrian selection of a morphological logic as the dominant form of national historical norm contributes both to the collective (i.e., interdependent) and conservative quality of its historical thought. In a morphological logic, all facts contribute to the form, each individual action plays its role in the mutually shared form to which all contribute. While a morphological thinker need not be a political conservative, there is a "conserving" aspect to all morphological thinkers in that historical forms never completely disappear, and for the most part are always in a phase of becoming.

The Germanies, on the other hand, had norms for historical life that for each individual stimulated more public assertion. The ceaseless competition that existed among the Princes in the hundreds of principalities, a competition that was dynastic and religious, set a conflict-oriented model of public life. Moreover, the patriciate of the towns had been in conflict with the princes since the late Middle Ages. The suburban artisans and peasants represented milieus that gravitated between alliances or conflict with the urban patriciate and the lower aristocratic landowners of the surrounding country. Every social class knew that only self-assertion could protect its rights. Thus arose an active citizenship in the Germanies, even against the aristocracy's attempts to frustrate the sharing of public power. The individual as an isolate will who found community only through common principle made law more salient than in the patrimonial state of Austria. In the years between 1200 and 1500 when citizen rights flourished in the German cities, the constant, often conflicting claims of autonomy, rights, and responsibilities between the city and the aristocratic ruler became normative. In that same time, citizen rights ended in Austria. The burghers of the Austrian cities from the rule of Emperors Rudolf I through Maximilian gradually lost all the medieval privileges they had gained under the Hohenstaufens.[16] Justice was increasingly a product of the Emperor's goodwill, rather than as became the Germanic bourgeois norm, justice wrought by the fair application of an impersonal law.

While the period between 1500 and the Enlightenment in Austria brought increasing control of every facet of public life by the Habsburg Emperors, in the Germanies Calvin's vision of "natural law," which bound ruler and ruled by contractual clarity, grew in its influence. Frederick William, the Great Elector of Brandenburg-Prussia, became a Calvinist, and his attention to the highly differentiated rights and responsibilities that already existed in the Hohenzollern domains was underscored by the Calvinist emphasis upon natural law.[17] The educated commoners of Brandenburg-Prussia and the other Germanies gravitated toward a natural-rights-conception of membership in the state that even more radically conceived the distribution of political authority than had Frederick William's circumspect understanding of the rights and responsibilities of ruler to ruled. Johannes Althusius articulated a natural rights individualism that enhanced the already existent norms where each social group asserted its traditional autonomy and rights.[18] Kant's fourth thesis in his essay on an *Idea for Universal History* restated this natural law emphasis for the bourgeois classes in its stress on individuality and law: "the means employed by Nature to bring about the development of all the capacities of men is their antagonism in society, so far as this is, in the end, the cause of a lawful order among man."[19] Individuals kept their own counsel, and acted as a rule with great self-direction. Ideas were more of a helpmate than other people. Ideas gave justification for going it alone, publicly and privately. Principles were the best company. Where Germans formed associations so that common, collective action could be made, these associatons were organized in their means and ends with clear role and scope so that an individual knew his or her place within them and could differentiate this engagement from the other aspects of their private and public commitments.[20]

The weakness of the German norms lay in the very strengths of their individual self-direction that was justified by idea, for this self-direction led to an overweening individualism taken to extremes of imbalance. One might compare Kleist's *Michael*

Kohlhaas or Goethe's *Faust* to Austrian heros such as the civil servant in Grillparzer's *Ein treuer Diener seiner Herrn* or Kafka's counter-example to the Kleisteian or Faustian heroes in his Karl Rossman of *Amerika* or K. of *Das Schloss*, all individuals who learn difficult but necessary lessons of interdependence. A healthy democratic society requires cooperative models as well as individualistic models. Individualistic self-assertion is reinforced for the Germans by a historicism whose expression sharpens individual encounter, contrast, and contradiction.

Nietzsche is unable to grasp the multiplicity of other lives in their separate integrities because of this German convention of integrating multiplicity into a common, transcendent medium. When he connotes the nature of experience with Austrian wisdom, as he does in his respect for Franz Grillparzer and Adalbert Stifter, he inevitably distorts the Austrian comprehension of multiple integrities. For example, in his *On the Advantage and Disadvantage of History for Life* he quotes Grillparzer on the multiple causes in any historical experience:

> Grillparzer goes so far as to say: "what else is history, after all, than the way in which the spirit of man apprehends what for him are *impenetrable events*; unites elements of which God only knows whether they belong together; replaces the unintelligible with something intelligible; introduces its concepts of externally oriented purpose into a whole which surely admits only purposes with an inner orientation; and again assumes chance where a thousand little causes were at work. Every person at the same time has his individual necessity so that millions run in directions parallel to each other in crooked and straight lines, cross, support and restrict each other, strive forward and backward and in this assume the character of chance for each other, and so, leaving out of account the influences of natural events, make it impossible to demonstrate a penetrating all-inclusive necessity of events.[21]

Nietzsche uses this observation to point to the lazy generalizations of most historians in determining propositions about events. However, his own solution also departs from Grillparzer's multiplicity; Nietzsche sums up his deliberations by saying: "to describe with insight a known, perhaps common theme, an everyday melody, to elevate it, raise to a comprehensive symbol and so let a whole world of depth of meaning, power and beauty be guessed in it" (36). Thus, again the lifting of differing causes, differing integrities, into one common, transcendental medium. Nietzsche's reading of Adalbert Stifter is similarly warped to a German historical-logical viewpoint. Adalbert Schmidt asserts that, in *Thus Spoke Zarathustra*, Nietzsche's conception of "The Stillest Hour" is derived from Stifter. Nietzsche states: "Die stillsten Worte sind es, welche den Sturm bringen. Gedanken, die mit Taubenfüßen kommen, lenken die Welt" ("It is the stillest words that bring on the storm. Thoughts that come on doves' feet guide the world").[22] Stifter, of course, does not see any one event, especially a dramatic one, as the most significant moment of human episodes. He is the last to wish to bring on a storm with a still word. He writes on his "soft law" in *Bunte Steine*:

> The force which causes the milk in the poor woman's crock to rise up and overflow is like that which drives forth the lava from the volcano, and leaves it on the surface of the mountain to flow down. Only the latter

> appearance is more obvious, compelling the glance of the uninformed and the inattentive [...] And as it is in outer nature, so it is in the inner of humankind. An entire life full of justice, simplicity, self-control, understanding, effectiveness in one's circle, admiration of the beautiful, united with a calm, resigned dying, I hold as great: powerful movements of dispositions, frightful manifestations of anger, the desire for revenge, the inflamed spirit that strives for activity, and in its excitement, compels, disturbs, and even throws away its own life, I hold not as great, rather as less significant, since these things are only manifestations of the single and one-sided forces as the occurrence of storms, fire-spilling mountains, and earthquakes.[23]

Stifter's "soft law" is the unity realized by the interrelation of all small interconnected cause-effect moments. The "law" is that complex, interconnected form. Stifter does not speak of the most salient principle or the one cause, but always the sequence of small moments that develop the whole. Thus, he as an Austrian eschews any transcending (or reduction) of differing individual moments to a univocal and abstract leaven. The irony is that the Austrian was and, I contend, still is caught in the web of morphological form, thus the personalism and interpersonalism has an inherent univocality, nonetheless. Stifter, in his essay-report of the solar eclipse on July 8, 1842 surprises the twentieth century reader by predicting a kind of painting where color escapes from the forms of material content – a prediction of abstract expressionism, as well as a prediction of atonal musicfree of traditional structure. Actually this is not formulated as prediction, but rather a yearning to escape morphological form. The eclipse is tracked through its several phases until it is complete. In the heart of darkness of the two minutes when the solar orb is completely eclipsed, the flames of the sun's penumbra shoot colors outward and a silence becomes the background of the slight sounds of animal and human restlessness. Stifter writes:

> Couldn't one invent a music for the eye by the simultaneity and succession of light and color as well as a tonality for the ear? Until now light and color have not been independently applied, rather fixed in designs; for fireworks, transparencies, and illuminations are only the raw beginnings of a light music [...] Wouldn't a whole composed only of light accords and melodies, and similarly (aural) tones engender power and shock? In any case, I can't name one symphony, oratorio or anything in that vein that is so exalted as the two minutes of light and color in the heavens [...] (*Stifters Werke*, 2: 950-51)

Stifter asks not only for a release from form, but also for the excitement of the monumental moment – for shock. The German way may be the Austrian antidote if Austria's intersubjective strengths can be preserved and reformulated to include a more individualistic public practice. Franz Brentano, Sigmund Freud, Ernst Mach, Christian von Ehrenfels, Edmund Husserl, Anton Marty, Franz Kafka, Ludwig von Wittgenstein, John von Neumann, and other Austrians of the late nineteenth and twentieth centuries gave their culture and ours the tools to deconstruct form and liberate being human for new constellations of intersubjectivity. Austria today has a rich heritage for liberating itself from its still morphological historical logic.

¹ I translate the word "sanft" as "soft" – rather than "gentle," as it has been translated by some critics – because Stifter means the English equivalent of soft as "unobtrusive, quiet." Stifter sees the "sanftes Gesetz" as that law of natural processes that underlies the more striking symptoms of its presence. The most exact term of the "sanftes Gesetz" would be the Germanic use of "sanft" as an inhering process that is natural to persons and things. See Jakob und Wilhelm Grimm's definition of "sanft" as "von zuständen und verhältnissen, die ihrer entwicklung und beschaffenheit nach in der natur ihres trägers selbst begründet oder mit ihr eng verbunden sind, hinsichtlich ihrer rückwirkung auf körperliches befinden, aber auch auf das innerliche leben"; *Deutsches Wörterbuch*, Volume 8 (Leipzig: S. Hirzel, 1893), 1779.
Stifter's description of the process of the "sanftes Gesetz" as a "Walten" substantiates my translation. He wrote of the lawful regulating of natural and human processes in this sense to Aurelius Buddeus as a "Walten," a "regulating action," "a way of connecting things" (*Stifters Werke*, 1: 72). The Grimms write of "walten" in these senses: "eine regelnde, bestimmende thätigkeit bezeichnen" and "anknüpfung durch"; *Deutsches Wörterbuch*, Volume 13 (Leipzig: S. Hirzel, 1922), 1384 and 1385.
² Adalbert Stifter, *Bunte Steine* in *Stifters Werke in Zwei Bänden* (Salzburg/Stuttgart: Das 'Bergland Buch', N.D.), vol. 2, 13-17.
³ Adalbert Stifter, *Der Hochwald* in *Stifters Werke in Zwei Bänden* (Salzburg/Stuttgart: Das 'Bergland Buch,' N.D.), 1: 212.
⁴ Günter Fellner, *Ludo Moritz Hartmann und die Österreichische Geschichtswissenschaft, Grundzüge eines paradigmatischen Konfliktes* (Vienna-Salzburg: Geyer, 1985), 92.
⁵ Robert Musil, *Beitrag zur Beurteilung der Lehren Machs* (Reinbeck bei Hamburg: Rowohlt, 1980), 43. See also Mark E. Blum, *The Austro-Marxists 1890-1918: A Psychobiographical Study* (Lexington, KY: UP of Kentucky, 1985), 157-158.
⁶ Franz Brentano, *Grundzüge der Ästhetik* (Bern: Francke Verlag, 1959), 133-134.
⁷ Brentano writes in this regard: "Gewiss ist, dass die Welt von einheitlichen Gesetzen durchdrungen und zu einem Ziele zusammengeordnet ist, den Stempel eines einheitlichen Werkmeisters an sich hat. Ohne solche Einheit wäre kein Kunstwerk eine kleine Welt. Gewiss auch, dass, wie die Welt nur durch jene Gesetze wissenschaftlich erfassbar ist, so auch das Kunstwerk durch solche Einheit fasslicher wird. Aber hätte die Welt überhaupt einen Wert, ohne Psychisches in sich zu begreifen? Und hätten Symmetrie und Wiederholung in der Mannigfaltgkeit?" (*Grundzüge der Ästhetik*, 134).
⁸ Franz Stuckert, *Theodor Storm. Der Dichter in seinem Werk* (Tübingen: Max Niemeyer, 1966), 72.
⁹ Franz Brentano, *The Foundation and Construction of Ethics*, trans. Elizabeth Hughes Schneewind (New York: Humanities Press, 1973), 2.
¹⁰ Franz Grillparzer, *King Ottocar, His Rise and Fall*, trans. Henry H. Stevens (Yarmouth Port, MA: The Register Press, 1938), 8.
¹¹ Albion W. Small, *The Cameralists, The Pioneers of German Social Polity* (Chicago: University of Chicago Press, 1909), 484.
¹² See Erhard Dittrich, *Die Deutschen und Österreichischen Kameralisten* (Darmstadt: Wissenschaftliche Buchgesellschaft, 1974), 52-54; see also Louise Sommer, *Die Österreichischen Kameralisten in dogmengeschichtlicher Darstellung* (Vienna: Carl Konegen, 1920; Aalen: Scientia Verlag, 1967), 162-164.
¹³ See Joseph von Sonnenfels, *Über den Geschäftsstyl; die erste Grundlage für angehende österreichische Canzleybeamte* (Vienna: Kürzbock, 1784/1820).
¹⁴ See Louise Sommer on the late-eighteenth-century German cameralist theorists Jakob, Soden, and Hufeland who were influenced by Adam Smith, albeit preserving their statist

bias; Sommer, "Cameralism," in *Encyclopedia of the Social Sciences*, vol.3 (New York: Macmillan, 1951), 160.

[15] Reinhard Merkel, *Strafrecht und Satire im Werk von Karl Kraus* (Baden-Baden: Nomos Verlagsgesellschaft, 1994), 90-92.

[16] See Heinrich Schuster's discussion of the Austrian bourgeois loss of public authority to the Emperor between 1273 and 1512 in "Die Entwicklung des Rechtslebens, Verfassung und Verwaltung," in *Geschichte der Stadt Wien*, (Vienna: Adolf Holzhausen, 1897), vol. 1, 368-376.

[17] See Ferdinand Schevill, *The Great Elector* (Chicago: University of Chicago Press, 1947), esp. 96-97 for the traditional awareness of legal limits to authority in the Hohenzollern lands, as well as 249 and 409ff for the impact of Calvinism on Frederick William.

[18] See Otto von Gierke, *Natural Law and the Theory of Society, 1500-1800*. Trans. Ernest Barker (Boston: Beacon Press, 1957), 70ff.

[19] Immanuel Kant, "Idea for a Universal History from a Cosmopolitan Point of View," *On History*. Trans. Lewis White Beck (Indianapolis: The Bobbs-Merrill Company, 1963), 15.

[20] See Otto von Gierke's description of the early German cooperative community whose means of coherence were the specific public functions that were a right of the person. Public life as a collective was the integration of these individual, separate functions: "Das Recht löste sich im Rechte auf, bis es nur noch in der Idee ein gleiches ungemeines Recht, in Wirklichkeit nur die zahllosen individuellen Rechte, Freiheiten, Privilegien und Sonderbefugnisse der Stände, Herren und Genossenschaften, der Marken und der Höfe gab"; *Das deutsche Genossenschaftsrecht*, 2 vols. (Graz: Akademische Druck u. Verlagsanstalt, 1954), vol 2, 128.

[21] Friedrich Nietzsche, *On the Advantage and Disadvantage of History for Life*. Trans. Peter Preuss (Indianapolis: Hackett, 1980), 35.

[22] Nietzsche, "Die stillste Stunde," *Also Sprach Zarathustra* in *Friedrich Nietzsche. Werke in Zwei Bänden* (Munich: Carl Hanser, 1967), vol. 1, 645ff; translation taken from Walter Kaufmann, *The Portable Nietzsche* (New York: Viking Press), 258. See Adalbert Schmidt's observations on Nietzsche's indebtedness to Stifter for this thought in *Das sanfte Gesetz. Vom dichterischen Vermächtnis Adalbert Stifters*. Antrittsvorlesung gehalten am 14. März 1967 an der Universität Salzburg (Salzburg/Munich: Anton Pustet, 1969), 12; Schmidt refers to Ernst Bertram, "Nietzsche, die Briefe Adalbert Stifters lesend," in *Möglichkeiten. Ein Vermächtnis* (Pfullingen: Neske, 1958), 201-222.

[23] Adalbert Stifter, *Bunte Steine*, 15 [see endnote 2].

MATHEMATICS IN MUSIL

Randall R. Dipert

U.S. Military Academy (West Point NY) / University at Buffalo (SUNY)

1. Introduction

In a recent review in *The New Yorker*, John Updike writes of "the scarcely scalable volcanic cones which time and lessening literacy have made of Joyce, Musil, Mann, and even Kafka."[1] It is true that Musil has been dealt with harshly during the past few decades. Interest in Robert Musil seems to have peaked in the nineteen-seventies, and in this sense, the following essay arrives some decades too late.

Musil, I will argue, is a philosopher's novelist, and perhaps that explains his vast readership. In this essay, I will pay special attention to the extremely important role that mathematics, mathematical objects, and mathematizing have in Musil's major works of prose. One of the most important writers of fiction after the Enlightenment, Robert Musil is almost unique in having extolled mathematics, precision, and the methods and conclusions of the natural sciences as a cure for the intellectual and especially emotional ills of the contemporary soul. Others in Musil's milieu, notably Karl Kraus, advocated precision in language as a moral matter. Kraus, however, exemplified this perfect language without describing it, as did Musil. Nevertheless, in Musil's novels and essays, philosophers get more than they want. Most philosophers view novels as a form of entertainment, or perhaps at best as exalted high art, but certainly not as a proper mode of philosophizing. But for Musil, novels were the ideal form of philosophizing.[2] And despite the association of his name with scientific philosophy and the Vienna Circle, Musil's account of mathematical objects is nothing like the positivistic one; in fact, one can categorize him as anti-empiricist in several important ways.

Robert Musil, the legendary Austrian writer of fiction and several essays, was born in 1880 and died in exile in Switzerland in 1942. He is best known for the novelette *The Confusions of the Fledgling Törless*, and the very long novel *The Man without Qualities*, which, because of its length and unfinished state at the time of the author's death, it is something of a German *Remembrance of Things Past*. *Törless* had a second life as one of the first films of Volker Schlöndorff (*Der junge Törless*, 1964) and thus as a progenitor of the German New Wave Cinema. In addition to the writers of fiction Updike cites, Musil is also often associated with fellow Austrian Broch and the Germans Döblin and Hesse; nevertheless, the comparison of Musil to

Writing the Austrian Traditions: Relations between Philosophy and Literature.
Ed. Wolfgang Huemer and Marc-Oliver Schuster. Edmonton, Alberta:
Wirth-Institute for Austrian and Central European Studies, 2003. pp. 143-159.

any of these writers remains a contentious issue. Unlike other novelists, such as Thomas Mann, Musil was not known outside the German speaking world, even to literary professionals, until well after his death.[3] In 1990, with the publication of the fine and aptly titled *Precision and Soul*, Musil the essayist gained some recognition in the English-speaking world, long after general interest in Musil had peaked. His reputation as an essayist in the German- and English-speaking worlds has lagged far behind those of Karl Kraus or Walter Benjamin, to name an incongruous pair.

Musil was born in Klagenfurt, Carinthia; the male members of his family pursued military, medical, and, especially, engineering professions.[4] His father was a professor of engineering in Brno – the family was originally Czech, as the name suggests – and Musil himself was sent to military schools in his Gymnasium years. He subsequently studied engineering. Breaking with family tradition and wishes, he departed for Berlin, where he studied philosophy and psychology at the university and completed a doctoral dissertation on epistemology and Mach in 1908.[5] Before World War I, he had already ventured into writing fiction and edited *Die neue Rundschau* in Berlin. After the war, he remained in Vienna mostly and published the first volume of *The Man without Qualities* in 1930 to some acclaim, especially in Germany. He maintained a serious interest in science and scientific philosophy, and he was a member of a salon circle associated with Richard von Mises in Berlin; he had some contact with the Vienna Circle, mainly Neurath, and by association, with Wittgenstein. Although he suffered to some extent from agoraphobia, Musil frequented the famous coffee houses and was especially well acquainted with the dramatist Hofmannsthal. The young Wittgenstein lived, for a briefly overlapping period in the early nineteen-twenties, in the same building as Musil, on Rasumofskygasse in Vienna's Third District, but in a different section of the building with a different staircase.[6] There is no record of any personal interaction, but it is likely that they passed each other on the street, and Musil must surely have noticed the construction in 1926-1928 of what we know as the outrageously conspicuous Wittgenstein Haus only a block away. In any case, Musil had by 1933, if not earlier, become aware of Wittgenstein's *Tractatus*.[7]

Incongruous as it might seem, philosophers with any taste at all for fiction could be tempted to view Musil as the literary face of the Vienna Circle. One might correctly surmise that Musil was a knowledgable and sympathetic proponent of a largely Viennese type of "scientific philosophy." The rubric "scientific philosophy" can, in my view, be extended to include Mach, early Wittgenstein, the Vienna Circle, and even the symbolic, mathematics-style logic of Frege and his heirs.[8] Musil's 1908 dissertation on Mach gives weight to this suggestion. The opening sentences of the dissertation express the view that philosophy cannot possibly address crucial questions without attending to theories in science, especially basic notions of mathematical physics, and without considering the impact of methodological and epistemological issues of the sort Mach had pioneered. He also believed that science would have to take into account "philosophical" topics – even if the origins of these topics ultimately derive from the work of scientists thinking about science. And, at least in the early part of the century, the professional lives of Einstein and Bohr (and perhaps Dirac as well) are a vindication of Musil's thesis that philosophy must impact physics. What we call Anglo-American or "analytic" philosophy, brought to England and North America by German-speaking refugees and also surviving to some extent in Austria and Germany), confirms his thesis that the exact sciences can profitably impact philosophy.

For a novelist and essayist to have expressed these views in 1908 strikes the contemporary philosophical mind as intriguing to say the least. One expects to find disciplined, scientifically-educated "philosophical" novels that avoid the usual paeans to love, feeling, and a-rational ethical and political conflict. A novel for Quine, so to speak. Even if fiction must ultimately be about non-existent entities (at least Musil did not write poetry, surely a sign of good analytic-philosophical taste), one still has reason to hope that Musil's essays contain a wise, succinct exposition and defense of scientific philosophy, maybe even an original philosophical theory. One imagines a German-speaking Bertrand Russell, much more disciplined of course, and without such a feirce need for funds and popular influence.

It is certainly true that Musil did not adapt his style and subject matter to appeal to popular taste. But this virtue led to grinding poverty and personal tragedy, especially during his years of exile in Switzerland. He ended in the hopeless professional situation of having his writings banned for ninety percent of its potential readers, but without the international cachet of a name such as Mann or Broch. Writing in German for an educated audience, but one which at the time was scattered and reduced in numbers, affected writers of the German-speaking diaspora differently, but few were hit harder than Musil and Zweig.[9]

Musil has nevertheless deeply failed to accommodate the myth that has been erected around him, for several reasons. First, he is philosophically elusive. His fictional characters do not go about declaiming his or any precise philosophical views – they are too "real" for that,[10] and his irony ubiquitous; similarly, his essays are extremely digressive and lack all hint of systematic philosophical exposition or argumentation.[11] In style at least, he remains firmly a man of letters – without degenerating into the mere *Feuilleton* writer as criticized by Kraus. A craftsman-like art alone guides his fiction and essays, not organized truths and arguments. Second, he does not disparage or outcast as nonsensical the aesthetic, ethical, religious, and especially emotional components of human life as the Logical Positivists so famously proposed doing. In this respect he is closer to the Wittgenstein of the *Tractatus*. But perhaps quite unlike Wittgenstein, Musil proposed analyzing feelings and desires[12] in a liberal way, with recourse to science and literature, even in the analysis of a mass murderer's motives. Musil was more philosophical psychologist than mystical philosopher. Third, the methods and "mystical" objects of mathematics function in a very important, partly allegorical way in his writing. Mathematics serves for Musil a perfect model of human thought, with no suggestion of tautology or the lack of substance associated with positivistic, analytic, or formalist accounts of mathematics and its objects. Understanding mathematical reasoning and its objects is critical to understanding Musil, since mathematical issues lead us most directly to what we can regard as his philosophical theory.

II. Musil as Man of Letters

With regard to the predominantly "literary" character of Musil, it has often been said that Ulrich, the mathematician-hero of *The Man without Qualities*, is Musil's mouthpiece. I am extremely wary of this assumption. Although Ulrich's utterances do overlap considerably with Musil's own views, Ulrich is to some extent intentionally portrayed as a naif. It is uncertain where Musil ends and Ulrich begins: what represents the admirable efforts of a scrupulous and detached mathematician and what represents bumbling or merely emotionally detached behavior. While Musil clearly considered a mathematical type of approach a valuable instrument in our understanding of the whole phenomenal world, I am sure he did not see this as an easy and straightforward procedure and wanted to stress the difficulties. Not all applications of "mathematics" – perhaps not even many – are plausible, and some are purely comical. The comic, the ironic, and the serious and philosophical are rarely seen in pure and isolated form in Musil: his is an art designed to obstruct and sabotage stupid critics. The teenage Törless is of course a still more unlikely and at best partial spokesman for Musil himself.[13]

With Musil's essays, too, we are frustrated in our search for a "philosophy," although for different reasons. There is no question of who is speaking in his essays; there are no distinct voices and less irony. Indeed, we find titles that are more than faintly philosophical: "The Religious Spirit, Modernism, and Metaphysics," "The Mathematical Man," "Commentary on Metapsychics," and "Mind and Experience" as translated in *Precision and Soul* as well as essays such as "Analysis and Synthesis," "Form and Content," and various essays suggestive of aesthetic and ethical themes in the collection of *Essays und Reden* (*Gesammelte Schriften* 8). In "The Religious Spirit, Modernism, and Metaphysics," we encounter instead of philosophical theorizing a kind of perceptive philosophical joke that sounds faintly like Woody Allen[14]:

> But however one goes about it, as soon as one goes beyond the boundaries science has drawn for itself, not much knowledge will be achieved; and all metaphysical systems are bad because they apply their reason in the wrong way [...]: proving the reality of the hereafter instead of (for a more demanding taste) first trying to make such a thing "possible." In this fashion the various metaphysics build bridges, but to a tiresome place. In Kantian terms: all metaphysics are transcendental, and the transcendent remains pure boredom.
> (*Precision and Soul*, p. 24; modified translation by RRD)

To an extent, Musil predates the Vienna Circle's attempt to do "without" metaphysics, but with a wisecrack. The essay "The Mathematical Man" is somewhat less mocking as we will see shortly.

III. Scientifically Analyzing Emotions through Literature

Musil is perhaps best seen as a neo-Enlightenment figure, who viewed rationality, especially as guided by mathematics and the natural sciences, as salvation from the worst ills that had befallen humanity. Almost to a unique extent since Goethe, the literary man Musil stands alone in this praise of rationality and also in his knowledge and embrace of contemporary scientific thinking. Few of his commentators and admirers in the twentieth century, and especially in the last decades, have shown clear signs of sharing this vision and Musil's own appreciation and knowledge of the exact sciences – especially mathematics.[15] Appreciation of him has focused instead on his style (especially his irony and distance); on his place in European, Viennese, and German-speaking cultural history; and on his effort to give rich psychological portrayals of his characters. However, his very idea of psychology and how to practise it, and indeed of the makeup of what he persisted in calling the *soul* (*Seele*), far outstrip most conventional conceptions of psychology, which are still overshadowed in the contemporary literary world by the figure of Freud. Musil is not to be read as one would read Kafka or Schnitzler; for one thing, he contemptuously rejected psychoanalysis.

Musil's overall attitude to this investigation is nicely summarized in the quotation that inspired Pike's and Luft's volume of translations, *Precision and Soul*:

> We do not have too much intellect and too little soul, but too little precision in matters of the soul.

This remark is strikingly out of step with the prevailing view, in both the world at large and in the arts and humanities, that modern life has displaced feeling, intuition, and depth with cold calculation and thereby impoverished life, or even that the exclusive cultivation of rationality naturally results in a Fascist monster. This is based upon a fashionable opposition of rationality on the one hand and our emotional and conative lives on the other. The twofold nature of humankind was already a theme in Romantic thought, but Freud's dramatization of the "irrationality" of our deepest impulses – whatever we may ultimately think of the merit of his theories – has pushed these ideas still deeper into our collective consciousness. A Musilian vision that avoids this false – deeply and perniciously false – opposition is contrarian and of vital importance.

We might first contemplate the "standard" model of human life and action in contemporary analytic philosophy. It holds that our actions and world-view spring from two sources: our beliefs on the one hand, and our desires and emotions on the other. Belief formation and revision, as cognitive science calls it, are held to have their ideal in rational mechanisms that are describable by various forms of rules in logic. However, our desires and emotions arise from who-knows-where, as a kind of arbitrary given: arising from instinct and bodily compulsion, perhaps, acculturation, whim, and so on.

According to my reading of Musil's model of human life, mental life has desires and emotions that are almost entirely intentional, triggered by beliefs from the realm of reason, and directed toward cognitive objects that are shared with our beliefs.[16] Furthermore there is a normativity, various dimensions of what I call an orthotic quality (a "correctness"), that is as active in our emotional life as it is for beliefs. For one thing we can have, or lack, clarity in our emotional objects no less than in the object of our beliefs; likewise, a case can be made that some emotions are appropriate or well-founded in much the same way that beliefs are justified.

These two claims[17] "rationalize" desire and emotion. Second, as contemporary philosophers of science since Kuhn and Feyerabend have controversially sought to demonstrate, what count as good, even wise, scientific beliefs and inferences may have a-rational components that defy strict or complete algorithms. I would add that beliefs, precisely like desires and emotions, invariably involve feelings that vary widely in both quality and intensity. Even to pursue a life in science, one needs a motivation – an attraction, fascination, or passion about the science's objects. Together, these maneuvers have the effect of giving emotion and desire some form of "logic," and of injecting feeling and a complex evaluative procedure into belief (and related doxastic states such as hope and myth).

Musil believed in the kinship and intertwined complexity of beliefs, logic, sensations, desires, and emotions as atomic feelings; the characters in his fiction are a working out of these theories and a "combinatorial" portrayal of how we should see human beings. My primary evidence is a remarkable document, "Profile of a Program," originally dating from 1912 (it exists in two versions and was heavily annotated, perhaps at much later dates). It begins with these remarks:

> The Soul is a complex interpenetration of feeling and intellect[18] [...] The element of growth in this pairing lies in the intellect. To talk about depth, [...] greatness, or charm of feeling is misleading; notice from what primitive relationships these metaphors are still borrowed. It is intellect that brings these quarter-tone gradations upwards into feeling. (pp. 10-11; modified translation by RRD)

I interpret these remarks as follows. First, our conceptualizations of feelings and their differentiable texture are entirely derived from their relationships as understood through the intellect. We do not have simple names or simple thoughts for simple feelings. In contemporary and infinitely misleading parlance, the life of our feelings is "constructed." If we admit sensations as a type of feeling in this wide sense, we have the beginnings of a view that is not likely to agree with the fundamental sense-data and protocol sentences of later logical positivism. Second, I would also like to see this as inching toward the "Austrian" view of the intentionality of all mental life: even or especially our emotions and desires are directed toward complex thought-objects.[19]

For the purpose of tying together my second and third themes, the literary analysis of feelings together with mathematics as model, I quote a later passage from Musil's "Profile of a Program":

> Mathematical daring, dissolving souls into their elements and unlimited permutation of these elements; here everything is related to everything else and can be built up from these elements. But this construction demonstrates not "this is what it is made of," but "this is how its pieces fit together. (p. 13)

Here we see a cautious "phenomenalist" atomism, and in his fiction we see the combinatorics of this theory in action. Musil's case for the application of exactness (*Exaktheit*) – methodical care and precision in matters of the soul – reaches its climax in Part I, Chapter 61 of *The Man without Qualities*, namely in Ulrich's idea of the "Utopia of Exactness." But even here, the exaggerated rhetoric ("utopia") sounds a note of irony and distances Musil himself from what may be the flawed excesses of Ulrich's particular application of the method.

IV. The Fledgling Törless and Mathematics

The Confusions of the Fledgling Törless is a coming-of-age novel, set in a stifling military school. It is the story of Törless initially taking part in, then rejecting, the exceptionally cruel torture of a weaker fellow student, Basini. One might say it is part Hesse, but also part Kafka: there are dark, mysterious forces at work. It is a haunting story of youth, complicity, brutal physical-sexual male dominance, and hapless adult educators. Its dominant theme is moral-emotional confusion that parallels Törless's conceptual confusion about, of all things, i: the square root of -1.

Although a very early work (from 1906, when Musil was 26), *Törless* is both precursor and miniature of the massive *Man without Qualities*. Törless himself is variously described as both over-sensitive and over-thoughtful. He is even described as "without character," as someone whose personality and views were products of his friends' influence and whatever he happened to be reading. As an only child, he suffers greatly at the initial separation from his parents in experiencing *Sehnsucht*. Musil describes Törless's feelings, poorly understood by his teachers, at length and with great precision. Törless is described as having a hole in his emotional personality. His "confusions" accumulate and intensify with respect to his relationships with his friends Beineberg and Reiting, with the victim Basini, as well as his own swirling sensations and feelings, and his awareness of the vaguest of sexual feelings. Precisely in the middle of the chronology of these confusions, and also intellectually mirroring them, is his confrontation with imaginary numbers. Törless expresses the difficulty this way: "Every number, whether positive or negative, when squared yields a positive number. Thus there cannot be any actual number that is the square root of something negative" (p. 70). Beineberg is patient but does not share Törless's quandary. Lacking Törless's "oversensitivity," Beineberg is completely untroubled; for him, that is just the way it is done. Beineberg says that there are, of course, no such actual numbers, and that is why they are called "imaginary." It is as if we set the table for a deceased person, knowing he will not actually arrive and eat. We just pretend – for whatever reasons – that there are such numbers. This has its own use and if one did not accede to this idealistic, virtual element, then there could not be mathematics! Törless gradually concedes the metaphysically unresolvable problem about imaginary numbers. But now a deeper mystery arises for him. How do most people come to accept this with so little trouble? Where does the power come from to hold on to such a figment of one's imagination so that one ends up right? How can people set aside the scruples of reason, the usual standards of reason that applied mathematics enshrines, with only the consolation that it "will work out" (p. 71)? This becomes a meditation on the inapplicability of the dully real and the usefulness of the merely imaginary.[20]

With trepidation, Törless makes an appointment with their young and accomplished mathematics teacher. The talented teacher is, however, far more impatient than Beineberg and is made nervous by Törless's difficulties. He describes the reality that these imaginary numbers have as a "necessity of reason" (*Denknotwendigkeit*), but he is unwilling to demonstrate this necessity, instead saying that it is beyond Törless's present ability to understand. In order to explain the problem, the teacher would have to spell out, in a strict (*streng*) and intellectually-disciplined (*wissenschaftlich*) way all the involved assumptions (*Voraussetzungen*). And to understand these, Törless would need to understand ten times more than he presently understands about mathematics. Furthermore, the instructor does not have the time to begin this enterprise and advises Törless that, for the moment, he must simply have "faith" (*Glauben*).

Törless sits silently and is unwilling to leave, awaiting further explanation. As a last resort, the instructor grabs a book of Kant's on ethics and says that the problem is clearly explained in the book. When you try to reach the basis for understanding ethics, the teacher says, you encounter the "necessities of thinking." Mathematics is likewise, and that is the proof of imaginary numbers! Törless is still not satisfied, grabs the book on Kant's ethics, and starts to look through it. The instructor retreats, interjecting that the volume of Kant was not itself the required proof but only an example of the kind of proof that was needed. Törless subsequently buys this book and others that he has seen in the mathematician's room. He tries to read them, but he cannot make sense of them and recalls the copies of Kant in his father's office, which, like some relics in the Holy of Holies, were admired but only on special occasions actually touched. "One esteems [such books] only because one is glad that, thanks to their existence, one doesn't actually have to worry any more about such things" (p. 75). Beineberg's justification is pragmatic, the mathematician's justification is both transcendental and, as a last resort, an appeal to authority. Musil scorns them all.

A casual reading of the story of Törless might suggest that Musil is drawing a parallel between the metaphysical status of objects of mathematics and those of theology, and advocating a similar attitude of faith in both. Mathematics might then cast an indirectly positive light on religion – or religion a suspicious light on mathematics. Musil denies this affinity, however (although he tempts us with its presentation). It is Beineberg, not Törless, who first recognizes the parallel between religion and the mathematician's account of the proper attitude toward imaginary numbers. Törless is earlier described as having a near total contempt for religion and traditional piety.[21] In the academy's inquisition concerning Basini's torture that closes the book, Törless declares that the only thing similar to his confused attitude toward Basini and his complicity in the torture of the latter, is his attitude to the imaginary numbers. He is naturally asked to explain this strange connection. He explains by appealing to his thoughts about what is awe-inspiring and unimaginable ("Ungeheuerliches [...] nicht Vorstellbares," p. 130f), and the need to grapple with issues for which our thought is inadequate, and which require quite another, inner certainty than is provided by thinking (p. 131). The academy's faculty-jury, prompted by the priest-theologian's understanding of this language, provides an escape route for Törless, namely that he was motivated in the Basini affair by a misguided religiosity. Törless emphatically denies this.

V. *The Mathematical Man (Der mathematische Mensch, 1913)*

One widely quoted remark of Musil's is that after reading overwrought contemporary German literature, one should solve some problems in integral calculus in order to regain one's balance. Musil has had the misfortune, probably more now than in his own time, of having few readers and critics who are mathematically educated and share his mathematical sympathies. My survey of the secondary literature reveals that, remarkably, several major works do not mention the topic of mathematics, most at best closely paraphrase Musil's remarks, and some feel the need to explain in footnotes what would have been obvious to the reader whom Musil had in mind.[22] Musil has by and large received the attention only of students of German and comparative literature.[23]

"The Mathematical Man" is a remarkable popular essay. Even its title is remarkable. Although Hermann Broch concerned himself extensively with philosophical topics in his last years,[24] his "mathematical man," the mathematician of his essay "Methodisch konstruiert" (published first in 1917 and reprinted as the second in his collection of stories, *The Guiltless: Novel in 11 Short Stories*)[25] is a pathetic figure by comparison. While Musil's essay is indeed penetrating, it is also subtle and elusive; it characteristically avoids giving the curious reader the desired glib portrayal of mathematics.

Musil mainly sees mathematics as a "triumph of intellectual organization" that allows one to perform operations quickly and correctly that would otherwise be error-prone and take days (this seems to be a twist on Mach's theme of the "economy of research"). Musil bristles at the suggestion that some of the branches of pure mathematics have as yet no application and are therefore worthless: he sees mathematics as an enormous savings account that we have wisely stored in the bank. Mathematics is "incomparable. For our entire civilization has arisen with its assistance; we know no other way; the needs it serves are completely satisfied by it, and its aimless abundance is of the uncriticizable kind of irreducible facts" (Pike and Luft, pp. 40-41). According to Musil, most of us, even engineers and physicists, know little about mathematics nor do we appreciate it. For the professional mathematician, however, it has many rooms and its "windows do not open to the outside, but into adjoining rooms." For the professional mathematician it is a matter of a "total surrender and a passionate devotion." Mathematics was brought to "the most beautiful state of existence," but the mathematicians themselves discovered that it was without foundations, and that this foundationlessness could not be corrected (Musil possibly has in mind the discovery of non-Euclidean geometries and especially the difficulties in giving calculus a basis through analysis and eventually set theory, or Russell's Paradox; his views echo Törless's misgivings and anticipate the final *coup de grâce* in Gödel's theorems). "But the machines work! [...] The mathematician endures this intellectual scandal in exemplary fashion, that is, with confidence and pride in the devilish riskiness of his intellect."

What appears to have been the rejection of Beineberg's casual mathematical pragmatism in *Törless* has here become a modest endorsement: "the machines work." Despite this later view, I do not think that Musil is suggesting that their "working" alone justifies belief. Rather, as the context makes clear, their successful application should make us hesitate before impulsively sweeping imaginary numbers aside despite their foundationlessness. After the Second World War, the engineer in Musil realizes that this same mathematics that he admired plotted the trajectories of poison-gas shells. But as Phillip Payne notes about the relevant Part I Chapter 11 of *Man without Qualities*, "neither mathematician nor non-mathematician escapes unscathed [...]. There, with even handed criticism, the narrator leaves the matter" (p. 151). The "humanist" criticism of mathematics and engineering as a typically amoral or even immorally detached form of thought steadily rose between the world wars and then especially after mathematics' crucial involvement in the development of nuclear weapons. However, one might as well denounce writing and journalism – or pens and loudspeakers – for their misuse, an argument toward which Plato points perhaps. Musil probably could not have grasped such a point at all nor understood the appropriateness of Payne's remark about "even-handedness." Only exceptionally weak and mathematically ill-informed minds could regard mathematics and mathematical thinking – clear thinking itself – as harmful.

What follows is, in my view, the most important and beautiful passage in Musil's essays. It is nothing less than the appropriate antidote to the twentieth century's often anti-intellectual "humanism":

> After the Enlightenment the rest of us lost our courage. A minor failure was enough to turn us away from reason, and we allow every barren enthusiast to inveigh against the intentions of a d'Alembert or a Diderot as mere rationalism. We screech in favor of feeling over intellect and forget that – apart from exceptional cases – feeling is by itself utterly incomprehensible. In this way we have ruined our imaginative literature to such an extent that, whenever one reads two German novels in a row, one must solve an integral equation to balance out one's diet [...] [The way of mathematicians] is a parable for the intellectual of the future. (p. 42; modified translation by RRD)

VI. *Musil and Contemporary Philosophy*

To an extent, I believe I have tried to do what I earlier suggested was impossible: to extract from Musil's fiction and non-fiction a "philosophy," particularly a philosophy of mathematics that serves as a template for the rest of philosophical theorizing. Perhaps the best method of continuing this difficult task is the *via negativa*, discussing what Musil does *not* endorse, despite the rumors and false associations to the contrary. He is clearly neither a Machian positivist nor a full-fledged logical positivist. His dissertation on Mach is already more critical of an epistemology based purely on sense-experience than one would expect. He does not see sense-experience as a priviliged feeling, as a type of human experience on which all other constructs are to be based. Likewise, he does not see the laboratories for the natural sciences as solely those places in which we record and organize sense experiences alone: the literary realm can also distinctively contribute to our knowledge of humanity and the world by being a laboratory for all forms of human experience. This train of thought puts him at a point surprisingly distant from twentieth-century positivists. He leaves their sense-observation laboratories and roams the streets and minds of the cities. He observes souls, not the skin of bodies. The literary and the aesthetic, rather than being an often distracting nonsense-buzz, become instead necessary laboratory instruments for serious observation. Musil's motivation is "scientific" but by putting art at its center, his conclusion is almost an inversion of the verificationist theory of meaning.

Musil is also not a strident foundationalist. While he extols the now typical model of analysis of human experience into parts, he is unwilling to characterize these parts – as sense-data, for example. Similarly, he does not believe that such reductions demonstrate the importance of these "ultimate" elements. Instead, they show us about the relationships of the parts. In this respect he has more in common with the neutral monists than the later phenomenalists (who were perhaps idealists in some stage of denial). Also, given his "kaleidoscope" approach to the combinatorial analysis of the soul, there is reason to suspect that he did not believe that there was a single, uniquely correct analysis, but many different analyses that altogether cast light on explaining the phenomena of human understanding. Unlike the monistic analyzers such as Carnap, he is possibly suggestive of later pluralists such as Feyerabend.

Although Musil was a fierce critic of traditional religions, there is a kind of ghost object of the activity of having faith that remains with us. He remains a traditionalist in refusing to endorse the Nietzschean proposal that some of us are now so advanced that we have risen above the need for such attitudes. In mathematics at least, he was pragmatist enough to agree that there are propositions that cannot be justified – and perhaps are even implausible or contradictory. Because of our need for such propositions, in order to have beliefs at all, as well as because of the peculiar accident that "they work," we must in a sense accept them. He clearly saw this as a kind of ironic and grudging embrace of mysticism.[26] This is antithetical to the Vienna Circle and also rare in the wider movement of scientific philosophy. As I have portrayed Musil's views, they are more than a little similar to the views of Wittgenstein's *Tractatus* (although the publication dates of *Törless* and "The Mathematical Man" preclude any possible influence from Wittgenstein), but are also suggestive of the view of the very late Wittgenstein in *On Certainty*.

Although an outspoken defender of the Enlightenment, Musil must also be seen as a peculiar and troubled rationalist. First, there is the unempiricist, unpositivistic nature of the criterion for enlightened belief – namely, not just through the senses. Second, there is the view that some propositions lack justification in the usual, non-pragmatic sense. And finally, there is the more remarkable view that these propositions are difficult to accept or are even contradictory. They have a kind of necessity but are, in isolation, repugnant to reason. Musil is not a happy rationalist, but a frowning one.

Musil is obviously cognizant of the same developments in mathematics and logic as were the logical positivists. But his interpretation of them is quite different. Törless's taste for logic is precisely what eventually leads to his perplexity. Logic, in a very broad sense, is not the more basic of the two disciplines. Instead, logic presents obstacles for the acceptance of mathematical propositions, which are more inspiring, more curious, and also more useful than logical truths.

Within the epistemological discussions of mathematical truths, the empiricist tradition had always had a difficulty with mathematics. Both the modal character (their neccesity) and the acquisional feel (how we think we came to accept them; why we accept them) appear quite distinct from those of empirical propositions. One just comes, usually in a flash that is little like sense observation, to recognize their abiding truth. The early empiricists, as well as their twentieth century kin, struggled to reconcile these metaphenomena. Their resolutions of this difficulty were various. Mathematical truths are definitionally true; these truths are built into our definitions of human-constructed mathematical concepts, although not self-evidently so. A variant of this view is that mathematical truths derive from metaphysically and epistemologically deeper truths of logic. Some had earlier argued that these formulations are the only consistent arrangements of these mathematical concepts, and this gives them their truth-like status.

Empiricist theories of mathematical truths in fact have been dealt a series of blows in the last two centuries. Non-Euclidean geometries, spreading rapidly to algebra and even number theory, have taught us that there is no single consistent theory of such objects. The logical positivists rejected both empiricist and Kantian views of mathematics as synthetic *a priori*. This leaves only the position that mathematics – that is, every mathematical truth – is ultimately definitionally, analytically true.[27] Mathematical propositions are tautologies, if they are true. Logicism, the promising early twentieth-century view that deeper truths of logic metaphysically or epistemologically anchored mathematical truths, has died a more agonizing death. First, the intuitive logical truths of Frege and Cantor turned out to be more infested with contradiction than any decent mathematical theory ever had been. This led to more complicated and artificial efforts, that we now know as set theory, in order to obtain a unifying approach to mathematical truths. While the result – modern foundations of mathematics – is an artful and often helpful creation, few have noticed that the original desideratum of a metaphysical or epistemological obviousness and anchoring quality seems to have become forgotten. Furthermore, these foundations have arbitrary components, and Gödel turned on his Viennese colleagues to show that logical truth would never be able to anchor mathematical truth in the way they had hoped. Gödel himself abandoned this project of analytically anchoring mathematics through tautologies of logic and became an outright mathematical Platonist. He believed we have a peculiarly stable insight into mathematical truths, but that this is neither observational nor logico-definitional in origin and character.

Musil appreciated fully only the early stages of these developments, but it is interesting that he *never* was enamored of the wrong-headed view that mathematical truths are in some ways either definitionally true or disguised truths of logic. However, I do not think that Musil precisely took Gödel's route either. While our attitude toward deities is in some ways *like* our attitudes toward (fringe) mathematical objects, this is not to say that these numbers do exist.[28] Instead, I propose that Musil's approach is one of justifying individual – especially slightly repugnant – mathematical truths through the systematic workability of the whole mathematical edifice. For various reasons I prefer to call this a "holistic theory" of mathematical truth rather than a "pragmatic theory."[29] This is not to claim that these propositions are precisely *truths*, and perhaps not to say that we should precisely *believe* them. Whatever it is, Musil's conception is very distant from the views of Mach or the Vienna Circle.

V. Conclusion

The ideal for thinking about both ourselves and the world that Musil puts before us is a kind of scientific humanism. His vision is in some ways an optimistic Enlightenment vision that reaches back to the eighteenth century rather than being part of nineteenth- or twentieth-century thinking. While Musil is surely a pessimist about the present states of our modern souls and about our present modes of analyzing souls – from psychotherapy to logical positivism – he is ambitious and optimistic about our ability to do so and the prospects for success. His proposal is manifestly not eliminativist or dismissive in, for example, seeking to dismiss all of our experience or to suggest that it is probably reducible to physical explanation. For sense perception and what it confirms as true is only one mode of human experience, and is not privileged. Modern reductivism and eliminativism have succeeded in diverting us from an effort to analyze and understand our psyches. Rather, they promise that eventually our psyches can be ultimately explained by physics, somehow. In contrast, Musil's approach is a "psychological realism," taking the swirling and ill-understood myths, hopes, emotions, and desires – those features of inner life that novels above all other art forms explore – as the data for theorizing (it is axiomatic since Kant that we must first understand the perceiver, including the perceiver's motives and limitations, before we can understand the perceived). To this realm we are then to apply the distance and discipline that mathematics alone provides. We analyze our souls, we analyze relationships, and we construct plausible combinations of feelings. Novels are then the large-scale, "realistic" thought-experiments of this new mathematics of the soul.

I find it hard not to be smitten with this vision. It reconnects C.P. Snow's "two cultures." It puts back together the Humpty Dumpty of our fractured humanist/scientist modes of thought. It demands the precision and discipline that one sees (only) in the sciences, especially in mathematics. There is no place for political posturing, for merely fuzzy feeling,[30] or glorifying our ignorance or accidental career choice (such as being ignorant of, having failed, or having a distaste for calculus). But likewise Musil's vision does not seek to ignore the obvious. It does not claim that the world is just the clean Moosbrugger-less world of protocol sentences or quarks.[31] It underscores that our feelings are "real"; they are as real or more real than subatomic particles or the square root of -1. But this is only a paraphrase of Musil himself:

> The misfortune is that people who are concerned with such questions today [i.e., such as mysticism and the spirit] have little understanding of

the virtues of clear thinking [...]; while others, who would have such understanding, have for the most part no intimation that there is something here that has been grasped at a great depth but been lost again on the way back to the surface. [...] With us, artistic and scientific thinking do not yet come into contact with each other. The problems of a middle zone between the two remain unresolved.[32]

---

[1] April 3, 2000, p. 89; he contrasts these writers with the more approachable Proust.

[2] Thus like Wittgenstein, and unlike the Vienna Circle, Musil represents a break with the traditional style of expository writing — in an artistic direction.

[3] David S. Luft, "Introduction," in Robert Musil, *Precision and Soul: Essays and Addresses*. Ed. and Trans. by Burton Pike and David S. Luft, Chicaco: University of Chicago Press, 1990, p. xvi.

[4] My colleague at West Point, LTC Elliott Gruner, alerted me to the probability that our shared terms of employment had unconsciously prodded me into renewing my interest in Musil, a one-time officer, reportedly having a military bearing, and the author of the notorious *Törless*. Gruner reports considerable cadet interest in Musil at the time he attended West Point (though not a single work by Musil is in the library); he has used Musil's books as texts for a course at the U.S. Air Force Academy on military academies in fiction.

[5] *Beitrag zur Beurteilung der Lehren Machs*, reprinted in 1980. Musil's examining committee was composed of the well-known Stumpf ("sehr gut"), Riehl ("befriedigend"), Rubens in physics as *Nebenfach* ("sehr gut"), and Schwarz in mathematics ("befriedigend"); see Marie-Louise Roth, *Robert Musil: Ethik und Ästhetik. Zum theoretischen Werk des Dichters*. Munich: Paul List Verlag, pp. 346-347.

[6] Musil lived at 20, Wittgenstein at 24 Rasumofskygasse; Janik and Veigl err when they say Musil was "one stairway further"; it was two (Allan Janik and Hans Veigl, *Wittgenstein in Vienna: A Biographical Excursion through the City and its History*. Vienna: Springer, 1998, p. 184).

[7] Janik and Veigl, *Wittgenstein in Vienna*, p. 185.

[8] Musil himself includes the logico-mathematical tradition in a remark from 1912 that echoes the first sentences of his dissertation: "But all intellectual daring today lies in the natural sciences. We shall not learn from Goethe, Hebbel, or Hölderlin, but from Mach, Lorentz, Einstein, Minkowski, *from Couturat, Russell, Peano*..." (Musil, *Precision and Soul*, p. 13; my italics). Pike and Luft translate – here not precisely enough for my purposes – "exakte Wissenschaften" as "natural sciences"; however, "natural sciences" would exclude mathematized economics and maybe even mathematics itself.

[9] While not Jewish, Musil had left Berlin after a stay from 1931-33 largely because of distaste with political developments. Further printing of his books in Austria and Germany became impossible in 1938, presumably because of the Jewish owners of Musil's last publisher, Bermann-Fischer (Wilfried Berghahn, *Robert Musil in Selbstzeugnissen und Bilddokumenten*. Reinbek bei Hamburg: Rowohlt, 1963, p. 128). He was encouraged to seek a lifting of the ban through special pleading to the Propaganda Ministry, but rejected this option and left Austria, ostensibly for health reasons, first traveling to Italy and then to Zurich and Geneva.

[10] In order to present a philosophy in a narrative life such as a novel, with actions and feelings as well as thoughts and utterances, one would have to have a philosophical view that was thoroughly integrated with human life. The philosophy has to be liveable and not merely utterable in order to join mental life – both cognitive and emotive – with outward action. Perhaps Socrates' life and philosophy would work but Wittgenstein's later life would have, for example, problems in both plot and narrative, so to speak. The pregnant silences are too numerous. A negative model of what I have in mind as a philosophical novel also involves much speechifying, such as one encounters in, say, Galt's speech in Rand's *Atlas Shrugged* (at least, however, hers is a philosophy of thought and action.) Likewise, one might say that Camus's Meursault is a plausible union of thought (at least pensiveness) and inaction as a kind of action. Kantian, Schopenhauerian, and more generally idealist novel-heroes are scarcely imaginable to me. Likewise I cannot imagine a Carnapian or a Quinean novel-hero, for how can we have a novelistic development when action and ethics, emotions, desires, and aesthetics are such sidestepped mysteries?

[11] See Luft, "Introduction" to Robert Musil, *Precision and Soul*: "he believed that most of the inherited fund of philosophical argument was locked into words and concepts that hardly touch the life and feelings of the average person in our civilization. He believed, indeed, that the proper philosophy of our time is to have no philosophy" (pp. xix-xx). I doubt if Musil was so concerned with the "average person" and I think one can argue that the available philosophies and terminology were the problem – philosophy as choosing from the smorgasbord of the history of philosophy – not philosophy itself.

[12] It is risky to summarize Wittgenstein's attitudes toward these conative realms, but the extremely lean aesthetic of the *Tractatus* and his architecture, and to a certain extent his known literary tastes, suggest a neo-Stoical effort to banish strong feelings of the sort we see in Romantic, late Romantic, and *fin-de-siècle* literature, not to "understand" them.

[13] Schlöndorff departs from Musil's mask of literary integrity by drastically changing Törless's final speech before the military academy's inquisition into a thinly-veiled criticism of the gullible and rudderless masses who followed the Nazis. This altered speech may be significant in postwar history as one of the first signs of serious, internal denazification in the FRG, but it is more editorial than art – a serious aesthetic flaw in the works of Schlöndorff and Grass, I believe. (I nevertheless do not think it is *impossible* to combine art with political expression, even serious German-Austrian postwar *meae culpae*.)

[14] See Woody Allen, "My Philosophy," in *Getting Even*. New York: Vintage Books, 1978, pp. 21-25.

[15] Ulrich's "he loved mathematics because of the kind of people who could not endure it" (I, 11; p. 37). For example, Roth's summary of the point of "The Mathematical Man" – which does not mention the details of imaginary numbers – is the banal "Ratio und Irratio berühren sich" (p. 84). Roth also cites the appearance of a volume *Mathematik und Dichtung* (1969) as proving Musil's prophesy (p. 367). I view it as an exception that proves this generalization still holds. See also Cay Hehner's *Erkenntnis und Freiheit* (Munich: Wilhelm Fink Verlag, 1994), in which there is no mention of mathematics even under a discussion of "logic." I have not examined Thomas Sebastian's forthcoming *Beyond Epic Simplicity: The Intersection of Literature, Philosophy, & Science* (Camden House, forthcoming June 2000), Wilhelm Klingenberg's *Mathematik und Melancholie: Von Albrecht Dürer bis Robert Musil*, or Gerolf Jässl's "Mathematik und Mystik in Robert Musils Roman *Der Mann ohne Eigenschaften* (Eine Untersuchung über das Weltbild Ulrichs)," Dissertation, Munich 1963 (cited in Hyams, note 1, p. 96); see also the bibliography in Wilfried Berghahn, *Robert Musil*.

[16] In The *Man without Qualities* (Volume II, "From the Posthumous Papers," Chs. 52, 54-55, 58), Musil does address these issues. He rejects behaviorism (equating emotions with behaviors). He might be taken to criticize the intentionality of emotion (as a "widely held

prejudice"; p. 1271), but the target is the "unified whole" provided by the "inner relation." The subsequent notion of "appearing to be appropriate" is close to my "orthotic" quality.

[17] One notes shared mental content, the other notes parallel normativity in mechanisms or "inferences."

[18] Compare the following passage from "Mind and Experience" (1921): "A person is not only intellect, but also will, feeling, lack of awareness, and often mere actuality, like the drifting of clouds in the sky." *Pace* Luft (xxi), this is a very complicated and subtle remark. It surely echoes the interpenetration remark of "Profile," but its twist, perhaps its emphasis, is on including in a person the surprising "lack of awareness" and "mere actuality." This passage continues in a way that echoes the previous subordination of feelings to intellect: "But those who see in people only what is not achieved by reason would finally have to seek the ideal in an anthill or beehive..."

[19] I know of no passages in Musil referring to Brentano or Meinong by name.

[20] Cf. "Le réel et l'imaginaire," in Jean-Pierre Cometti, *Robert Musil de Törless à L'homme sans qualités* (Brussels, 1986), pp. 93-105.

[21] In the collapse of his friendship with and worship of the young prince (p. 20).

[22] Such as Robert Musil, *Precision and Soul*, p. 297, note 1.

[23] A more subtle appreciation of Musil's view on mathematics is, however, to be seen in some works such as the chaotic *Musil-Kommentar* (1980) by Helmut Arntzen, p. 39.

[24] Some of this work is not without value, such as his remark that the positivistic tendency of the Enlightenment is a "mode of thought that stands outside the realm of faith and must pursue, not truth but experience" quoted in T. Quinn, "'Dialektik der Verzauberung': Mystification, Enlightenment, *The Spell*," in *Hermann Broch*, ed. Stephen D. Dowden, p. 121 (quoted from Broch's "Geist und Zeitgeist," *KW* 9/2, p. 183). For a discussion of works that compare Musil and Broch, see Robert L. Roseberry, *Robert Musil: Ein Forschungsbericht* (Frankfurt a.M.: Athenäum Fischer Taschenbuch Verlag, 1974), p. 148. Broch's later work in philosophy is portrayed in the somewhat superficial *Die Philosophie Hermann Brochs* by Ernestine Schlant (Bern: Francke Verlag, 1971). Broch's views on mathematics and logic (Schlant, pp. 82-90) are of less interest than one might hope, since they appear to be an eclectic assortment of views expressed by various philosophers in the twentieth century. As summarized by Schlant, there is, for example, a formalist conception that the thoughts and their expressions in mathematical formulation are isomorph; one also finds the Russellian idea that mathematics can be defined as the theory of all possible relations between things without (monadic) properties.

[25] "Unterrichte [der "Gymnasialsupplenten"] Mathematik und Physik, kraft einer kleinen Begabung für exakte Betätigungen [...]. Denn der aus Mittelmäßigkeiten konstruierte Charakter macht sich über die Fiktivität der Dinge und Erkenntnisse wenig Gedanken" (p. 33). Appearing after *Törless* (1906), the mention of the anti-hero's "constructed character" and of the "fictional nature of things" is suggestive.

[26] Cf. B.F. Hyams, "Was ist 'säkularisierte Mystik' bei Musil?" in U. Baur and E. Castex, eds., *Robert Musil: Untersuchungen*, pp. 85-98.

[27] See Rudolf Carnap, "The Old and the New Logic," esp. pp. 140-143, and Hans Hahn, "Logic, Mathematics and Knowledge of Nature," in A.J. Ayer, ed., *Logical Positivism* (New York: Free Press, 1959). A.J. Ayer's *Language, Truth and Logic* (New York: Dover, 1952) is useful, too, especially Chapter IV. Carnap and Ayer retain the more usual view that mathematical truths are "a priori" and "necessary" without much inspection of what *that* means. Ayer separates two notions of analyticity in Kant: meaning-inclusion and (unique) logical consistency. However, since inclusion (from Leibniz) was metaphorical, and might more properly be analyzed as saying that if the predicate P1 is included in the meaning of P2, this is just to say that "x is P2 but not P1" is contradictory, Kant is perhaps ultimately

vindicated. Ayer argues for the position that the truth of 7+5=12 is merely a consequence of the meanings of "7," "5," "12," the operation "+" and perhaps the meaning of the relation "=." This leaves him with the formidable task of explaining how the truth of some mathematical propositions, despite being simply expressed and consisting of what appear to be simple terms whose meaning we fully understand, can be so difficult to determine (Fermat's Theorem, Goldbach's Conjecture), and the process seemingly more like discovery than like examining a lexicon.

[28] "Ohne Zweifel war er [i.e., Ulrich] ein gläubiger Mensch, der bloß nichts glaubte" (p. 826).

[29] Perhaps the correct attitude to some of these objects is not precisely "faith" but rather a grudging resignation. This would explain Musil's own seeming ambivalence between scorning faith in Törless and endorsing it in "The Mathematical Man."

[30] The "banal zärtliche Vorstellung[en]" of the novels that Törless read (p. 11).

[31] I find it odd that Musil does not quote or refer to Terrence's famous epigram that had earlier so captured Montaigne (in many ways a kindred spirit to Musil): "Nihil humani a me alienum puto."

[32] Musil, "Commentary on a Metapsychics," in *Precision and Soul*, ed. Burton Pike and David S. Luft, 1990, pp. 57-58; the "us" refers to Germans with the exception of Nietzsche, but the passage surely applies more widely.

OEDIPUS ENDANGERED:
ATREAN INCEST AND ETHICAL RELATIONS IN MUSIL'S
DER MANN OHNE EIGENSCHAFTEN

Jill Scott
University of Toronto

In his 1931 essay, "Der bedrohte Oedipus," Robert Musil provokes the ire of the psychoanalytical establishment with this bold prediction: "Soweit ich weiß, steht heute der vorhin erwähnte Oedipuskomplex mehr denn je im Mittelpunkt der Theorie; fast alle Erscheinungen werden auf ihn zurückgeführt, und ich befürchte, daß es nach ein bis zwei Menschenfolgen keinen Oedipus mehr geben wird!" (504). Oedipus, it would seem, is the Everyman of human psychological development, an archetype, an icon, a bastion of our collective mythology.[1] The stain of this master narrative appears to seep to the very core of twentieth-century cultural consciousness. This paper argues, however, that Musil's narrative masterpiece, *Mann ohne Eigenschaften*, threatens the privilege of the psychological autocracy of the Oedipus myth.

The myth of Electra runs through the novel like a musical leitmotif, and the sibling incest mimed by Ulrich and Agathe provides the framework for the first threads of a new relational ethics as a space of intersubjectivity. I propose that Musil invokes Ernst Mach's theories of the provisional ego and sensation body in his interpretation of the Atrean myth to challenge the singular, masculine-gendered subject position of the Oedipal model. The novel's narrative trajectory eventually transcends Mach's "unrettbares Ich" and moves beyond the cliché of a Viennese crisis of identity. Through an investigation of *Körpersemiotik* and experimentation with gender in the form of androgyny, hermaphrodism, and the "new woman," Musil engages in a larger argument with modernity and the culture of militarism and morality. At the end of the aforementioned Oedipus essay, the author ventures the question: "Werden wir statt des Oedipus einen Orestes bekommen?" (504). In *Mann ohne Eigenschaften*, Musil answers this query in the affirmative.

Musil's life and work from about 1924 until his death in 1943 (exiled in Switzerland) was solely dedicated to the production of one mammoth masterpiece of literary modernism, which, by the author's own admission, had become a historical novel in the process of its creation (5, 1941).[2] *Mann ohne Eigenschaften*, a precise silhouette of the waning Habsburg Empire, is suffused at first with biting irony,

---

Writing the Austrian Traditions: Relations between Philosophy and Literature.
Ed. Wolfgang Huemer and Marc-Oliver Schuster. Edmonton, Alberta:
Wirth-Institute for Austrian and Central European Studies, 2003. pp. 160-180.

which is suddenly replaced by a poignant, almost sentimental lyricism that risks descending into the worst kind of kitsch. The seemingly endless dialog and diatribe on such lofty subjects as love,[3] morality, freedom, mysticism and social deviance, contrasted with political intrigue aimed at the general glorification of a pathetically outdated empire, is strategically crammed into the anticipatory pre-war year of 1913.

Tension also mounts around Musil's protagonist, Ulrich, whose main claim to fame is his *Eigenschaftslosigkeit*, the total absence of any defining characteristics or traits. At the age of thirty-two and entirely lacking in professional ambition, this son of a prominent Austrian aristocrat suddenly decides all at once to take a year off from life, during which time he hopes to make some meaningful discovery about the nature of humanity and the world. As time slows down and the plot all but grinds to a halt, bogged down in numerous pages of idle contemplation, the reader's patience and the writer's capacity are stretched to the limit.[4] The novel is infuriatingly masterful in taking on subjects of grand scale that hold great promise and result in ever larger circles that lead to an inevitable vortex; *Mann ohne Eigenschaften* is about something and nothing at the same time. And yet the resulting creative intensity is never resolved, for the work remains a novel fragment.[5] It is as if the characters have been cut off in mid-sentence as the anxiety of pending war is frozen in the air. The author never has to orchestrate the suicide, murder, or *Liebestod* of the protagonist and his sister, for they are figuratively terminated in the dangling threads of the novel's refused conclusion.

I. Peripeteia and Pierrot

Mann ohne Eigenschaften presents its anti-oedipal polemic in very subtle ways. The pervasive paradigm of Oedipus and his complex are never directly challenged, rather his position is usurped by his other: Electra. Halfway through the novel, when Ulrich's attempt to transform himself and the world has proven entirely unsuccessful, the narrative is abruptly shaken by the death of Ulrich's father. This precipitates a dramatic upheaval in the protagonist's life and initiates a significant shift in tone. The narrator dispenses with clever, ironic ploys that poke fun at everything from the self-satisfied society dames with their lavish wardrobes and secret affairs to the petty and obsequious ways of the Austrian civil service with its ludicrous and antiquated bureaucracies.

A new narrative voice emerges as the Atrean myth of Electra seeps through the pages of the third book and stains the characters with the painful legacy of patricide and sibling incest. This is no parlor joke – the patriarch's sudden death, precipitating haunting reverberations of Agamemnon's ghost, coupled with the much anticipated reunion between Ulrich and his long-absent sister, Agathe, constitutes the *peripeteia* in the novel. Electra's story is unearthed in this poignant recognition scene. Never mentioned by name, the myth has been scraped to its bare bones, reduced to a few crucial clues. The first of these is the death of the father.[6] The children seem almost pleased at the passing of their overbearing father. However, the recurring sense of loss and confusion in the second half of the novel is akin to that felt by the Atrean children at the senseless murder of Agamemnon.

The other major element of the myth's structure is precisely the *anagnorisis* of Electra and Orestes. During the much-anticipated recognition scene, the earth ought to cease rotating on its axis for one long moment of gaping silence. Musil heightens the suspense of this encounter by maneuvering his subjects into place and then delaying their meeting in much the same way as does Sophocles in his Attic version. And yet, there is something almost artificial and contrived about this first meeting. As I will show, this is merely a trial run for the real recognition scene, which appears much later in the novel.

Ulrich arrives at the family home following his father's death, exhausted and dishevelled after a train journey, only to learn that Agathe, whom he labels his "unbekannte Schwester" (3, 674), is indisposed and cannot see him right away. He is confused by this inhospitable reception and does not know what to make of it since he barely knows his mysterious sister (they have barely seen each other since early childhood). Conscious of the power dynamic in play, Ulrich surmises that her reluctance to rush to greet him gives Agathe the upper hand in the situation. Finally, after an agonizing hiatus, the siblings are poised to enter the scene. Unlike the Electra myth of antiquity, in which Orestes disguises himself as the messenger of his own death, here brother and sister both know what is at stake in this reunion. Or at least they think they do.

In subtle rebellion at having been abandoned upon his arrival – "Sie hätte mich doch wenigstens in der Wohnung gleich begrüßen sollen!" – Ulrich decides to wear "eine[n] große[n], weichwollige[n] Pyjama, den er anzog, beinahe eine Art Pierrotkleid, schwarz-grau gewürfelt" (3, 675). Little did he know that his sister has taken the same exaggeratedly casual attitude toward her dress and has donned almost identical pyjamas. When Ulrich enters the room, he is confronted with a Pierrot, "der auf den ersten Blick ganz ähnlich aussah wie er selbst" (3, 676). Equally flabbergasted, Agathe exclaims: "Ich habe nicht gewußt, daß wir Zwillinge sind!" (3, 676). Though certainly suspenseful and anxious, this recognition scene differs fundamentally from the Greek myth. While the protagonists in the Hellenic versions display emotions ranging from shock and dismay to disbelief and bittersweet tears, Ulrich and Agathe seem more awkwardly surprised and somewhat clumsy in their first interaction. They must wait patiently for the second *anagnorisis* to truly recognize each other. Once they get over the incredible coincidence of their matching outfits and the uncanny *doppelgänger* experience, the siblings resort almost immediately, as if out of adolescent shyness, to conversational banalities such as the sports they prefer.[7] Still, the meeting is not without lasting consequences. Even if they are as yet blind to the true nature of their bond, Ulrich and Agathe begin to function as one indivisible unit. From this point forward, they progressively refer to their status as "Hermaphroditen" and "Siamesische Zwillinge," and consider that they are inextricably linked in some kind of platonic, one might even say "mythical," union.

II. Oedipus Meets Mach

And so it is that Ulrich and Agathe in turn mime this artful meeting of Pierrot with him/herself.[8] Their extraordinary encounter constitutes an identity crisis for Musil's protagonist, from which, it seems, he will never recover. The mere possibility of an Oedipal scenario is forever banished from the novel, since Ulrich's consciousness is now unmistakably and irreversibly split, as if severed at the root into two distinct, platonic halves. Oedipus, Freud's Oedipus at any rate, has as his sole purpose the pursuit of a unified and developmentally complete consciousness. Oedipus may, in his emergent state, waffle somewhat in his object choice, but this ambiguity gives way in the end to a secure and singularly masculine subjectivity. Freud is adamant on this point: "Anyone who fails [to master the Oedipus complex] falls a victim to neurosis" (149). According to this view, the relationship between Ulrich and Agathe is a sign of neurosis, for it is the successful mastery of the Oedipal stage that awakens and installs the incest taboo.[9] Contrarily, I would argue that the siblings are able to negotiate an ethical pact precisely because they do not fall victim to the restrictive social initiation of the Oedipus complex.

Though Musil initially followed the father of psychoanalysis in setting up sexual relations as a crucial cultural model, his system diverged significantly from that of Freud because of his insistence on the coexistence of eros and intellect as a move toward a revolutionary, sexual ethics.[10] Moreover, he repudiated the cult-like status and seemingly unscientific approach of the psychoanalytic establishment. While Musil seems to have set out, in part, to refute the primacy of Freud's principal paradigm, these theories were by no means his sole reference point. In fact, he had written his doctoral dissertation, *Beitrag zur Beurteilung der Lehren Machs*, on the pre-Freudian psychology of Ernst Mach (1838-1916), a physicist who had given the Austrian public a new formulation of the monist doctrine of positivism.[11] Mach's famous dictum proclaiming the unsavable self, "das unrettbare Ich," became a powerful catchphrase and dominated the psychological landscape of Viennese modernism. Adopted by the influential cultural critic, Hermann Bahr, it became an axiom for the crisis in language and the crisis of identity itself. As Mach himself said: "[das] Ich [ist] keine von der Welt isolierte Monade, sondern ein Teil der Welt und mitten im Fluss derselben darin" (quoted in Frank 325). As such, and this is Mach's central argument, subjectivity can exist only as a bundle of sensations and as a fiction of its own perceptions of the world. Or as Musil interprets it: As soon as one attempts to analyze the self, "löst es sich in Relationen u[nd] Funktionen auf" (8, 1403). This is demonstrated in *Mann ohne Eigenschaften* when all that appears tangible and malleable in its characters slips through one's fingers like the finest silt.

I propose that *Mann ohne Eigenschaften* simultaneously engages with and critically evaluates Mach's theories and that the Electra myth serves as a platform for this dynamic dialog. The novel denies Freud's exclusive Oedipal narrative, all the while leapfrogging Mach's deconstructive metaphysics and opening up a space for alternative ethical relations. The encounter of the mythological siblings in the guise of Ulrich and Agathe, together with Musil's experimentation surrounding their negotiations of subjectivity and positionality, provide the basis for a new ethics to emerge.

The author makes no attempt to outline a systematic theory of ethics. In fact, an ethical *system* is an oxymoron: "Wo eine Regelmäßigkeit sich einstellt," laments Musil, "dort hat sich eine Moral gebildet" (8, 1305). In *Mann ohne Eigenschaften*, morality is shown to be static and artificial, whereas ethics functions as a continuous, fluid, and relational project. "Moral ist in ihrem Wesen als Vorschrift nach an wiederholbare Erlebnisse gebunden" (8, 1093), whereas Ulrich states in the novel: "Das Unmoralische gewinnt sein himmlisches Recht als eine drastische Kritik des Moralischen!" (3, 959). Later in the novel, such statements become bolder and more anarchic in tone, and as Musil himself comments in connection with the relationship between Ulrich and Agathe: "Nichts ist fest. Jede Ordnung führt ins Absurde" (5, 1834). In much of this enigmatic section, the narrator speaks in axiomatic phrases, spitting out philosophical vignettes and leaving the reader to decipher his code. Unwittingly, we become schooled in the doctrines of Mach, which will then be mutated through Musil's clever manipulation of character and narrative development.

III. Recognition Scene Turned Seduction Scene

While Musil at times forgets he has vowed never to analyze a character, he usually allows his protagonists the freedom to experience their own fluid shifts. One scene in particular demonstrates Musil's narrative technique and relational theory. In the chapter "Beginn einer Reihe wundersamer Erlebnisse," near the beginning of the *Nachlaß*,[12] Ulrich and Agathe are preparing for yet another evening out with friends. Already late, they are dressing hastily, and Ulrich is assisting his sister in the absence of qualified maidservants. The narrator outlines in the minutest detail this scene, in which Agathe puts on a silk stocking. Her body becomes the object of an artist's gaze: "am Hals rundete die Spannung des Vorgangs drei Falten, die schlank und lustig durch die klare Haut eilten wie drei Pfeile" (4, 1082). Her brother loses his cool distance and is helpless in the face of the powerful kinetic force connecting him to his sister; the painting "schien ihren Rahmen verloren zu haben und ging [...] unvermittelt und unmittelbar in den Körper Ulrichs über" (4, 1082). Suddenly, Ulrich leans over his sister from behind and bites into one of the folds on her tenderly exposed neck.

This moment, marking a turning point in the sibling relationship, is one that I characterize as the *second recognition scene* in the novel. In the antique myth of Atreus, *anagnorisis* is a single event, and there is no need for Orestes and Electra to reenact their first meeting.[13] However, according to my reading, Musil's rendition suggests that Ulrich and Agathe never really *saw* each other during the Pierrot scene. They were too absorbed in establishing the pecking order of the sibling hierarchy. Ulrich was still acting his spoiled playboy routine and Agathe was preoccupied with plotting the end of her marriage. Only at this point does the narrative's veneer of irony finally fall away to reveal the quasi-mystical union of two souls.

At frequent intervals following the first recognition scene, Ulrich and Agathe critically evaluate themselves as the two halves of Plato's original human (3, 903), as Pygmalion, as the Hermaphrodite (3, 905), and as the Siamese twins (3, 908; 3, 936; 3, 945); they even refer to themselves as hermits (3, 801). Very early on, Ulrich comes to understand the nature of his dependent relationship with Agathe; she is the sister who will allow him to love himself. His self-analysis reveals a deficiency that she can apparently fulfill:

> Ich weiß jetzt, was du bist: Du bist meine Eigenliebe! [...] Mir hat eine richtige Eigenliebe, wie sie andere Menschen so stark besitzen, in gewissem Sinne immer gefehlt [...] Und nun ist sie offenbar, durch Irrtum oder Schicksal, in dir verkörpert gewesen, statt in mir selbst! (3, 899)

After a great deal of debate and reflection, Ulrich refines this hypothesis:

> Aber auch ich muß doch etwas lieben können, und da ist eine Siamesische Schwester, die nicht ich noch sie ist, und geradesogut ich wie sie ist, offenbar der einzige Schnittpunkt von allem! (3, 945)

This kind of analysis abounds in the chapters leading up to the second recognition scene, and the tone is cerebral and sterile. Ulrich may have softened around the edges since the arrival of his sister, but his thinking is still mired in an intellectual, even clinical, quagmire. What this second *anagnorisis* reveals is clearly on a different plane.

Following the initial description of Ulrich lunging in a vampiric maneuver toward Agathe, the whole scene is repeated in extreme slow motion, this time emphasizing the somatic distortions of this single gesture. In a cinematic frame-by-frame analysis, we learn that Agathe has been liberated into weightlessness and has lost her balance. The event has called all muscles into play, but simultaneously paralyzes their limbs (4, 1082). The siblings abandon ordinary language for a kind of corporeal code, such that "der geschwisterliche Wuchs der Körper teilte sich ihnen mit, als stiegen sie aus einer Wurzel auf" (4, 1083). Indeed, they suddenly recognize their collective blindness as if a cloudy film has been peeled back from their eyes:

> Sie sahen einander so neugierig in die Augen, *als sähen sie dergleichen zum erstenmal*. Und obwohl sie das, was eigentlich vorgegangen sei, nicht hätten erzählen können, weil ihre Beteiligung daran zu inständig war, glaubten sie doch zu wissen, daß sie sich soeben unversehens einen Augenblick inmitten dieses gemeinsamen Zustands befunden hätten, an dessen Grenze sie schon so lange gezögert, den sie einander schon so oft beschrieben und den sie doch immer nur von außen geschaut hatten. (4, 1083; my emphasis)

Ulrich and Agathe are granted the gift of a special vision, which gives them insight into the nature of their relationship as they stand on the crest between their past and their future. They see that they have been hovering at this precipice since the night of their first meeting. They had been trying all along to articulate in ordinary language what they have now experienced physically as a "shared condition" or "anderer Zustand."[14] What had been an accident of bodily gesture has become a catalyst for something more. Even when Ulrich picked up the phone and canceled their engagements for the evening he showed no signs of sobering up (4, 1083). Far from being an isolated incident, this moment has set the scene for the next phase of Ulrich's and Agathe's collective being.

IV. *Romanticism Revisited*

For what seems like an eternity after Ulrich's daring overture, the siblings remain silent. Only their glances meet as they navigate through unknown territory using a new somatic language. They sense that their movements are censored by some warning, a higher force that has nothing to do with moral codes (4, 1083). When they finally regain the use of their voices, they speak in a forgotten tongue, borrowing vocabulary and imagery from early Romantic poets such as Tieck, Schlegel, and Novalis. As if from nowhere, Ulrich blurts out to Agathe: "Du bist der Mond [...] Du bist zum Mond geflogen und mir von ihm wiedergeschenkt worden" (4, 1084). With these prophetic words, he places his sister in the role of female redeemer in the Romantic tradition.[15] She is his mirror image, thereby strengthening their hermaphroditic bond. Agathe been given back to Ulrich, and he implicitly has been given back to himself, and has found love for himself through his love for his other half.

Breaking the spell in the most annoying manner, the narrator interrupts our romantic scene – "Verläßt man hier das Gespräch der Geschwister [...]" (4, 1084) – to inform us that we are in the midst of an artificially altered reality and must not fully integrate into this magical world. Soon, however, the narrator forgets his task of waking the reader and carries on with such clichéed romantic epithets as the all-encompassing corporeality of the night far from the harsh light of day, which facilitates a state of "grenzenlose Selbstlosigkeit" (4, 1085). If this scene were removed from its context, it might seem to be extracted from Novalis's *Hymnen an die Nacht*, with its lovers "in dunkle Nacht gehüllet," or from Wagner's *Tristan und Isolde*,[16] where the magical couple feels their love threatened by the jealous and deceitful day.[17]

Musil's sexual imagery has clearly been borrowed from his Romantic predecessors. The sensual moon, icon of intoxicating desire, beckons irresistibly and invites the siblings into a magical union of the flesh. And yet, like a magnet that attracts and repels with equal intensity, the moon seems to draw them together and keep them apart (4, 1085). Still, they are aware of love's fever in their bodies (4, 1086), and gaze longingly toward the celestial sphere, as if transplanted from Caspar David Friedrich's Romantic painting about two lovers mesmerized in lunar observation. Just when their metaphysical union threatens to dissolve into a sexual consummation, Ulrich adds a puzzling corollary by comparing Agathe to "Pierrot Lunaire." The narrator again severs the bond with any romantic paradigm with a clinical analysis of this archetype: "In der bleichen Maske des mondlich-einsamen Pierrots [...]; es drückte also die Vorliebe für Mondnächte beträchtlich ins Lächerliche hinab" (4, 1086). For a number of reasons, the siblings are kept from expressing their love in a sexual union of the flesh: one reason is Ulrich's admission that their scene has slipped into a sentimental debauch, trivialized to the point of kitsch (4, 1086). Then the Pierrot allegory returns from the first recognition scene bringing with it the overtones of androgyny, hermaphroditism and general confusion around sexual identification. But a more significant deterrent is the unknown force that has marked the siblings for some "höhere Ahnung" (4, 1083).[18]

With the return of a rather pathetic image of Pierrot, the siblings realize they are nothing but characters in their own plot. Nevertheless, brother and sister both understand that they have experienced, even for a fleeting moment, a hint of what Ulrich names: "Seligkeit des Gefühls" (4, 1086). In a posthumous note, Musil writes: "U[lrich] weiß sich u[nd] Ag[athe] [als] eine Art letzte Romantiker der Liebe" (5, 1844), thereby making their allegiance explicit.[19] In many ways, the siblings' journey to another reality comes across as clichéed and sentimental, but it is rescued from descending into kitsch at the last minute by common sense that breaks through the veneer. Having recognized that they are characters in their own play or figures in a painting, they take the necessary steps to close the scene. Agathe unexpectedly calls "Gute Nacht!" to her brother and then, as though waking suddenly from a slumber, she closes the curtains so quickly that the tableau of the two of them standing in the moonlight vanishes suddenly and completely (4, 1087). The Romantic dream is eclipsed as quickly as it emerged.

In a larger sense, Ulrich's and Agathe's romantic encounter illustrates Musil's attempt to compensate for a loss of authenticity in the world around them. Their collective mourning for what was and their yearning for what might be colors the narrative as they linger on the cusp between genuine meaning and irony, between sincere love and debauched vulgarism. But like the mythological characters whose roles they restage, they too must make a decision and move forward. Typically, a traditional recognition scene is followed by stunned silence at having *seen* for the first time, and yet Electra and Orestes both know they cannot gaze forever into each other's eyes. They have a task before them; their love alone will not redeem the kingdom of Argos, and they take up their swords and go to battle. So, too, Ulrich and Agathe must confront their future together.

V. *Sensation Body and Provisional Fictions of the Ego*

In the middle of the prolonged romantic scene, Ulrich feels the need to theorize their relations, and he explains: "Wir hatten unsere Körper vertauscht, ohne uns zu berühren" (4, 1084). The body emerges as a central metaphor for their relationship, be it a physical body or a "sensation body," as postulated by Mach. It is no coincidence that the catalyst that finally allows Ulrich and Agathe to understand the depth of their connection is a single physical gesture. What cannot be understood on a cognitive level must be approached on the corporeal level.

In a very early work, *Die Analyse der Empfindungen* (*The Analysis of Sensations*), Mach relates that in his youth he had come across Kant's *Prolegomena to All Future Metaphysics* in his father's library, and this precipitated his later inquiry into the "superfluity of things in themselves." He explains that one day "the world, including my own selfhood, suddenly appeared to me as a coherent mass of sensations, in which my sense of self was only and simply a stronger cohesion" (24). In his later work, *Erkenntnis und Irrtum* (*Knowledge and Error*), Mach further outlines his theory of the ego's construction through its fundamental interdependence with the body's spatial surroundings and its experience of sensations: "There is something all but unexplored standing behind the ego, namely our body" (8). Inasmuch as the body is the only vehicle for knowledge of the self, it is equally vulnerable to errors of perception: "the imagination rounds off incomplete findings [...] thus occasionally falsifying them" (7). In other words, the dependence upon outside forces and the processing of these forces as internal circumstances of sensation can lead to delusion. This propensity to confuse knowledge and error based upon a misunderstanding in the interpretation of incoming data renders the self a fundamentally unknowable entity; in consequence, "an isolated ego exists no more than an isolated object: both are provisional fictions of the same kind" (9). As a "provisional fiction," the self is nothing more than a sensation cluster, connected to plants, animals, and objects through its sensory perceptions. Essentially, humans are not too different from machines, argues Mach: "some kind of weird and wonderful automata" (18). Far from despairing at this seemingly fatalistic view of the ego, the psychologist insists that this model of human development is actually liberating because it frees us, first, from the mind/body dichotomy and then from a static, fossilized notion of self.

Mach's phenomenological and pragmatic approach to the perception of the self is important for Musil's project in a number of ways. For one thing, as we have observed, the characters in *Mann ohne Eigenschaften* are shown to be fluid entities, without ground. Initially, it seems that remedying this would be a reasonable task, and Ulrich tells his sister optimistically: "Wir suchen einen Grund für dich" (3, 959). Eventually, however, the narrator recognizes the impossibility of such a project, and describes another version of being, "welches wir im Grunde nicht begründen können" (5, 1752).

Another important factor for Musil's characters is Mach's theory that emotions are part of the overall experiential phenomena of the body. He explains:

> At first glance, feelings, affects and moods of love, hate, anger, fear, depression, sadness, mirth and so on, seem to be new elements. On closer scrutiny, however, they are less analyzed sensations linked with less definite, diffuse and vaguely circumscribed elements of internal space: they mark certain directed modes of bodily reactions known from experience. (1976, 17)

Ulrich echoes Mach's theory when he elaborates his own thoughts on the emotion of love to Agathe: "Da ist erstens ein körperliches Erlebnis, das zur Klasse der Hautreize gehört" (3, 941). Love is, for Ulrich, first and foremost a physical-mechanical experience rather than one of the soul; this is illustrated by the fact that their mutual experience of love entails sharing and even exchanging bodies. Ulrich describes a sensation that affects his body when he is close to a woman, "als sei ihm da selbst ein zweiter, weit schönerer Körper zu eigen gegeben worden" (3, 898). Being twins is not enough; they must be Siamese twins and physically connected so that all sensations are shared. The narrator begins to utter Mach-like phrases on the coexistence of emotion and physical sensation, such as Ulrich's dream "zwei Menschen zu sein und einer" (4, 1060).

Clearly, Musil is engaging with Mach's theories in order to understand the nature of his characters' subjectivity. But he eventually goes beyond Mach's corporeal aesthetics and challenges his mentor. Musil supports the notion of the ego as an unstable cluster of physical sensations, essentially a nothingness, which is at every moment being redefined according to new spatial and sensational circumstances. He parts company with Mach when he develops from this model a complex set of *social* relations. Not only is the ego a fluid entity, but it intermingles and interferes with other sensory beings. Ulrich and Agathe are determined by their respective somatic perceptions; however, they also codetermine each other's beings through their interactions.

Further exceeding the limits of Mach's theories, Musil seems dissatisfied with a notion of the "unrettbares Ich" and the pessimistic view that the ego is really nothing but an accident of error and false perception. Instead, he proposes and demonstrates an alternative, some would say utopian, perspective. Ulrich and Agathe embark upon a path of discovery, recognizing the inherently unsettled nature of their collective being as a cluster of sensations, and they do so through the catalyst of love. Without love, their status as Siamese twins or shared hermaphrodite would be at best ridiculous and at worst pathetic. Love itself compels them to seek a better alternative to the status quo. "Aber das Reich der Liebe," affirms the narrator, "ist ja in allem die große Anti-Realität" (4, 1319), and this is the inspiration for the siblings' quest to imagine a reality beyond the limits of morality. Indeed, they risk everything and enter into their ethical pact, an experiment of gargantuan proportions.

Ulrich is more articulate than Agathe about their desire to meld fully with each other. Throughout the novel, he repeatedly voices the wish to abandon his masculine identity and become his female other. He recalls how, even as a child, when he saw his sister dressed up for a birthday party, he longed desperately, "ein Mädchen zu sein" (3, 690). Later in the novel, his love for Agathe awakens in him "Sehnsucht, sie zu sein" (4, 1311); he yearns to be his sister at any cost. But to be his sister is far more than simply wishing to unite completely like Siamese twins. It becomes a code word for a particular way of being that Ulrich and Agathe begin to cultivate consciously after their mystical recognition; they step deliberately beyond the confines of moral codes and strict social structures and withdraw into what they call "ein zweigeschlechtiges Mönchtum." Ulrich asserts this alternative definition of sorority: "die 'Schwester' [ist] ein Gebilde, das aus dem 'anderen' Teil des Gefühls ersteht, der Aufruhr dieses Gefühls und das Verlangen, anders zu leben" (4, 1314). Together, Ulrich and Agathe acknowledge their existence as that of the "third sister," the intermingling of "I" and "you."[70]

VI. The New Woman

Ulrich's desire to embody womanhood itself in the form of his/a sister is foregrounded by the rise of a new ideal of femininity in the novel. Very early on, we find evidence of a dichotomy between two categories of women, characterized by body type: the round, soft, maternal woman and the hard, tight, boyish girl. The female characters in the novel are equally divided among these two categories: Diotima, Bonadea, and Leona all fall into the maternal group, while Clarisse, Gertha, and Agathe are more androgynous and boyish. Diotima, Ulrich's confidante and cohort in the *Parallelaktion*, is described as embodying "ein Schönheitsideal [...], das hellenisch war [...] mit ein bißchen mehr Fleisch" (1, 109). She has a large, warm body with feminine curves and several rolls of voluptuous fat on her neck. On the other hand, Clarisse's "kleiner, nervöser Leib" (1, 53) is hardly maternal, but rather "hart und knabenhaft" (1, 354). Over time, this tendency accelerates until she becomes an emaciated rack of bones, devoid of feminine flesh.

In his slow eradication of the maternally connoted female body from the novel, Musil refers tacitly to the legacy of Johann Jacob Bachofen or even Otto Weininger. In Bachofen's anthropological study of mythology, *Mutterrecht*, the primitive, maternal principle finally gives way to the laws of paternity precisely when Electra decides to avenge Agamemnon's death. And the misogynist Weininger, who abhorred all things maternal, saw in women the roots of social disease. He was disgusted by the so-called bisexuality of culture and the feminization of the ego, and considered this phenomenon a symptom of decadence and social decay. Musil can hardly be said to uphold either of these theories. He observes and comments upon the same phenomenon of gender ambiguity and experimentation; however, he introduces this new construction of femininity in order to celebrate women's liberation from their maternal responsibilities and their newfound ability to interact with a free-floating set of gender signifiers.

Musil theorizes this concept in his essay, *Die Frau gestern und morgen* (1929), where he begins by describing an outdated version of femininity. Women's bodies become caricatures in his descriptions: "Der ideale Mund hatte die Größe und Rundung eines Stecknadelkopfes und die Händchen und Füßlein saßen mit der Ohnmacht kleiner Falter am üppigen Kelch des Leibes" (642). Female bodies were prudishly buried beneath wads of fabric, which had the opposite of the desired effect, creating "eine ungeheuer künstliche Vergrößerung der erotischen Oberfläche" (641). In an early chapter of *Mann ohne Eigenschaften*, the narrator expounds upon these same points almost word for word, postulating that the extensive clothing of the traditional woman was something of a civilized aphrodisiac. Maternal and corpulent, these women were sexual beings.

The ideal of woman changed, proposes Musil, with the Great War. The new woman shed her camouflaging layers and her maternal role all at the same time: "[Sie] wendet sich vorläufig an die Knabeninstinkte des Mannes, ist knabenhaft mager, kameradschaftlich, sportlich spröd und kindisch" (645). She remains physically immature and is principally concerned with matters of how to prevent reproduction. This fact is made evident in the novel when Ulrich's friend and confidante, Clarisse, maintains a self-imposed chastity in spite of her husband's tireless pleading for conjugal relations. Another of the protagonist's female companions, Gertha, also denies herself and Ulrich the pleasures of the flesh when, at the height of passion, a twisted scream hurtles from her body in a violent purging of all sexual impulse.

Agathe, too, falls squarely within the bounds of the new woman,[21] such that when Ulrich sees her for the first time in feminine attire, he mistakes this costume – "vor die schlanken, hohen, den seinen ähnlichen Beine [...] hatten sich Röcke gesenkt" – for a disguise (3, 694). Women's clothing is a foil more jarring than the Pierrot pyjamas of their first meeting. Her body is "groß und schlank," and her shoulders are "von einer gesunden Breite" (3, 896), all of which contributes to Ulrich's confusion surrounding her gender status. In fact, his very first remark about her appearance notes the sexually ambivalent and immature nature of her body: "Ihre Brust ging nicht in Brüsten verloren" (2, 676). He is so shocked that he is incapable of determining whether his initial fascination with her arises out of curiosity or sexual desire.

This pre-pubescent, androgynous and perhaps asexual image of Agathe acts as a mirror for Ulrich's construction of his own masculinity. Musil never writes an essay on "Man Today" or the nature of the new man. But Ulrich's own self-conscious analysis of his character and his relationship to Agathe speak to a larger shift in the development and manifestation of masculinity, a shift that I would posit as a threat to the Oedipal scenario. This is not a man whose sexual development is either predictable or complete. He refuses to identify with or emulate the kind of man his father was and purposefully casts off the shadow of the domineering man. The absence of his biological mother precludes any Oedipal mother-son conflict. And, while he appears to go through a period of infatuation with maternally connoted women, Ulrich does not take part in the ritual of usurping the power of the maternal in order to assert his masculine, sexual supremacy. Mother figures simply fade away when the new woman takes center stage as the dominant cultural and corporeal aesthetic.[22]

My point here is that the demise of the Oedipal scenario is inversely proportionate to the rise of the Electra myth. When Ulrich is finally ready to turn his back upon his father's world for good, the myth of Atreus is introduced. The son leaves behind the security of paternal inheritance and the solid Oedipal subjectivity it connotes. Following the father's death and the recognition scene, Agathe and Ulrich slowly begin their retreat from the world; they abandon the life of Viennese high society and begin their self-imposed exile as recluses. The two of them lose any clear sense of identity they might have had and enter a zone of liminal subjectivity. By the end of the *Nachlaß*, the two have practically fused into one being, so complete is their union. Agathe describes a dream she has, in which she entered her body lying on the bed, only to discover that it was her brother's body. She is startled by this uncanny sensation, which takes the *doppelgänger* motif of Siamese twins one step further. The dream continues with her taking her brother's body into her arms, lifting it up high in exaltation. Their bodies melt into each other such that they are indistinguishable. The dream represents a state of utopian bliss, a simultaneous stasis and complete fusion of subjectivities that Ulrich first mentioned in the moonlit scene. There is a religious sense of awe to this scene, as though Agathe were Mary Magdalene lifting Christ's dead body to become one with it.

Agathe's dream also signals a shift in her overall role in the novel. She becomes the driving force behind their collective actions, exemplified by Ulrich's repeated desire to become her, to meld with her. As Ulrich casts off his allegiance to Oedipus, Agathe accepts the role of Electra, courageous and defiant.[23] She asserts her independence and sets her own agenda, and Ulrich, like Orestes, seems happy to follow. Though her task is not that of orchestrating a literal matricide, her characterization as the new woman acts as a figurative matricide. She extinguishes the maternal element in herself, just as Musil postulates its erasure from the cultural imagination.[24]

Agathe's new role is foreshadowed by Ulrich's own suggestion, shortly after their first meeting, that the siblings might also take on the roles of Isis and Osiris as they perform the alchemy of becoming symbolically one. Musil explores this theme elsewhere in poetic form: "Isis und Osiris" (1923) reveals the grizzly story of Isis stealing her husband's male member: "Und die Schwester löste von dem Schläfer / Leise das Geschlecht und aß es auf" (597). In exchange, she gives him her heart, which he in turn consumes. The poem parallels the siblings' quasi-incestuous relations in *Mann ohne Eigenschaften* in that Osiris, like Ulrich, is figuratively emasculated. Unlike his mythological counterpoint, however, Ulrich is a willing victim. In both cases, the brother/lover's sacrifice is rewarded when he gains access to the coveted trophy: his sister's heart. Such a metaphor of cannibalistic ritual is perhaps a more profound symbol of the depth of their union than sexual consummation itself.

The novel starts off with Ulrich as a solitary and singular protagonist in a quasi-*Bildungsroman* quest for a purpose and meaning in life. By the end of the unfinished work, we are on much less solid ground. Agathe and Ulrich have melted into each other to the extent that they function as one character, with Agathe or the androgynous new woman as the dominant force. Oedipus has been abandoned, and Electra and Orestes have become one. Musil is not alone in his explorations of this scenario. In his 1977 play, *Hamletmaschine*, Heiner Müller presents us with a similarly subtle critique of Oedipus. In fact, the author suggests elsewhere that Oedipus has long outlived his usefulness: "Im Jahrhundert des Orest und der Elektra, das heraufkommt, wird Ödipus eine Komödie sein" (*Projektion 1975*, 16). Müller replaces Oedipus with a failed Hamlet in disguise, who wavers on the edge of an abyss, a crisis in consciousness of such proportions that he, too, declares his desire to abandon his masculinity: "Ich will eine Frau sein" (15). He does not want to be just any woman; he wants to be Electra. Like Ulrich, Müller's Hamlet figuratively fuses with and is transformed into an Electra-character,[25] albeit a disabled one. Müller's disfigured and wheelchair-bound Electra also enacts a symbolic matricide in her denial of her own fertility, threatening to annihilate all her unborn children.

Unlike Müller's Electra, whose anarchic view privileges destruction as the only ethical stance, Musil's characters embrace the possibility of creating and nurturing an alternative reality through their own ethical relations. As I have already argued, Musil refutes Freud's Oedipal subject in part by looking to Mach, whose metaphysical scepticism constructs the subject as a provisional fiction of physical sensations. Mach's pessimistic pragmatism, however useful as a provisionary model, does not provide all the building blocks for Musil's project. He does not want his version of Electra and Orestes to end up in a void or in a relational *cul-de-sac*.

VII. Nietzsche and the Abyss

It is to Nietzsche that Musil looks to complete his vision of an alternative relational ethics. The philosopher is present as a backdrop throughout *Mann ohne Eigenschaften*, first introduced through Ulrich's close friend, Clarisse. He had given her the complete works of Nietzsche as a wedding present, and indeed she begins to embody the spirit of Dionysus. The narrator remarks upon the unspoken force that threatens her stability: "Etwas Unbestimmbares riß sich dann los in ihr und drohte mit ihrem Geist davonzufliegen" (1, 62). Clarisse even proposes a "Nietzsche Year" as a parallel to the ridiculous jubilee year planned for Emperor Franz Joseph. Her obsession reflects the extent to which this philosophy dominates the landscape of cultural consciousness in Musil's Vienna. However, Clarisse's rather shallow reception of Nietzsche – she cherishes the weighty tomes but seems not to have read them – and her worship of him as a statuesque icon act as a counterpoint to Musil's larger conversation with the philosopher toward the end of the novel. The author's allegiance to Nietzsche is more implicit than explicit, but it permeates his prose, especially in the third book and *Nachlaß*.

"All ordered society puts the passions to sleep," asserts Nietzsche in *The Gay Science*, a message paralleled by Musil's conviction that morality is a narcotic that lulls even sharp minds into a dull, sleepy trance. The author sees in Nietzsche the potential for a different kind of drug, perhaps one that stimulates productive insomnia to "reawaken the sense of comparison, of contradiction, of joy in the new, the daring, and the untried" (Kaufmann, 1963, 93). The characters in *Mann ohne Eigenschaften* are engaged in a Nietzschean experiment of audacious joy, through which they escape ordered society to imagine something new. Agathe and Ulrich risk everything to break free from social mores, and their actions echo Ulrich's aphoristic bluntness: "alles ist moralisch, aber die Moral selbst ist nicht moralisch" (3, 1024).

While Musil does not expressly mention Nietzsche in the novel's treatise on morality, the creative tension of the characters' unfinished and permeable subjectivities recalls the philosopher's invitation to move beyond one's own self in an explosion of Dionysian excess. Musil demonstrates his theory of ethical relations through the perpetual metamorphosis of his characters and their courageous endeavors to harness their love and sketch a new vision of intersubjective being. In so doing, he provides a model for modern individuals to recreate themselves constantly and to embrace the chaos of the changing world around them.[26]

Agathe and Ulrich may engage in a Nietzschean experiment of joy, which leads to a hermaphroditic fusion of Electra and Orestes; however, their coexistence does not culminate in the kind of Dionysian frenzy that consumes Hugo von Hofmannsthal's Electra as she performs her famous *Totentanz*. Instead, their challenge is to walk an ever-narrowing precipice between two extremes: utopia and anarchy.[27] Like Nietzsche's tightrope dancer in *Also Sprach Zarathustra*, they are confronted on either side by a cliff and a bottomless abyss. Perhaps the impossibility of succeeding at such a feat is what prohibits Musil from completing his masterpiece. The novel refuses to end with Electra and Orestes walking hand in hand into the sunset. On the contrary, it simply peters out as Ulrich and Agathe teeter ever closer to the edge of the abyss. In order to stay alive, they must reject the slumber of moral stagnation and stay awake to imagine new ways of being in the world.

[1] Freud states that the legend of King Oedipus from classical antiquity has universal validity and that "every new arrival on this planet is faced by the task of mastering the Oedipus complex" (149). Indeed, by the time Musil began serious work on his novel, the theory of the Oedipus complex had gained such notoriety in the field of psychiatry and among the general public that this might have seemed to be true.

[2] The first volume, published in 1930, received so much praise that Musil began to dream of a Nobel Prize. Under pressure from his publisher and his readers, the second volume was divulged in 1933 and was less of a success, due in part to the political climate as well as Musil's own view that it was a less polished piece. *Mann ohne Eigenschaften* was banned in Germany and Austria in 1938, and censorship would eventually extend to all his works. In dire financial straits throughout the remaining years of his life, Musil labored increasingly over the manuscript, though with little progress.

[3] After meditating and hypothesizing upon the nature of love in conversations mostly with Agathe, but also with anyone who will listen (Clarisse, Bonadea, Diotima), Ulrich boils the problem down to its essential questions: "wie man seinen Nächsten liebe, den man nicht kenne, und wie sich selbst, den man noch weniger kennt [...], wie man überhaupt liebe," and "was Liebe 'eigentlich' sei" (4, 1223-24). These are not only important questions with regard to his relationship with Agathe, but Ulrich feels compelled to include "millions of loving couples" in his equation. This is just one example of how our protagonist ensures his own failure by setting himself impossible tasks. His musings on other subjects are of equally preposterous proportions.

[4] Indeed, the praise for *Mann ohne Eigenschaften* has not been unanimous. Peter Handke called the work "ein bis in die einzelnen Sätze größenwahnsinniges und unerträglich meinungsverliebtes Werk" (quoted in Luserke 96).

[5] Critics use the word "fragment" when referring to *Mann ohne Eigenschaften* (Luserke 103, Rogowski 75), and rightly so, though I prefer the label "incomplete." In the strict sense of the word, of course, the work is a "fragment," but I simply cannot bring myself to use this term to describe a novel that runs to almost two thousand pages including all the extensive unpublished posthumous papers, depending on the edition. Fragmented it is, and increasingly so toward the end, though it is debatable whether this is a result of the unfinished nature of the project or rather a factor of an intentional aesthetic transformation within the text. I tend to support the latter interpretation: Musil struggles to provide narrative closure, in part due to the lack of plot towards the end. His characters have abandoned their social roles, but they have not replaced their former lives with any clear plan of action. Though many critics and scholars have insisted upon a clear distinction between the published segments of *Mann ohne Eigenschaften* and the *Nachlaß*, I have chosen to treat Musil's latter drafts and notes as part of the whole. These chapters may be rough and unpolished, but they nevertheless provide important clues to the direction of the author's considerations on a number of key points.

[6] And here, we can include Ulrich's and Agathe's biological father, the patriarchal figure of the aged Emperor Franz Joseph, as well as the terminally ill Habsburg Empire itself. The seventieth jubilee celebration of Franz Joseph's accession to the throne, planned for December 2, 1918, is the subject of the great *Parallelaktion*, an elaborate planning committee with which Ulrich becomes involved. The whole scheme revolves around the attempt to overshadow the German celebration of Wilhelm II's jubilee in June of that year. Ulrich's father explains: "Da der 2. XII. natürlich durch nichts vor den 15. VI. gerückt werden könnte, ist man auf den glücklichen Gedanken verfallen, das ganze Jahr 1918 zu einem Jubiläumsjahr unseres Friedenskaisers auszugestalten" (1, 79). This scheme reveals the full extent of the ludicrous activities within the government (especially as the whole *Parallelaktion* dissolves into a social club) and the lengths to which the Austrians will go to uphold their historical supremacy over the Germans. The campaign is a ridiculous and desperate attempt to resuscitate a dying tradition and the prestige it once evoked, and a symptom of a larger philosophical problem of the "nonempty gap" (Ryan 216) that invades much of the rest of the novel in different forms.

[7] Surely it is no coincidence that the identical disguise is that of Pierrot, the notoriously ambiguous circus figure, descended from early European *commedia dell'arte* theatre. He has been known as *Pulcinella, Punch, Pedrolino,* or *Petrushka*, the simpleton and fool who exposes and ridicules his masters. This melancholy clown suffers slightly from schizophrenia, appearing at once mischievous and playful, then sinister like the jealous and cynical operatic figures of Rigoletto and Pagliacci. But the aspect of Pierrot's personality of most interest to us is the ambiguity surrounding gender identification in Ulrich's and Agathe's chance meeting. Traditionally gendered male, in the late-nineteenth and early-twentieth centuries Pierrot was increasingly played by women, the most famous of which is undoubtedly Frank Wedekind's Lulu character. This double articulation of Pierrot as feminine man and masculine woman irreparably alters the nature of the siblings' reunion. They can no longer be identified as man and woman, with all the erotic overtones implicit in the Attic recognition scenes. Instead, they meet as brother and sister, as twins, perhaps even as each other's alter ego.

[8] Perhaps Musil knew of Mallarmé's fascination with the self-identical play of murder, incest, and suicide orchestrated by Pierrot, the mime. In a brutal and bizarre drama, Pierrot illustrates his murder of the unfaithful Colombine. He ties her to the bed while she is sleeping and tickles her feet, so that her "ghastly death bursts upon her among those atrocious bursts of laughter" (quoted in Derrida 199). Pierrot simultaneously plays the murderer and his female victim, thus initiating the simultaneous collapse of both gender and subject/object boundaries. A single character takes on a form of oscillating androgyny, in an illustration of what Derrida calls a "masturbatory suicide." While it is certain that Musil's invocation of Pierrot has a different aim, the analogy is a useful one.

[9] It is important to establish the metaphorical nature of sibling incest between Agathe and Ulrich. Their bond is not really of a sexual nature. Rather, they use the fuel of eros to orchestrate their quasi-transcendent union.

[10] Musil parts company with Freud on the fundamental issue of biology. Freud insists upon the "biological foundation of the Oedipus complex," thereby rendering it an essential part of human sexual development. For Musil, this is a simplistic view, which fails to take into account the significance of social, psychological, and indeed ethical factors.

[11] A genius of many talents, Mach was, among other things, a physicist, an engineer, a psychologist, and a philosopher. He is known for his theories on epistemology and positivism, and for his experiments in optics, acoustics, electronic induction, physiology, and photography. He held posts alternately as Professor of Mathematics, Physics, and Philosophy, and was inducted into the Fluid Mechanics Hall of Fame as one of the leading

pioneers of supersonic aerodynamics. He is perhaps most famous for his discovery of the unit of the speed of sound, appropriately labeled the "Mach."

[12] The *Nachlaß* is divided into two sections: the first is a group of twenty chapters which appear relatively intact and have undergone the first stages of the intense polishing to which Musil subjected all his work. The second section consists of notes, sketches, and drafts for future chapters or versions of other chapters. There is much repetition and the writing is disjointed and almost fantastic in nature. We witness an unraveling of character and plot such that all of the first three books of Musil's masterpiece almost appear to come apart at the seams before our eyes. Upon reading this section, everything that has come before these pages seems like fiction, and the dream-like, visionary quality of these final musings becomes the real novel. Here Musil experiments with various alternative scenarios, including the possibility of Ulrich having sexual relations with a number of the women in the text: Agathe, Diotima, Clarisse. This testifies to Musil's own complaints that publishing the work piecemeal limited him severely; he considered the novel a continual work-in-progress, experimental in nature, and felt that the release of early chapters distorted the entire work (Pike xii). Perhaps one of the most important contributions of the *Nachlaß* is the light they shed on Musil's concept of mysticism and what he called "anderer Zustand."

[13] Classical and neo-classical drama often include a recognition scene as a means of driving the plot forward. Aristotle accorded it great importance and developed criteria for *anagnorisis*, which included some kind of false inference. Whether deliberately contrived or not, there is necessarily a misunderstanding concerning the true identity of a character (Dupriez 433-34). While Ulrich and Agathe do not appear to fall prey to such Aristotelian false inference, there is indeed, I would argue, a misunderstanding. For they never get beyond the Pierrot costume to see the true nature of their relationship. Thus, this chapter constitutes a second recognition, one that seems to run almost the entire course of the novel without full resolution. Ulrich and Agathe are in a constant state of *seeing* each other for the first time.

[14] Musil introduces the term "anderer Zustand" in the third book to refer to Ulrich's and Agathe's experiment in creating an alternative, imaginary social reality. The author never clarifies this ambiguous epithet, perhaps because defining it might ruin the magic of the quasi-utopian twosome the siblings attempt to nurture and sustain.

[15] We need only think of examples such as the "beloved" in Novalis's *Hymnen an die Nacht*, Lucinde in Schlegel's novel of the same name, or the many Wagnerian redeemers: Senta, Elisabeth, Brünnhilde, and Isolde. These women all sacrifice themselves to facilitate the transcendence of the male hero, often an artist struggling to realize his creative potential. While Agathe's role in *Mann ohne Eigenschaften* does not fit easily into this paradigm, there are elements of this tradition at play in the novel, especially in this critical chapter. Ulrich does most of the talking, and Agathe acts more as facilitator to his experience of discovering self and subjectivity. As we shall see, this model breaks down when it becomes clear that Ulrich cannot simply overcome his existential angst even when he finds his Platonic mate. From Ulrich's mature perspective, Wagner's predictable plots will seem foolishly simple. In the final sections of the narrative, Agathe emerges as the dominant force in the guise of the new woman.

[16] Novalis is no stranger to the world of *Mann ohne Eigenschaften*. Agathe is in the habit of quoting Novalis – "Was kann ich also für meine Seele tun, die wie ein unaufgelöstes Rätsel in mir wohnt?" (3, 857) – even though she denies belief in the soul. She leaves it to her brother to answer such questions. Wagner, too, figures prominently in the novel; his music is the source of tension between Clarisse and Walter, Ulrich's childhood friends. They play duets of his music on the piano and are enchanted by its romantic fervor; Walter even compares their suffering to that of Tristan and Isolde. Wagner also functions as a backdrop in

the novel (Clarisse's brother is conspicuously named Siegfried), representing a now defunct world where authenticity was still sought and sentimentality was not regarded as kitsch.

[17] Along with the ubiquitous romantic characterization of night as a refuge from the harsh realities of the light, both Novalis and Wagner speak of a new kind of sight: for Tristan and Isolde, to be "nachtsichtig" (80) means being able to see the lies of the strict moral and social codes imposed by day. And Novalis's lovers have access to the night's loving sun, "liebliche Sonne der Nacht" (151), a secret inner piercing light fueled by passion. Ulrich's and Agathe's new extended vision features some of these same characteristics, allowing them access to a higher plane, but also freeing them from a static and repressive moral system.

[18] That Ulrich and Agathe do not consummate their love is in some ways a strange reversal of Wagner's erotic philosophy in *Tristan und Isolde*. While Wagner was an unabashed fan of Arthur Schopenhauer and his philosophy of will-negation, he allowed himself certain liberties in its application. The *Liebestod* makes for a perfect Schopenhauerian climax, with Isolde as otherwordly redemptress, and yet their physical union of the flesh contradicts the philosopher's doctrine of asceticism. While Musil's motives are clearly not the same as Wagner's, his decision to deny Ulrich's and Agathe's sexual desires contradicts the romantic imperative of erotic love and paves the way for them to transcend their earthly existence (and here this might be translated as the strict moral codes of Viennese society) and move toward the construction of a relational ethics, with Schopenhauer's will-negation acting as the driving force.

[19] Manfred Frank interprets *Mann ohne Eigenschaften* as part Romantic allegory and part Romantic critique. He points to the appropriation of key concepts regarding the construction of the self and argues that Musil adopts Novalis' critique of Fichte's self-determining self in favor of a self that is determined by a non-self. He demonstrates that Ulrich's and Agathe's foray into Romanticism represents a quasi-religious aspiration, which abolishes totalizing systems and unfolds as an anarchic project.

[20] Near the end of the *Nachlaß*, three sisters are mentioned, referring to the trio of Ulrich, Agathe, and the fictional world they have created, which itself is granted object status. Musil's notes are by this point chaotic and convoluted. The author contemplates Ulrich's and Agathe's respective thoughts of suicide, albeit not without a glimmer of hope. Ulrich vows that they will not kill themselves until all other avenues have been exhausted.

[21] In fact, Ulrich is annoyed that she is not more assertive in her role as a new woman: "Diese männliche Machtvorstellung von der weiblichen Schwäche ist heute noch recht gewöhnlich, obwohl mir den einander folgenden Wellen der Jugend daneben neuere Auffassungen entstanden sind, und die Natürlichkeit, mit der Agathe ihre Abhängigkeit von Hagauer behandelt, verletzte ihren Bruder" (3, 684). As the novel progresses, Agathe becomes increasingly independent, even straying from Ulrich's sphere of influence and the situation is reversed altogether when, one day, he has no knowledge of her whereabouts. When he finds himself unneeded, Ulrich no longer wants her to embody the new woman. Instead, he behaves like a selfish and jealous husband.

[22] Walter Sokel suggests that Musil veers away from his essayist persona in his fictional treatment of women: "Als Essayist und Philosoph neigte Musil dazu, den Mann und Bruder siegen zu lassen. Als Romanschreiber und Erzähler erlaubt er der weiblichen Hauptfigur einen ästhetischen Triumph davonzutragen. Das zeigt, dass Musil seine eigene stereotype Idee von der Frau imstande war zu transzendieren" (1983, 127). Sokel seems here to confuse the issue somewhat. The triumph of the feminine aesthetic may be a victory on the level of cultural values, but it has little to do with the portrayal of Musil's character, Agathe.

[23] Ever since the Attic tragedies of antiquity, Electra has been synonymous with a non-traditional version of womanhood. She is not described in any of the extant versions of Aeschylus, Euripides, or Sophocles as either particularly feminine or beautiful. An outcast in

the Kingdom of Argos, she is often described as a haggard figure dressed in rags. Similarly, her actions do not fit the traditional status of a single woman, be it in antiquity or more recent times. She is fierce, vengeful, courageous, and defiant, full of rage and determination – attributes for which she is condemned and ridiculed. In Musil's immediate literary memory is Hofmannsthal's influential adaptation of Sophocles' *Elektra*, in which he takes these elements to the extreme and portrays his Elektra as a hysterical maniac.

[24] Such figurative matricide need not be seen in a negative light. Musil uses Agathe to question and redefine the nature and role of femininity. But, ultimately, he sees her emergence as the "new woman" as one of strength and rejuvenation. In building a bridge of re-gendered ethical relations, Agathe's expression is allowed to extend beyond the confining limits of maternity.

[25] Müller, too, borrows from the legend of Isis and Osiris when he has Elektra offer Hamlet her heart as a tasty morsel. The ultimate symbol of a true union of souls has always involved consumption of the flesh.

[26] Though Nietzsche's thought offers utopian possibilities for Musil's characters, if left on this course the siblings risk falling victim to a vacuous and apolitical sentimentality. Mach's theories constitute the pragmatic anchor for this ideal couple on the margins of society and lend much-needed leverage to the symbolic silence of their self-imposed exile.

[27] Critics (e.g., Schärer, Luserke) have accused Musil of indulging in utopian fantasies, which provide no real political alternative for the corrupt and decrepit society he seeks to undo. Musil counters this criticism with this diary entry: "Das Kontemplative des Anderen Zustandes ist aber etwas anderes als der Trance... Es ist ein europäischer Versuch, ohne Bewußtseinsverlust usw." (*Tagebücher* 786; see Kochs 187). The author prevents his characters from succumbing to the utopian trance by having them tread a thin line between their ideal vision in a self-exiled alternative reality and the threat of their dream imploding in destructive anarchy. In the end, it is the continual encounter with the/one's other that keeps Ulrich and Agathe alive to the challenge of resisting the status quo and attempting to embrace a different version of reality.

References

Bachofen, Johann Jacob. *Mutterrecht und Urreligion*. Ed. Hans G. Kippenberg. Stuttgart: Alfred Kröner, 1984.
Bahr, Hermann. "Das unrettbare Ich." *Zur Überwindung des Naturalismus. Theoretische Schriften 1887-1904*. Ed. Gotthard Wunberg. Stuttgart: Kohlhammer, 1968. 183-192.
Baumann, Gerhart. *Robert Musil. Ein Entwurf.* Freiburg: Rombach, 1997.
Böschenstein, Bernhard, and Marie-Louise Roth, eds. *Hommage à Musil. Genfer Kolloquium zum 50. Todestag von Robert Musil*. Bern: Peter Lang, 1995.
Brooks, Daniel J. *Musil's Socratic Discourse in* Der Mann ohne Eigenschaften. *A Comparative Study of Ulrich and Socrates*. New York: Peter Lang, 1989.
Cellbrot, Hartmut. "Schwellenerfahrungen in Robert Musils *Der Mann ohne Eigenschaften*." *Geschichte der Österreichischen Literatur. Teil 2*. Ed. Donald G. Daviau and Herbert Arlt. St. Ingbert: Röhrig, 1996. 483-492.
Derrida, Jacques. *Dissemination*. Chicago: U of Chicago P, 1981.

Dupriez, Bernard. *A Dictionary of Literary Devices.* Trans. Albert W. Halsall. Toronto: University of Toronto Press, 1991.
Ego, Werner. *Abschied von der Moral. Eine Rekonstruktion der Ethik Robert Musils.* Freiburg: Herder, 1992.
Eisele, Ulf. *Die Struktur des modernen deutschen Romans.* Tübingen: Niemeyer, 1884.
Frank, Manfred. "Auf der Suche nach einem Grund. Über den Umschlag von Erkenntniskritik in Mythologie bei Musil." *Mythos und Moderne.* Ed. Karl Heinz Bohrer. Frankfurt a.M.: Suhrkamp, 1983. 318-362.
Freud, Sigmund. "Three Essays on the Theory of Sexuality." *The Penguin Freud Library. Vol. 7.* Penguin: London, 1977. 45-170.
Hirsch, Walter. "*Der Mann ohne Eigenschaften* oder Dasein im Spiegelbild." *Das Drama des Bewusstseins.* Würzburg: Königshausen & Neumann, 1995. 119-130.
Kochs, Angela Maria. *Chaos und Individuum: Robert Musils philosophischer Roman als Vision der Moderne.* Freiburg: Verlag Karl Alber, 1996.
Large, Duncan. "On the Use of the Negative in *Der Mann ohne Eigenschaften*." *Musil-Forum* 17/18 (1991/1992): 38-62.
Le Rider, Jacques. *Modernity and the Crises of Identity.* Trans. Rosemary Morris. New York: Continuum, 1993.
Luserke, Matthias. *Robert Musil.* Stuttgart: Metzler, 1995.
Mach, Ernst. *Knowledge and Error.* Boston: D. Reidel Pub. Co., 1976.
—. *Die Analyse der Empfindungen.* Jena: [no publisher], 1911.
Meisel, Gerhard. *Liebe im Zeitalter der Wissenschaften vom Menschen. Das Prosawerk Robert Musils.* Oplan: Westdeutscher Verlag, 1991.
Müller, Heiner. "Hamletmaschine." *Hamletmaschine. Heiner Müllers Endspiel.* Köln: Promethverlag, 1978. 11-23.
—. "Projektion 1975." *Theater der Zeit.* Berlin: Akademie der Künste, 1996. 16.
Musil, Robert. *Der Mann ohne Eigenschaften* [=*Gesammelte Werke. Band 1-5*]. Reinbek bei Hamburg: Rowohlt, 1978.
—. "The Posthumous Papers." *The Man Without Qualities.* Trans. Burton Pike. New York: Vintage, 1995. 1413-1770.
—. "Isis und Osiris." Robert Musil. *Gesammelte Werke in Einzelausgaben. Band 3.* Reinbek bei Hamburg: Rowohlt, 1955. 597.
—. "Die Frau gestern und morgen." Robert Musil. *Gesammelte Werke in Einzelausgaben. Band 2.* Reinbek bei Hamburg: Rowohlt, 1955. 640-646.
—. "Der bedrohte Oedipus." Robert Musil. *Gesammelte Werke in Einzelausgaben. Band 3.* Reinbek bei Hamburg: Rowohlt, 1955. 502-504.
—. *Tagebücher.* Reinbek bei Hamburg: Rowohlt, 1983.
Novalis. *Hymnen an die Nacht. Werke, Tagebücher und Briefe Friedrich von Hardenbergs. Band 1.* Munich: Carl Hanser, 1978. 147-77.
Pekar, Thomas. *Die Sprache der Liebe.* Munich: Wilhelm Fink Verlag, 1989.
Pike, Burton. "Preface to the Posthumous Papers." *The Man Without Qualities. Vol. II.* New York: Vintage, 1996. x-xvi.
Precht, Richard David. *Die gleitende Logik der Seele: Ästhetische Selbstreflexivität in Robert Musils Der Mann ohne Eigenschaften.* Stuttgart: M&P Verlag, 1996.

Puppe, Heinrich. *Muße und Müßiggang in Robert Musils Roman* Der Mann ohne Eigenschaften. St. Ingbert: Röhrig, 1991.
Rogowski, Christian. "'Die alten Tragödien sterben ab': Musils Schwärmer als Kritik des zeitgenössischen Theaters." *Modern Austrian Literature* 26,2 (1993): 63-85.
Rosenkranz-Kaiser, Jutta. *Feminismus und Mythos: Tendenzen in Literatur und Theorie der achtziger Jahre.* New York: Waxmann, 1995.
Ryan, Judith. *The Vanishing Subject. Early Psychology and Literary Modernism.* Chicago: University of Chicago Press, 1991.
Schärer, Hans-Rudolf. *Narzismus und Utopismus. Eine literaturpsychologische Untersuchung zu Robert Musils* Der Mann ohne Eigenschaften. Munich: Wilhelm Fink, 1990.
Sokel, Walter. "Agathe und der existenzphilosophische Faktor im *Mann ohne Eigenschaften.*" *Beiträge zur Musil-Kritik.* Ed. Gudrun Brokoph-Mauch. Bern: Peter Lang, 1983. 111-128.
–. "*Der Mann ohne Eigenschaften* und das achtzehnte Jahrhundert." *Das neuzeitliche Ich in der Literatur des 18. und 20. Jahrhunderts. Zur Dialektik der Moderne.* Ed. Ulrich Fülleborn and Manfred Engel. Munich: Wilhelm Fink Verlag, 1988. 293-302.
Stephen, Inge. *Musen und Medusen: Mythos und Geschlecht in der Literatur des 20. Jahrhundert*s. Köln: Böhlau, 1997.
Wagner, Richard. *Tristan und Isolde.* Ed. William Mann. Essex: Friends of Covent Garden, 1968.
Wagner-Egelhaaf, Martina. *Mystik der Moderne: Die visionäre Ästhetik der deutschen Literatur im 20. Jahrhundert.* Stuttgart: J.B. Metzlersche Verlagsbuchhandlung, 1989.
Weininger, Otto. *Geschlecht und Charakter.* Vienna: Braumüller, 1908.

A SYMPOSIUM AS ORNAMENT?
HERMANN BROCH'S SCHLAFWANDLER TRILOGIE AND THE
DISCOURSE OF ART AND PHILOSOPHY IN THE MODERN NOVEL

Mark Grzeskowiak
University of Toronto

> Es hat seit dem Expressionismus, ja vielleicht überhaupt in der ersten
> Hälfte dieses Jahrhunderts wohl kaum einen deutschen Dichter ge-geben,
> der die Probleme der Moderne und insbesondere der modernen Dichtung,
> genauer: des modernen Romans, in so vielfältiger und um-fassender
> Weise durchdachte wie Hermann Broch. (Brinkmann 347)

It would be fair to say that Richard Brinkmann's 1957 evaluation of the Austrian author Hermann Broch maintains a degree of verity in German literary scholarship. Along with Thomas Mann, Alfred Döblin, and Robert Musil, Broch's oeuvre is still considered to be exemplary of late-modernist prose in the German language. His novel, *Die Schlafwandler: Eine Romantrilogie*, in particular, has become a standard for those interested in delineating the "Deutsche Roman der Moderne"; both in terms of its topic and in terms of its narrative form (Durzak 287; Petersen 38). Broch claimed that in writing *Die Schlafwandler*, he had attempted to create a new *type* of novel, one similar to experiments by contemporaries such as James Joyce, John Dos Passos, and André Gide. Central to Broch's conception of this new novel is the unity of reflection, plot, and style, and in fact it is on the basis of what he termed this "einheitliche Geschlossenheit" that he felt the form of the novel could be renewed. I would like to look at how this unity is achieved in *Die Schlafwandler* by considering the philosophical and architectonic status of "Das Symposion oder Gespräch über die Erlösung," a dialog passage that appears in "Huguenau oder die Sachlichkeit."

Die Schlafwandler was written by Broch between 1928 and 1931, and it comprises three books. Each book is set in a different historical period – 1888, 1903, and 1918, respectively – and each presents a different story. Characters from the first two run over into the third, however, and there is a unity, as I mentioned above, to the trilogy's theme. Before I enter into a discussion of the symposium dialog and its relation to this theme, it might be best to provide a cursory review of the main points of the novel's plot.

Writing the Austrian Traditions: Relations between Philosophy and Literature.
Ed. Wolfgang Huemer and Marc-Oliver Schuster. Edmonton, Alberta:
Wirth-Institute for Austrian and Central European Studies, 2003. pp. 181-188.

The first book, "Pasenow oder die Romantik," is set in and around Berlin at the end of the nineteenth century. Lieutenant Joachim von Pasenow is the son of a Prussian landowner. The military and social traditions that have come to define his life are beginning to unravel around him. It is a gradual dissolution depicted in the book through his relationships with his father, his friend Eduard von Bertrand, and Ruzena, a girl from a local theatre with whom he has fallen in love. Joachim has a brief affair with Ruzena, but eventually ends their relationship and marries the daughter of a neighbouring landowner. His decision to marry Elisabeth Baddensen is a culmination of the romanticism to which the title refers; like the antiquated customs and habits that structure his life, Joachim's marriage is an empty formality and an attempt to escape from the changing realities of the world around him.

The second book is set in the industrial milieu of Cologne and Mannheim at the turn of the century. "Esch oder die Anarchie" centers on August Esch, a bookkeeper who develops an idiosyncrasy following his dismissal from a shipping company; he feels that the world is full of tiny, bookkeeping errors. Esch's attempt to trace these errors to what he perceives to be their origin fails, and he retreats into a world of utopian plans and dreams. He develops an idealized image of America and decides to go there to escape the pressures of his lower-class life, and he even invests his savings in a variety show, hoping that the profits will help him to leave Germany. Esch's restlessness and his constant desire to bring about some sort of social revolution constitute the "anarchy" to which the title of the second book refers. These impulses lead Esch to a confrontation with Bertrand, now an industrialist, and into an almost mystical relationship with Mutter Hentjen, the owner of a small tavern. Eventually Esch loses everything invested in the variety show and marries Mutter Hentjen.

Events in the third book take place toward the end of the First World War, in a little town on the Mosel. Both Esch and Pasenow reappear in "Huguenau oder die Sachlichkeit" (the former as the owner of the town's newspaper, the latter as its military governor), and so too do Bertrand and Mutter Hentjen. A deserter, Wilhelm Huguenau, arrives in the town and immediately proceeds to manipulate Esch out of his ownership of the newspaper and subsequently attains a certain prominence among the townspeople. But Huguenau lives in fear that his desertion from the army will be discovered, and the story that unfolds in the third book centers for the most part on his attempt to win the favor of Major Pasenow and to prevent any friendship from developing between the latter and Esch. "Huguenau oder die Sachlichkeit" includes various other story lines running parallel to, and at times crossing, the principal story of Huguenau, Esch, and Pasenow. Each of these secondary story lines concerns a different character in the town. Lieutenant Jaretzki, for example, has lost an arm in battle and tries to come to terms with his situation through alcohol. Hannah Wendling is a young woman who slowly loses her sense of connectedness to her husband, to her marriage, and finally to the world around her. Gödicke is a soldier who had been buried alive in the trenches and whose "resurrection" is in effect a gradual reconstruction of his identity. Also embedded in this third book are a narrative and an essay. The narrative, "Geschichte des Heilsarmeemädchens in Berlin," is recounted by a convalescent in the Berlin home of a group of Jewish refugees. As the third book unfolds, we discover that this convalescent is actually Bertrand, and that he is also the author of the essay, "Zerfall der Werte." Broch later wrote that in putting together the complex narrative of "Huguenau oder die Sachlichkeit" he intended to weave all of the separate stories together like a carpet:

> im *Huguenau* ist eine neue Technik versucht [...] Das Buch besteht aus einer Reihe von Geschichten, die alle das gleiche Thema abwandeln, nämlich die Rückverweisung des Menschen auf die Einsamkeit – eine Rückverweisung, die durch den Zerfall der Werte bedingt ist – und die Aufzeigung der neuen produktiven Kräfte, die aus der Einsamkeit entspringen, wenn sie tatsächlich manifest geworden ist. Diese einzelnen Geschichten, untereinander teppichartig verwoben, geben jede für sich eine andere Bewußtseinslage wieder: sie steigen aus dem völlig Irrationalen ("Geschichte des Heilsarmeemädchens in Berlin") bis zur vollständigen Rationalität des Theoretischen ("Zerfall der Werte"). Zwischen diesen beiden Polen spielen die übrigen Geschichten auf gestaffelten Zwischenebenen der Rationalität. Auf diese Art wird die Sinngebung der Gesamttrilogie erzielt, und ebenso wird der metaphysisch-ethische Gehalt [...] mit aller Deutlichkeit zum Ausdruck gebracht. (quoted in Durzak, 1966, 76)

The "Zerfall der Werte" that Broch describes is presaged by both Pasenow's romanticism and Esch's anarchism, and it culminates in Huguenau's "Sachlichkeit"; at the end of the third book, after coldbloodedly murdering Esch by stabbing him in the back, Huguenau later cheats Esch's widow, Mutter Hentjen, out of all her savings.

"Sachlichkeit" is in itself a difficult term to translate into English; it can be thought of as "objectivity," as "matter-of-factness," or perhaps even as "functionalism." All of the principal characters in *Die Schlafwandler* suffer from what might be called a disconnected perception of reality – with the exception of Huguenau. Unlike Pasenow and Esch, Huguenau is rooted in the objective here and now of the world. His relations with the other characters depend upon their usefulness to his plans, and he spends little time reflecting upon his actions. The problem, or idea, with which Broch was trying to come to terms in the character of Huguenau, was general to the period in which he wrote *Die Schlafwandler*. Huguenau not only confronts reality, but also creates it for himself by removing any secondary or ethical reflection from his actions. Broch is ambivalent when it comes to providing a final judgment of Huguenau and his Machiavellian attitude. At the end of the novel, Huguenau returns home and becomes a successful businessman. It is not that the novel is devoid of alternatives; in fact *Die Schlafwandler* is a perfect example of the interpretive possibilities that arise from what contemporary literary theorists have termed "the turn to narrative." My present concern, however, is with the actual structure or "Architektonik" of the novel.

Broch conceived his novel as a tangible structure and often used terms such as "Architektur" and "Architektonik" when describing the composition of *Die Schlafwandler*. As some of his readers have noted, it is not insignificant that a discussion of modernist architecture is included in the embedded essay in the third book, "Zerfall der Werte." Its author, Bertrand, begins the second part of his essay by commenting, "vielleicht ist das Entsetzen dieser Zeit in den architektonischen Erlebnissen am sinnfälligsten [...] hinter all meinem Ekel und meiner Müdigkeit steckt eine alte sehr fundierte Erkenntnis, die Erkenntnis, daß es für eine Epoche nichts Wichtigeres gibt als ihren Stil" (436). Paul Michael Lützeler has termed Broch the "kulturphilosophische Romanschriftsteller par excellence," and has provided the most detailed interpretation to date of the novel in relation to Broch's writings on the philosophy of culture. Like a number of authors of his generation, Broch was influenced by epochal theories of culture. Lützeler has shown how Broch's earlier thoughts on modernist architecture are repeated in "Zerfall der Werte," and he has also pointed to aspects of the "Architektur" of the novel that can be thought of as realizations of this theory. I would like to review some of Lützeler's arguments before I turn to the question of the "Symposion-Gespräch" (see Lützeler, 1996, 289-297).

At the turn of the century, the Viennese architect Adolf Loos helped to set the tone for the later development of modernist architecture when he advocated the removal of decorative ornaments and greater emphasis on functional considerations in the construction of buildings. Loos's criticism was directed at the type of aestheticism that had produced the various "neo" architectural styles (Gothic, Classic, Romantic) over the course of the nineteenth century. It is a criticism that was shared in certain respects by Broch himself. He used similar arguments to distinguish between art and kitsch, which he saw as "Mache" or "Dekorationsbombast" – an attempt to hide the lack of a central value through aesthetic decoration. But Broch also pointed to what he saw as the wider consequences of a total reduction of style to function. Loos was not simply describing architecture; he was writing from within that disintegration of a system of values he set out to criticize, and the problem, according to Broch, lay in Loos's evaluation of the ornament.

An ornament could be decorative and merely fulfill an aesthetic function, but for Broch it was also indicative of the style of a period in art history, and in this sense an ornament was not merely decoration; it completed a work of art by summarizing it and expressing its essence on a smaller scale. Accordingly, an approach to architecture that removed the ornament from its theoretical considerations, such as that proposed by Loos, could also reveal something about the epoch in which it appeared. In spite of his stated intentions, Loos's proposition was similar to a concept of art reduced to the aesthetic (*l'art pour l'art*) and to a system of values that had fractured into various independent systems of values with their own absolute logic. The author of "Zerfall der Werte" points out that the one quality which distinguishes modernist architecture from all previous architectural styles is the removal of the ornament, and that proponents of modernism have failed to recognize that the ornament is not merely an accessory; in its medial position, it provides the basis for any representation of a broader, or perhaps it would be better to say "deeper," unity between the two:

> "Baustil" ist Logik, ist eine Logik, die das Gesamtbauwerk durchdringt [...] und innerhalb dieser Logik ist das Ornament bloß das letzte, der differentiale Ausdruck im kleinen für den einheitlichen und einheitsetzenden Grundgedanken des Ganzen. (437)

The ornament is the only art form that cannot exist autonomously; as such, it provides the starting point for Bertrand's thoughts on the broader collapse of a universal system of values.

Lützeler has suggested that Broch incorporated his thoughts on the ornament by including "textual" markers in the novel that can be thought of as realizations of Bertrand's thoughts in the essay (299-303). In the first book, the military uniform assumes the role of ornament, and in the second book the variety show fulfills this function. Both motifs, according to Lützeler, are decorations; they hide the loss of a central value rather than help to bring expression to it. And both are restricted to the level of the diegesis. In the third book, it is the essay itself that takes on this role, but Lützeler believes that in this case, it represents an authentic ornament as it is conceived by Bertrand (and, ultimately, Broch):

> Das Gebäude findet seine ästhetische Vollendung im Ornament, und der Roman *Die Schlafwandler* findet seine Abrundung im "Zerfall der Werte". So sinnlos ein Ornament ohne Gebäude, so sinnlos "Der Zerfall der Werte" ohne die Romanhandlung. (Lützeler 298)

The essay grows out of the novel by integrating and discussing on a theoretical level all of the problems associated with the disintegration of values in the story. There are two other major compositional moments in the third book: "Geschichte des Heilsarmeemädchens in Berlin" and "Das Symposion oder Gespräch über die Erlösung." I would like to discuss now whether the latter can be considered as an ornament or decoration on the basis of what I have just described.

"Das Symposion oder Gespräch über die Erlösung" takes place in the home of Esch and Mutter Hentjen. The editor, his wife, Major Pasenow, and Huguenau are seated at a table. The narrator introduces the dialog, which ensues as a "Theaterszene" (551), and the form of the "Symposion-Gespräch" is the same as we would expect to find in a dramatic script or perhaps even the libretto of an opera. Dialog is rendered directly, although there are italicised passages that might pass for stage directions or prompts. The narrator also lets us know that this "Theaterszene" is a symbol. In fact, in the atomized and mediated world of *Die Schlafwandler*, it is the symbol of a symbol, a symbol "zweiter, dritter, n-ter Ableitung" (551).

In the opening dialog, Esch asks the Major if he would like another glass of wine. He declines, and Huguenau remarks, pretentiously, that it is a harmless wine and that the most the Major would have to fear from it is "einen einfachen natürlichen Rausch..., man schläft ein, wenn man genug hat, das ist alles" (552). Esch interjects that to be drunk is never natural: "ein Rausch," he says, "ist eine Vergiftung" (552). Huguenau, interpreting this as a taunt, replies in kind that he can recall times when Esch himself had drunk more than his share of wine in the local tavern. And looking over at Esch, he adds "übrigens [...], gar so unvergiftet kommen Sir mir nicht vor" (552). The Major, sensing perhaps that this denigration of Esch is being staged for his ears, tells Huguenau that his comments are deplorable. Huguenau persists, and goes so far as to call Esch a wolf in sheep's clothing, "ja, dabei bleibe ich... und, mit Verlaub zu sagen, seine Räusche tut er im geheimen ab" (552). What follows in the "Symposion-Gespräch" corresponds to the dramatic pattern set out in these opening lines. Huguenau, self-centered, sarcastic, and trying to draw the Major away from Esch, is himself excluded from the increasingly esoteric discussion between the other two men. Esch, following his own train of thought, breaks from it only occasionally to respond to Huguenau. The Major complements what Esch has to say, although it is clear from their exchange that he is also trying to draw Esch in a particular direction with his thoughts.

Numerous biblical references, and also allusions to other parts of the trilogy, are integrated into the "Symposion-Gespräch." The Major quotes the Lutheran Bible, and some of Esch's comments are reminiscent of his earlier conversation with Bertrand in the second book, when he visits the industrialist. Symbols are always difficult to interpret definitively, and I would like to suggest three possible ways in which the "Symposion-Gespräch" might be approached in relation to the theme of *Die Schlafwandler*.

First, in terms of the story, the dialog marks the point at which Huguenau becomes aware of both Pasenow's animosity toward him and the favorable opinion Pasenow has of Esch. The dynamic between Huguenau and Pasenow is one of the more interesting aspects of the third book, and it is never really clear if the former's mollification is self-serving or sincere. This fine line between rational and irrational action is, as Broch often pointed out, a principal element of *Die Schlafwandler*, and it finds its quintessence in Huguenau's attitude towards Pasenow.

Second, in respect of the essay, the dialog can be considered in relation to Bertrand's thoughts on religion. "Auf dem Tische," the narrator tells us in describing the scene, "das Brot und der Wein." Bread and wine are central to the Christian Holy Communion and are, at least since Hölderlin's famous poem, motifs associated in the German culture with a general unifying impulse. In the course of the dialog, Esch and Pasenow try to draw each other in a particular direction with their comments, and at the end they do reach a synthesis, but it is in the form of the song of the "Heilsarmee," something I will return to later.

Third, with regard to the novel's philosophy, and by that I mean Broch's comments on weaving the different story lines in the third book together like a carpet – what he would elsewhere call its polyhistoricism – the dialog is a "Symposium"-dialog. The Platonic original was rooted in the ancient Greek custom in which a group of men, after a meal and over wine, would discuss a topic chosen by a Symposiarch. Plato created an original philosophical genre based on this ritual, and it is this "Symposium" form, which the Romantics later imitated in their "Symphilosophieren" and to which the title of the dialog refers.

But is it an ornament or decoration? Most probably, it is a decoration. In spite of the fact that the "Symposion-Gespräch" condenses many of the principal themes of the novel, it ends in the song of "Heilsarmee." The "Zerfall der Werte" discusses architecture, philosophy, and also religion. Bertrand is extremely critical of Protestantism, and describes it as just another symptom of the disintegration of values. He does not consider it a religion (and therefore capable of instituting a new hierarchy of values), but rather as a sect, and he regards the Salvation Army itself as the quintessential Protestant sect:

> Religionen entstehen aus Sekten und zerfallen wieder in Sekten, keh-ren zu ihrem Ursprung zurück, ehe sie sich gänzlich auflösen. Am Anfang des Christentums standen die einzelnen Christus- und Mithraskulte, an seinem Ende stehen die grotesken amerikanischen Sekten, steht die Heilsarmee. (578)

Given the option of joining Marie, the Salvation Army girl, Bertrand chooses to stay with the Jewish refugees because he believes it is the most honorable choice available to him. If the "Symposion-Gespräch" is considered a decoration, however, then it might also give an indication of two directions in which the author of *Die Schlafwandler* did not see a possibility of renewal (at least at the time that the novel was written): in the Christian church and in Platonism. The ethical trajectory is similarly directed away from the past, but what distinguishes *Die Schlafwandler* is precisely this mixture of narrative and essay. Broch does not argue only from a position "beyond good and evil," he also depicts what he perceives to be its effects on the various characters in his novel. This "what he perceives to be" is perhaps the strongest argument that can be made against the ethical component of *Die Schlafwandler*.

In conclusion, I would like to touch upon a ubiquitous problem in recent literature on Broch, namely whether or not he should be considered a modernist or a post-modernist. At a recent conference, a novel by Thomas Mann was described as pre-postmodern. An elderly gentleman, somewhat perplexed, asked whether or not pre-postmodern simply meant modern; it is a question that might be asked of several German and Austrian authors whose novels are considered representative of late modernist prose. Lützeler has answered this question in favor of modernism for Broch, but in order to do this he focuses on Broch's Platonism. In Broch's insistence upon the need for a universal system of values, or at the very least his nostalgic recollection of it, Lützeler believes that Broch is on the other side of the philosophical divide when it comes to the central debate on the "grand narratives" (Lützeler 302). But I think that we could also take into consideration Broch's concept of a textual "Architektur" in this regard. The early theory of postmodernism was also informed by discussions about the larger role of architecture in society, and Charles Jencks's study *What is Post-modernism?* is a good example of this. Jencks hinted that one of the many revivals of postmodern architecture was the ornament, an ornament which not only grew out of the building to which it was attached but also helped to situate it in the broader community in which it was built. In this respect, Broch is not quite as modernist as he might seem at first glance, and I mention this only in order to suggest that the answer to a question that continues to perplex North American literary scholars – "What is a Postmodernist Text?" – might be found in the work of seemingly modernist authors such as Broch. The conclusion of *Die Schlafwandler* carries what would appear to be Broch's inscription: "Schluß der *Schlafwandler* / Wien 1928-31" (716). And this leads to a final question: Is the contemporary "return of the author," or what some critics refer to as "narcissistic narrative," an ornament or a decoration?

References

Broch, Hermann. *Die Schlafwandler: Eine Romantrilogie*. Frankfurt a.M.: Suhrkamp Taschenbuch Verlag, 1994.
Brinkmann, Richard. "Romanform und Werttheorie bei Hermann Broch. Strukturprobleme moderner Dichtung." *Deutsche Romantheorien: Beiträge zu einer historischen Poetik des Romans in Deutschland*. Ed. Reinhold Grimm, Frankfurt am Main: Athenäum Verlag, 1968. 347-374.
Durzak, Manfred. *Hermann Broch in Selbstzeugnissen und Bilddokumenten*. Reinbek bei Hamburg: Rowohlt Verlag, 1966.
–. *Hermann Broch*. Stuttgart: J.B. Metzler, 1968.
–. "Flake und Döblin. Ein Kapitel in der Geschichte des Polyhistorischen Romans." *Germanisch-Romanische Monatsschrift* 20 (1970): 286-305.
Hutcheon, Linda. *A Poetics of Postmodernism: History, Theory, Fiction*. New York: Routledge, 1992.
Jencks, Charles. *What is Post-modernism?* New York: St. Martin's Press, 1989.
Lützeler, Paul Michael. "Hermann Brochs Architektur-Theorie und ihre Auswirkung auf *Die Schlafwandler*." *Von Franzos zu Canetti: jüdische Autoren aus Österreich. Neue Studien*. Ed. Mark H. Gelber, Tübingen: Niemeyer, 1996. 289-303.
Petersen, Jürgen. *Der Deutsche Roman der Moderne: Grundlegung, Typologie, Entwicklung*. Stuttgart: J.B. Metzler, 1991.

SONNETS

by

Franz Josef Czernin

wasser, sonett

das meer, es wird durchkreuzt im eignen namen laut,
da im glas wasser stürmt, als öffnung vor zu schweben,
wie all die schäume sich mit lippen selbst beleben,
dass wasser unsre farben spielt, zusammen braut

sein bild als aug: aus blauem sich das durch uns staut,
blick bis zum rand zu füllen, da auf die see wir heben,
von grund auf schwall ausschöpfend, wir auch fliessend geben,
dem meer, den wellen wort, das unsern lauf rein schaut:

gestrichen wird, auch an wie aus, das ganze segel
an jedem punkt, dass tränen, tropfen sich durchdringen,
aus einem guss, in einem boot auf uns zu bringen,

ja lösend ruder, blatt mit dieser zunge: pegel
auf es und angibt mit der quelle, die in dingen
und zwischen zügen, zeilen fasst: stillt dies die regel?

wasser, sonett

was unter strömt und über schäumt, ich übersetze
durch dich, der wasser uns so hoch, so tief lässt reichen,
da es sich, fliessend, über trägt, noch im entweichen,
als das, was unter jeder hand gemein, knüpft plätze,

die ich uns, unter gründig, über mässig, durch die netze
da regnen lasse; was, uns schwall, in all den schläuchen
läuft unter, über neu durch dich, seh ich aus teichen
mit nassen augen, dass uns zwischen zeilen schätze

flüstern sich ein, die winken? wasser, das ins wasser geht,
uns über, unter, rauscht so wahr vom wein, der schenkt
sich ein bald, rein, da unter schwellig, es gelenkt

stets auf dich selbst, mir über fällig, wort an steht
da bis zum hals: wie es sich murmelnd schön her drängt,
uns mund schon wässrig macht, bis dir der trank gerät.

erde, sonett

aus grauem, masse wälzt es sich, uns rührt, wild dreht,
ja schleudert ding aus sich, hier mich heraus fest greifend,
dass heiss der brei hervor gebracht hat uns, gesät
als korn längst, wahr dran, doch jetzt auf den teig versteifend

sich dergestalt; so macht ich uns aus staub, der sich gerät
feucht ausser sich, in all den namen gliedernd, reifend,
dass es, in solcher fassung, sich bewahrt, da steht,
geformt, bezeugt durch uns, selbst schale so einstreifend

als kern wie sachlich: was das heisst, da wir durchdringen
uns leibhaft, dass es sauer, süss aufgeht, das maß
gebend, so ein wie aus, gleich voll: was uns schon stets besaß,

schürft lebhaft, tief hier? steine, brote, die verschlingen
einander uns, am wort, das hält, sich isst gelingen
auf ganz: ob jeder deut davon jetzt in sich las?

erde, sonett

aus nichts als punkten, tot, aus all dem staub, dem grauen,
da aufgewirbelt massenhaft, zeug dies so greift
heraus, rührt heiss sich bald, zu brei, an sich zu bauen,
aufgehend, ein- in solcher sache, ob es auch läuft,

ja über, ach, auf uns heraus; wie nackt, versteift
darauf, abtastend dergestalt wir dadurch schauen,
an ganz gehörig; so gefasst hält eins sich, reift,
dies gliedernd leibhaft, fest, jetzt endlich zu verdauen

am wort: das teilt mit unsrem korn, wahr dran, verkehrt,
(auch mit sich selbst), schalen, ja, kerne lässt zerspringen,
wie wir uns stets mit haut danach, mit haar verzehrt.

kein krümel bleibt auf einmal, nichts von all den dingen
als das, was sich aus unsren, freien stücken nährt,
da wir im eignen namen selbst durch uns ganz dringen.

waizen, spreu

da boden doppelt, so aufwühlend, zu mir fällt,
es stampft aus spreu und staub sich, lärm und all dem kot;
zusammen stoppelnd, stotternd sich, heraus dies stellt,
dass das, was wüst gesät, sich aufgeht, all dies schrot

in körnern, wahr an uns; dran sich es, wörtlich, hält,
da ich es mahle aus, so fruchtbar aus der not
beleibt, wie es uns schmerzlich fasst, bis wir gepellt
aus jeder schale frisch sind, neu, einander brot,

dies da mit teilend: kern gepflanzt, auch fort, gemessen
uns dergestalt wird zu, in jedem zeug bedingt
mit haar und haut, auskostend bitter, süss, wir fressen

uns auf, ganz sachlich: wie da an sich erde bringt,
hier jeden fussbreit mich, wir sind, von uns besessen,
im letzten krümel noch, was durch sich selber dringt?

erde, sonett

aus all dem dunklen, böden, staub gestampft, errichtet
einladend sich dies haus, anheim euch, fest gestellt,
dass prunkvoll türmend, doch bedacht gefügt, geschichtet,
die leeren plätze greifend, raum in räumen sich gesellt,

weit dafür eingenommen uns; was da höfe hält,
auch worte, weiss einleuchtend, ist so reich gewichtet,
trägt bis zum letzten stein, leicht über auch, sei zelt,
das uns anhimmelnd fernen ausmalt, fenster dichtet.

wie hell wir uns durch hallen wieder holen, spiegelnd
glanzvoll erschliessen; stufe über stufe schwingt
sich auf, uns hebt aus all den angeln, lauf beflügelnd,

vervielfacht tür ist, tor, gleich ein- sind, ausgeklinkt,
gekreuzt wird jeder gang mit sich: ob auf es springt,
das ganze schloss, eröffnend uns, sich selbst besiegelnd?

erde, sonett

voll pracht, hochherzig malend aus uns ganz, errichtet
leibhaft der bau sich, weitläufig an wie ausgelegt,
abstufend reich mir zu gestalten viel geschichtet,
auch heimlich räume greift es, haupt stumm, steinern prägt,

anhimmelnd so bedacht; euch eingefleischt ihr mich verdichtet,
dass wir uns bilden ein gesicht, da glanzvoll trägt
mich festlich, körper, über euch, wie schwer gewichtet
aus tiefen wieder hallen holt, zu ruhn bewegt

auf welchen säulen, bögen! ach, im grossen, zügen
zugänglich mir, doch uns auch übersteigt dies zelt,
hebt lauf auf keis um kreis, erschliesst, nicht nur verschwiegen,

den punkt, so hoch: ringsum ihr schallt, mich gleich euch stellt,
schön dar, dass wir von grund auf zu einander fügen,
da leuchtend ein dies haus erbaulich uns erhält?

erde, sonett

schwankend der ganze bau, von grund fest uns erschütternd,
da wir, so lückenhaft, falsch, schief, sind uns gelegt,
ja aus auch, unbedacht ent-deckt; ich, doppelt, zitternd
zieh böden weg euch, überstürzend kaum dies trägt,

wird stets entworfen. wie bin haltlos uns, zersplitternd,
stellt bloss sich dies, durch euch entrüstet, auf sich schlägt,
an selbst gemasst. in trümmer gehn, verlustig und verwitternd
malt mir dies dunkel an die wand , wie sehr bewegt

rührt blindlings uns. so wird auf dies stets gehoben,
aus all den angeln wir, da fehlend, doch in stücken,
an allen ecken, enden tür sind, tor, verschoben,

verschaukelt! wie ist frei der himmel, sich erblicken
leer lässt, ein loch zuletzt: getürmt prunkt staub, wir oben
wie unten sind da mit geteilt, haus zu entrücken?

erde, sonett

dies eingefleischte kleid, darin ich tief versenkt,
dass es sich, stoffe blühend, glanzvoll uns entfaltet,
prächtig erscheint, schön färbend; schleierhaft beengt
es mich, doch damit uns erwirkt, hier leibhaft waltet,

ja, schaltet: schalen sind um schichten mir verhängt,
da jede silbe auf sich drängt, sinnreich uns spaltet,
dass es die blüten streut, dies so besternt, umfängt,
schmerzlich bemäntelnd uns verblümt, doch wohl gestaltet!

ach, dunkel zu gefallen, uns dies überträgt
einander musterhaft, da sich, davon durchdrungen,
das blatt so teilt, selbst mit, bloss sich gewand jetzt legt,

staub aus, in unsren namen: wie wir sind verschlungen
im kern so herz-, ja sachlich, bis, doch neu geprägt,
dies platzt heraus, mit jeder faser nackt, entsprungen.

erde, sonett

da so ich angetanzt, wie ihr mir leibhaft gleicht,
in all dem zeug, einander wieder uns zu geben,
ich, stofflich eure pracht entfaltend, wechsle leicht
die seiten, als ihr, kleidsam mich so anzustreben,

mich dreht, mir schleierhaft, zum ding: behende reicht
mir das, ergreifend, euch, da wir uns selbst aufheben
in der verschlingung, bis ihr wendig euch entweicht,
auffächernd mich allein, doch so, wie ich vorschweben

in meinen namen lass mir uns: ja, dies gewand,
verkörpernd dergestalt, schön auslegt und beschreitet,
wie wir uns übertragen, zeigend rand um rand

so ungesäumt: stets jede masche sich ausweitet,
geht durch sich selbst, entsprechend, weit gespannt,
bis alle fasern nackt sind, wir ganz ausgedeutet.

luft, sonett

da es mich schrillt, verpfeift, bin aufgeschreckt, -gespürt,
heraustrompetet selbst verschreiend durch mich drehe;
umbraust, durchzuckt weh im verdonnern bin gerührt,
verschleudernd alles sausen lasse, flöten gehe,

bis es, zusammentrommelnd, packt mich, schlägt, abschwirrt,
mitreissend mich verzupft, verduften lässt, dass stehe,
nein, längst verweht bin, stets auf andrem blatt, verirrt,
entgeisternd mir, vergeigt, verschollen, ja, die böe,

weit fegt, hinweg...in schwebe bleibe, luft so liegen,
wie kreis, sich selbst beschreibend, mich lässt an sich deuten,
dass fern anklingend hohe bögen mich aufwiegen:

am höchsten punkt es lässt uns all dies hören, läuten,
bis wind, sich legt, auch aus-, wird still. so frisch erschwiegen,
sich wort hält atem an uns, neu mich zu besaiten?

luft, sonett

süss wird es eingeblasen, doch uns gleich geht flöten,
da wir gehörig sind erschüttert, stürmisch, lückenhaft,
sodass es auf mich, durch uns pfeift, all dies trompeten,
einpauken stopft die löcher nicht, sie schmerzlich klafft:

so sind gepackt, gerüttelt maß, wir wind gedrehten,
ja davon aufgewirbelt, es uns trommelt, rafft
zusammen, hochreisst laut, die so aus uns gewehten!,
bis selbst uns fern dies läuten hören lässt, geschafft

wer weiss wie sehr, wohin: was ist da aufgegangen,
dass wir entgeistert sind, vergeigt, doch auch erwogen
in atem haltend an uns, immerfort anlangen,

am höchsten punkt, so sehr verspielt, ja aufgeflogen,
doch rings voll anklang: ob wir uns so selbst einfangen,
in schwebe bleibt, ob aus, ob ein uns schliesst der bogen.

engel, zungen

wie lücken-, schleierhaft es antanzt, doch auch lichtend,
so leicht uns fächert auf: hauch zart besaitend luft
sich greift aus mir, dass stofflich, doch auch fein, gewichtend,
wir flöten gehn einander, sehr verlustig, kluft

uns anweht! reich, doch nebelhaft auch, sich andichtend,
hier süss aus jedem loch verpfiffen, aus dem blauen
es gibt uns wieder ein, dich zuträgt, bis, uns sichtend,
selbst wendig kreis drehn, wort, ja, atem halten, stauen:

allseits sind so posaunt heraus, hinein gewandt,
wie wir anhimmeln selbst aus heiterm uns vielkehlig,
da, insgeheim gelüftet, noch das fernste band

dich auslöst, ein: jetzt bin mir voll-, ach, überzählig,
antönend wohl dir zu gefallen, weit bis zum rand,
dem letzten deut uns froh entlocken, so saumselig?.

Diese Gedichte stammen aus *elemente, sonette,* aus einem Vorhaben, an dem ich seit einigen Jahren arbeite.

INDEX

Subject-entries are printed in italics; page-numbers in italics refer to endnotes.

A

Aeschylus, 3, *177*
aesthetic(s), 39, 41, 49–64, 82, 84, 92, 102, 112, 115, *116*, 121–23, 125, 134, 145–46, 153, *157*, 169, 171, *174*, *177*, 184
aestheticism, 125–27, 184
Allen, Woody, 146
analysis, 37, 68, 146–49, 155, *158*
Angell, James B., *29*
anti-liberalism, 94–96
anti-realism, 57, 169
anti-Semitism, *156*
Anzengruber, Ludwig, 42, 45
architecture, 25, 41, 44, 46, 79, *157*, 183–87
Aristotelianism, *35*, *98*, *176*
Aristotle, 2, 3, 17, 55, 60, 87, 132, *176*
association, method of, 3, 15, 17–18
Ayer, Alfred Jules, *158*

B

Bachofen, Johann Jacob, 170
Bahr, Hermann, 163
Baird, John Wallace, *30*
Barker, Ernest, *142*
Beardsley, Monroe C., 114
behaviorism, 14–15, *28*, *29*, 71, *157*
Benjamin, Walter, 144
Bergmann, Gustav, 13–21, *28*, *31*
Berkeley, George, 52
Bernet, Rudolf, 124
Bertram, Ernst, *142*
Blackburn, Simon, 54
Bloom, Harold, *64*
Blumenberg, Hans, 10
Bohr, Niels, 144
Boltzmann, Ludwig, 41, 73
Bolzano, Bernard, 45
Brentano, Franz, 4, 45, 134–35, 140, *141*, *158*
Breuer, Josef, 18, 21, 73
Brinkmann, Richard, 181
Broad, C.D., 15
Broch, Hermann, 9–10, 143, 145, 151, 181–90
Brouwer, L.E.J., 68
Bruckner, Anton, 45
Brunswik, Egon, 13, 14, 15, 17, 20–21
Burgess, Guy, 76
Busch, Wilhelm, 41
Bush, George, 77

C

Caesar, Julius, 107
Calvinism, 24, 138, 142
cameralism, 136
Camus, Albert, *157*
Cantor, Georg, 154
Carlyle, Thomas, 22–24
Carnap, Rudolf, 25–27, *32*, *35*, 153, *158*
Catholicism, 40, 42, 82, 94–96
causality, 15, 16, 22, 26–27, *33*–*34*, 44, 134
Chamisso, Albert v., 41
Chaplin, Charlie, 75
Christianity, 24, 38, 39, 69
civilization, 76, 79, 87, 151, *157*

clarification, 27, 41, 68-70, 73, 77, 79, 109
Claudius, Matthias, 41
Clinton, William, 77
Cohen, Robert S., *31*
Comte, Auguste, 38
conservativism, 3, *32*, 45, 95, 137
Cornish, Kimberly, 71-72, 76
Couturat, Louis, *156*
Crossman, Richard H.S., 8
Cuvier, Georges, 17

D

Darwin, Charles, 14, 38, 106
Daviau, Donald, 127
Defoe, Daniel, 115
Democritus, 4
Derrida, Jacques, 50, *175*
Descartes, René, 122, 123-24
Dewey, John, 14
Dirac, Paul A.M., 144
Döblin, Alfred, 143, 181
Doderer, Heimito v., 10
Dos Passos, John, 181
Dostoevskii, Fedor, 37-38, 42, 44
Doyle, Arthur Conan, 101, 113, *116*
drama, 125, 132, 136, 137, *175*, *176*
Drobil, Michael, 40
Dupriez, Bernard, *176*
Durzak, Manfred, 181, 183

E

Ehrenfels, Christian v., 133
Einstein, Albert, 106, 144, *156*
Electra, 160-80
emotion, 25, *98*, *143*, 145-49, 155, *157*
empiricism, 26, *32*, *35*, 39, 154
Engelmann, Paul, 41, 46, 94
Engels, Friedrich, 38
enlightenment, 8, 37, 85, 96, 131-42, 143, 146, 153, 155
Epicureanism, 22-24
Epicurus, 22, 23

epistemology, *35*, 144, 154, 175
Ernst, Paul, 7, 43, 133, 140
ethic, 78
ethics, 9, 22-23, 26, *34*, 68, 72, 75, 77, 84, 87, 88, 91, 143, 150, *157*, 160, 164, 173, *177*
Euripides, 3, *177*

F

falsification, 20
family resemblance, 69, 95
fascism, 79
Feigl, Herbert, 29, *32*
feuilleton, 73, 145
Feyerabend, Paul, 148
Fichte, Johann Gottlieb, *177*
Ficker, Ludwig v., 40, 94
Ficker, Ludwig von, 42, 67
fiction(ality), 50-52, 49-64, 101-20
Findlay, J.N., 129
Ford, Maddox Ford, *98*
Fox, George, 70
Frank, Manfred, 163, *177*
Franz Joseph I., 173, *175*
Frederick William, 138
Frege, Gottlob, 27, 37, 41, 68, 70, 73, 112-13, 144, 154
Freud, Anna, 13
Freud, Sigmund, 3, 4, 13-35, 73, 83, 87, *98*, 135, 140, 146-47, 163, 172, *174*, *175*
Friedman, Michael, *34*
Friedrich, Caspar David, 166

G

Gadol, Eugene T., *32*
Geach, Peter, 71
Gestalt, *35*, 44, 133
Gide, André, 181
Gierke, Otto v., *142*
Gladstone, William Erwart, 18
God(s), 6, 26, 39, 59, 82, 85-88, 91, 95, 139
Gödel, Kurt, 151, 154

Goethe, Johann Wolfgang von, 41, 68, 69, 71, 81, 139, 147, *156*
Golding, William, 114, *119*
Gomperz, Heinrich, 3-4, 6-7
Gomperz, Theodor, 3-6, 8-10
grammar, 69, 71-72, 77, 92
Grass, Günter, *157*
Greer, Germaine, *98*
Grillparzer, Franz, 2-5, 41, 45, 89, 95, 135, 138-39
Grote, George, 4-6, 8
Grünbaum, Adolf, 14, 17, 20-21

H

Habermas, Jürgen, 20
Habsburg, 132, 135, 138, 160, *175*
Hamlet, 103
Handke, Peter, *174*
Hänsel, Ludwig, 40, 68, 94
Harrison, Bernard, 49, 63
Hayek, Friedrich A. v., 38, *46*
Hebbel, Friedrich, *156*
Hegel, G.W.F., 2, 38, 132, 133
Hegelianism, 14
Hehner, Cay, *157*
Heidegger, Martin, *32*
Heine, Heinrich, 73
Hertz, Heinrich, 41, 73
Hesse, Hermann, 143, 149
Hilmy, S. Stephan, 43-44
Hintikka, Jaakko, 37, 69
historicism, 139
historiography, 133
Hitler, Adolf, 13, 24, 67, 75, 76, 73-77
Hobbes, Thomas, 17, *35*
Hofmannsthal, Hugo v., 94, 144, 173, *178*
Hofmannsthal, Hugo von, 121-30
Hölderlin, Friedrich, 1, *156*, 186
holism, 155
Holmes, Sherlock, 101, 103-14, 116, *118*
Horney, Karen, 15

humanism, 22, 49-64, 132, 152, 153, 155
Hume, David, 24-27, *33*, 115
Hussein, Saddam, 77
Husserl, Edmund, 121-30, 140

I

idealism, 10, 45, 52-53, 88, 153

J

Janik, Allan, 42-43, 126, 129
Jencks, Charles, 187
Jesus, 69
Jewish, 72
Jones, Ernest, 15, 16
Joseph II., 136, 137
journalism, 96
Joyce, James, 143, 181

K

Kafka, Franz, 143, 147, 149
Kant, Immanuel, 2, 10, 22, *32*, *33*, 45, 68, 81, 88-90, 95, 137, 138, 150, 155, *158*, 167
Kantianism, 14, 27, *32*, *35*, 88-90, 146, 154
Kaufmann, Walter, *142*, 173
Keller, Gottfried, 41
Kent, Clark (*alias* Superman), 103
Kern, Iso, 123-24
Keynes, John M., 67
Kierkegaard, Søren, 38, 39, 95
King John, 17, *30*
Kleist, Heinrich v., 41, 138
Kraus, Karl, 41-42, 67-79, 81-100, *98*, 143-44, 145
Kripke, Saul, 72
Kross, Matthias, 69
Kuhn, Thomas, 148
Kürnberger, Ferdinand, 42, 45

L

Lamarque, Peter, 51, *117*
Lange, Friedrich, 26–27, *33*, *35*
language, 2, 49–64, 143
language game, 40, 54, *64*, 69–70, 72, 126
Leibniz, Gottfried Wilhelm, *158*
Lenau, Nikolaus, 41, 45
Lenin, Vladimir Ilich, 38
Leopardi, Giacomo, 38
Lessing, Gotthold Ephraim, 41
Levinson, 8
Lewis, David, 101–20
Lichtenberg, Georg Christoph, 2
literature, philosophy of, 49–64, 103–14
Locke, John, 17, *35*
logic, 37, 55, 68, 71, 77–78, 101–20, 144, 153, 154, 185
Loos, Adolf, 40–41, 73, 75, 94, 184
Lorentz, Hendrik Antoon, *156*
Luft, David S., 147, *156*, *157*, *158*, 159
Luserke, Matthias, *174*, *178*
Lützeler, Paul Michael, 184–85, 187
Lysias, 5

M

Mach, Ernst, 7, 38, 133, 140, 144–45, 151, 152, 155, *156*, 160, 163–64, 167–69, 172, 173, *175*, *178*
Mahler, Gustav, 43, 46
Malcolm, Norman, 69, 70, 77–78
Mallarmé, Stephane, *175*
Mann, Thomas, 24, *32*, *34*, 143–44, 145, 181, 187
Marbach, Eduard, 124
Maria Theresia, 136–37
Marx, Karl, 23, 38, 133
mathematics, 143–59
Maudsley, Henry, 17–18, 22
McGuinness, Brian, 76
meaning, 7, 25, *29*, *31*, *33*, 40, 55, 56–60, 68, 69, 72, 92, 101–2, 131, 139, 153, 167, 172
Meinong, Alexius, 101–20, *158*
Merkel, Reinhard, 137
metaphysics, 1, 4, 8, 9, 22, 25–26, *31*, *35*, 59, 70, 77–78, 82, 146, 163, 166
Mill, John Stuart, 4–6, 23–24, 30, *31*, *34*, *35*
Milne, A.A., *30*
Milosevic, Slobodan, 77
Minkowski, Hermann, *156*
Mises, Richard v., 144
modernism, 187
modernity, 42, 43, 79, 160, 163
Montaigne, Michel de, *159*
Moore, George Edward, 23, 37
Mörike, Eduard, 41, 46
Müller, Heiner, 172, *178*
music, 37, 39, 43, 44, 46, 76, 79, 84, 140, *176*
Musil, Robert, 44, 143–59, 160–80, 181
Mussolini, Benito, 3
mysticism, 8, 153, 155, 161, 169, *176*

N

Naess, Arne, 13, *28*
Napoléon Bonaparte, 107
narrative, 63, *157*
National Socialism, 75
national-socialism, 24, *32*, *34*, *157*
neo-Kantianism, *34*–*35*
Nestroy, Johann, 41, 45
Neurath, Marie, *31*
Neurath, Otto, 13, 22, 23, 27, 28, 144
Newton, Isaac, 106
Nietzsche, Friedrich, 1, 7, 14, *32*, *33*, *34*, *35*, 38, 46, 88, 139, *142*, *159*, *178*
Nixon, Richard, 103–4
Novalis, 166, *176*–*77*
Nyíri, Janos Christof, 42–43

O

Oedipus, 160–80
ontology, 49–64, 101–20, *158*
Orestes, 160, 162, 164, 167, 172–74
ornament, 181–90
Othello, 61–63, *64*

P

Parsons, Terence, *116*, *118*
Pascal, Blaise, 38
Pašniczek, Jacek, *117*
Payne, Phillip, 152
Peano, Giuseppe, *156*
Petersen, Jürgen, 181
Pettit, Philip, 72
phenomenology, 115, 121–30, 134, 153
philosophy of science, 148
philosophy, analytic, 37, 39, 70, 145, 147
philosophy, German, 1–2, 14, 17, 20, 26, 28, *32*, *34*, 45, 88, 134
philosophy, Romantic, 14, 17, 20, 26, 28, *32*, *34*
philosophy, scientific, 143, 144–45, 153
Pierrot, 161–64, 166–67, 171, *175*, *176*
Pike, Burton, 147, *156*, 159, *176*
Plato, 51, 87, 88, 92, 152, 165, 186
pleasure, 22–24, 123
poetry, 25, 37–48, 63, 49–64, 73, 123, 127, 134, 145
politics, *32*, 67, 73–79
Popper, Karl R., 3, 8–10, 20
positivism, 143, 153, 163, *175*
positivism, logical, 28, 145, 148, 152–55
postmodernism, 187
pragmatism, 85, 150–55, 168, 173, *178*
Protagoras, 4
Protestantism, 82, 94–96, 186
Proust, Marcel, *156*

psychoanalysis, 13–35, 83, 92, 96, 147, 160–80
psychology, 2, 5, 71, 82, 86, 121, 123, 124, 144, 145, 147, 146–49, 153, 155, 160, 163, 168
Pufendorf, Samuel, 136
Putnam, Hilary, 54

Q

Quakerism, 70–72
Quine, Willard V.O., 145

R

Ramsey, Frank, 68, 106
Rand, Ayn, *157*
rationalism, 96, 152, 153
rationality, 9, 81, 146–49, *158*, 183, 186
realism, 49–64, 83, 115, 155
reason, 9, 26, *33*, *34*, 83–86, 88–89, 146, 147, 149, 152, 153, *158*
reduction, phenomenological, 121–30
religion, 3, 4, 9–10, 24–28, 39, 38–40, 45, 69, 87, 95, 138, 150, 153, 186
Ricoeur, Paul, 20
Riehl, Alois, *156*
Rilke, Rainer Maria, 41, 42
romanticism, 22, 38, 147, *157*, 166–67, *176*, 182, 183, 186
Rorty, Richard, 58
Rubens, Heinrich, *156*
Russell, Bertrand, 37, 39–41, 67, 68, 73, 78, 104, *117*, 145, 151, *156*

S

scepticism, 2, 51–53, 54, 58–63, 103, 122, 125, 127, 133, 172
Schalek, Alice, 96–97
Schalkwyk, David, 49
Schiller, Friedrich, 41
Schlegel, Friedrich von, 166, *176*

Schleiermacher, Friedrich, 2, 5
Schlick, Moritz, 22–24, 27, *31*, *32*, *34*, *35*, 68, 70
Schlöndorff, Volker, 143, *157*
Schmidt, Adalbert, 139, *142*
Schnitzler, Arthur, 147
Schopenhauer, Arthur, 37, 38, 41, 71, 73, 88, *177*
Schumann, Robert, 46
Schwarz, Hermann Amadeus, *156*
science, 7, 13–35, 38, 72, 75, 115, 122, 124, 133, 134, 135, 143, 144–50, 152, 155, *156*
semantics, 7, 52, 60, 101–20
sex(uality), 15, 50, 62, 81–94, 149, 163, 166–72, *175–77*
Shakespeare, William, 49, 61–63, *64*, 103
silence, 67–79, 162, 167, *178*
Silesius, Angelus, 39
Smith, Adam, *141*
Smollett, Tobias, 115
Snows, C.P., 155
Socrates, 1, 2, 5–7, *157*
Sommer, Louise, 136, *141*
Sonnenfels, Joseph von, 136
Sophocles, 3, 162, *177*
Spence, K.W., *28*
Spencer, Herbert, 38
Spengler, Oswald, 41, 44, 73
Sraffa, Piero, 41, 73
St. Simon Stylites, 23
Stifter, Adalbert, 95, 131–42
Stonborough, Margarete, 41
Storm, Theodor, 134
Stuckert, Franz, 134
Stumpf, Carl, *156*
style, 25, 37, 39, 43, 70, 73, 135, 145, *156*, 181, 184

T

Tagore, Rabindranath, 42
Thackery, William, 115
Tieck, Ludwig, 166

Tolstoi, Leo, 37–39, 42, 44, *46*, 109
Toulmin, Stephen, 42, 126
Trakl, Georg, 42, 46
truth, 6, 20, 26, *27*, 45, 51, 57–64, 70, 72, 74–75, 83–85, 89, 91, 101–2, 107–16, *118–19*, 145, 153–55, *158*

U

Uhland, Ludwig, 41
Updike, John, 143–44
utilitarianism, 22, *31*

V

value, 16, 43, 51, 78, 81–100, 102, 136, *177*, 183–85, 187
verification, 17, 106, 153
Vienna Circle, 9, 13–35, 143–44, 146, 153–55, *156*
Vigny, Alfred de, 38
Virgil, 57

W

Wagner, Richard, 166, *176–77*
Waismann, Friedrich, 70
Watson, John B., 14–16, *28*
Wedekind, Frank, 175
Weininger, Otto, 41, 73, 81–100, 170
Wieland, Christoph Martin, 1
Williams, William Carlos, *98*
Wimsatt, William K., 114
Wittgenstein, Ludwig, 7, 10, 37–48, 49–64, 67–79, 82, 91–92, 94, 140, 144–45, 153, *156*, *157*
Wright, Georg Henrik von, 37–38, 42–43

Z

Zohn, Harry, 73, 75
Zweig, Arnulf, 75
Zweig, Stefan, 145

CONTRIBUTORS

Mark E. Blum
Ph.D. in Modern European History, is presently Professor of History at the University of Louisville. Professor Blum has published a book on the *Austro-Marxists, 1890-1918*. His current interests include a comparison and contrast of the narrative logic of German and Austro-German culture in the modern era, particularly in the disciplines of history, literature, and the social sciences.

Franz Josef Czernin
Born 1952 in Vienna, studied from 1971 to 1973 in the USA. Since 1978 he publishes poems, novels, plays, essays, and aphorisms. He is member of the Grazer Autorenversammlung and the *Bielefelder Colloquium für neue poesie*. In 1993 he was writer in residence in Graz. Since 1980 he works on a project of a *kunst des dichtens*, an encyclopedic attempt to unite forms, techniques, and topics in one opus. He has received various awards and scholarships. The most recent are: 1997 Award of the City of Vienna for literature; 1998 Heimito von Doderer Award for literary essays; 1999 Anton Wildgans Award of the Austrian Industry.

Randall R. Dipert
C.S. Peirce Professor of American Philosophy at the University at Buffalo (SUNY); he taught, at the time of the writing of this essay, at the U.S. Military Academy at West Point; he has a longstanding interest in German-speaking and especially Austrian philosophy and literature. He has directed a program for study in Vienna, and the Austrian Studies Program at SUNY Fredonia. His other research interests include the philosophy of mathematics and logic, aesthetics, American philosophy, the philosophy of action and artefacts, and the philosophy of mind.

Newton Garver
Distinguished Service Professor at SUNY at Buffalo, is author of *This Complicated Form of Life*. The current paper is one of a series of papers tracing the metaphysical and practical implications of Wittgenstein's distinction between showing and saying. His other research interest is on philosophical aspects of violence and nonviolence; he recently contributed the article "Nonviolence" to the Scribners encyclopedia *Violence in America*. He can be reached at garver@acsu.buffalo.edu.

John Gibson received his Ph.D. in philosophy from the University of Toronto in May, 2001. His thesis, *Fiction & The Weave of Life*, is a study of the various problems literature raises for the philosophy of language.

Mark Grzeskowiak

He is currently a doctoral candidate at the Department of Germanic Languages and Literature at the University of Toronto. The title of his thesis is *The Symposium as Architext. A Study on Ernst Jünger's Approach to Narrative*. His interests are twentieth-century German literature, literary theory, history of poetics, political philosophy, intellectual history, and German-Canadian Studies.

Rudolf Haller

Rudolf Haller, born 1929 in St. Gallen, Austria; Professor Graz 1967; Visiting Professor: Peking University 1984, Stanford University 1985, Rome/La Sapienza 1988, University of Sao Paulo 1990, University of Hiroshima 1999. Author of 8 books and about 300 papers. Editor of the complete works of A. Meinong and O. Neurath, founder of *Grazer Philosophische Studien. An International Journal of Analytic Philosophy* (1975-2000; 60 vols.), and the series *Studien zur Österreichischen Philosophie* (1979-2001; 33 vols.).

Wolfgang Huemer

Wolfgang Huemer studied philosophy and German philology at the Universities of Salzburg, Fribourg, Bern, and Toronto. He finished his Ph.D. on phenomenology and philosophy of mind in 1999 and teaches currently at the University of Erfurt. He published articles on Brentano, Wittgenstein, and philosophy of mind and works currently on problems of perception and Husserlian phenomenology as well as the historical relations between phenomenology and analytic philosophy. His email address is: wolfgang.huemer@uni-erfurt.de.

Dale Jacquette

Professor of philosophy at The Pennsylvania State University. He has written books and numerous articles on central figures in Austrian philosophy. His recent publications include *Philosophy of Mind, Meinongian Logic: The Semantics of Existence and Nonexistence, Wittgenstein's Thought in Transition*, and *David Hume's Critique of Infinity*. Jacquette has also edited the Blackwell *Companion to Philosophical Logic* and is currently editing *The Cambridge Companion to Brentano*.

Wendelin Schmidt-Dengler

Professor for German literature at the University of Vienna; he has written several books and more than 200 articles on Austrian and German literature. He has edited works by Heimito von Doderer and Fritz von Herzmanovsky-Orlando. He is the director of the Archive of Literature of the Austrian National Library and member on the board of the Thomas Bernhard Stiftung. Schmidt-Dengler was Visiting Professor in Pisa (1984), Naples (1986), Klagenfurt (1975), Salzburg (1978), Graz (1982), and Stanford (1991).

Marc-Oliver Schuster
Studied German philology and philosophy at the University of Salzburg and Toronto. He wrote his Ph.D. thesis about *A Semiotic Study of Structuralist Imagination: H.C. Artmann's Aesthetics and Postmodernity*. Publications include articles on Doderer, Artmann, Celan, and Nietzsche.

Jill Scott
Assistant Professor in the Department of Germanic Languages and Literatures at the University of Toronto. Her dissertation, "Elektra after Freud: Death, Hysteria and Mourning," was the recipient of the Austrian Canadian Council Dissertation Prize. In 1999-2000, Jill Scott held a postdoctoral fellowship at the University of Chicago and began work on "Choreographing Modernity: Dancing Women in Performance and Text, 1850-1920." She has published articles on Novalis and Wagner, Benjamin and Hofmannsthal.

Barry Smith is the author of *Austrian Philosophy* (Chicago 1994) and editor of *The Monist*. He teaches philosophy at the State University of New York at Buffalo and has worked on topics ranging from Brentano and Kafka to ontological engineering and the aetiology of war.

Fred Wilson
Completed his Ph.D. under Gustav Bergmann at the University of Iowa in 1965 and has since taught in the Philosophy Department at the University of Toronto. He was elected a Fellow of the Royal Society of Canada in 1994. His research interests include studies in empiricism (Hume, John Stuart Mill), philosophy of science, and the history and philosophy of psychology.